BLOOD AND ORANGES

DISLOCATIONS

General Editors: August Carbonella, *Memorial University of Newfoundland,* Don Kalb, *University of Utrecht* & *Central European University,* Gerald Sider, *The Graduate Center* & *The College of Staten Island, CUNY,* Linda Green, *University of Arizona*

The immense dislocations and suffering caused by neoliberal globalization, the retreat of the welfare state in the last decades of the twentieth century, and the heightened military imperialism at the turn of the twenty-first century have raised urgent questions about the temporal and spatial dimensions of power. Through stimulating critical perspectives and new and cross-disciplinary frameworks, that reflect recent innovations in the social and human sciences, this series provides a forum for politically engaged and theoretically imaginative responses to these important issues of late modernity.

BLOOD AND ORANGES

European Markets and Immigrant Labor in Rural Greece

Christopher M. Lawrence

Berghahn Books
NEW YORK • OXFORD

First published in 2007 by

Berghahn Books

www.berghahnbooks.com

© 2007, 2011 Christopher M. Lawrence
First paperback edition published in 2011

All rights reserved.

Library of Congress Cataloging-in-Publication Data

Lawrence, Christopher M.
 Blood and oranges : European markets and immigrant labor in rural Greece /
Christopher M. Lawrence.
 p. cm. -- (Dislocations ; 2)
 Includes bibliographical references and index.
 ISBN 978-1-84545-307-7 (hbk) -- ISBN 978-0-85745-143-9 (pbk)
 1. Alien labor--Greece. 2. Xenophobia--Greece. 3. Social
integration--Greece. 4. Nationalism--Economic aspects--Greece. I. Title.

 HD8650.5.L39 2007
 331.6'209495091734--dc22
                              2007003838

British Library Cataloguing in Publication Data

A catalogue record for this book is available from the British Library

Printed in the United States on acid-free paper

ISBN 978-1-84545-307-7 (hardback)
ISBN 978-0-85745-143-9 (paperback)
ISBN 978-0-85745-285-6 (ebook)

CONTENTS

LIST OF ILLUSTRATIONS

LIST OF ABBREVIATIONS

CAP — European Union Common Agricultural Policy

DA — Democratic Army

EAM — National Liberation Front

EKAM — Special Interdiction Police Units

ELAS — Greek Liberation Army

ELGA — Greek Agricultural Compensation board

EMU — European Monetary Union

IKA — Institute of Social Security

KKE — Communist Party of Greece

KNE — Communist Youth of Greece

MAAE — Registry of Farmers and Farm Enterprises

ND — New Democracy party

OGA — Organization of Agricultural Insurance

OPLA — Units for the Protection of the Popular Struggle

PASOK — Panhellenic Socialist Movement

ACKNOWLEDGMENTS

There are many people who made this book possible and to whom I am grateful. First and foremost, I thank the people of Midea township, who offered me hospitality and suffered my endless questions with patience and humor. To all of them I offer my sincere gratitude, especially the families of Panos Papageorgopoulos, Kotsiba Papageorgopoulos, and Georgos Lekkas. In Nauplio, Nikos Vrachnos and Georgos and Jill Athineos provided me with support and friendship. In Athens, Roxanne Caftanzoglou of the National Centre for Social Research (EKKE) helped with introductions, and Aggeliki Athanasopoulou was gracious in sharing with me her own research on one of the villages in the area that I worked. I am also indebted to Charalambos Kasimis of the Agricultural University of Athens for the time he took to discuss my research with me. I also wish to thank the people who took the time to read and comment on various drafts, including Jane Schneider, Michael Blim, Augustos Carbonella, and Peter Loizos. In particular, I want to thank Gerald Sider, who has been an inspiration for me and whose unflagging enthusiasm and confidence sustained me through many periods of frustration and uncertainty. I also thank Natsuko Uesugi and Sophocles and Janine Stavri for their technical and artistic help. The final manuscript also benefited immensely from the careful copyediting of Jaime Taber.

It goes without saying that none of the people I thank here will agree with everything I have written. For any errors, I take full responsibility. Finally, I thank my daughters Selene and Thalia, who put up with quite a lot during the writing of this book.

For Thalia and Selene

PREFACE

In order to place my analysis of contemporary social relations in rural Greece in proper context, it is helpful for the reader to know something of my own background and the genesis of this work. As the product of a "mixed" marriage (my mother is Greek, my father American), I came of age straddling two cultures. As a young adult I lived for several years in Athens. Before I started fieldwork for this project I was already familiar with Greek society and had witnessed many of the transformations that have occurred there since the late 1970s. By the 1990s it was clear that as Greece integrated into the European Union a new period of history was unfolding. For me, as for many others, witnessing this development brought a heady mix of exhilaration and sorrow. While Greek society was finally catching up with the privileges and comforts of European life, it was also losing the simplicity and idiosyncrasy of daily experience. As an anthropologist, however, my attention soon turned to a development that few had foreseen: the sudden presence of a large number of desperate immigrants from Eastern Europe that seemed to be growing daily. The reaction of most Greeks to this influx was, for me, both fascinating and painful. Suddenly Greeks, who had years of experience dealing with foreign tourists, were publicly discussing things like "xenophobia" and the incompatibility of ethnic and cultural groups in a way that recalled for me the discourse of American racism. Friends I had known for many years who had in the past been politically "progressive" were increasingly enthralled by a new-found sense of nationalism. A new and more extreme form of social polarization seemed to be replacing the traditional inequalities of Greek society. The cultural heterogeneity of the "new" Europe was not supposed to look this way. By the early 2000s, after I had completed my graduate studies in social anthropology, I was determined to investigate this problem.

When I was finally able to begin fieldwork, immigration into Greece had become more regulated and institutionalized than in those early chaotic years. Most areas of the Greek economy had become dependent on immigrant labor, but a deep ambivalence about the presence of immigrants persisted. In studying this problem, I decided to focus on several small agricultural communities, where recent changes were much starker and the totality of social formations easier to grasp. I was introduced to the villages of Midea township through contacts I had in the nearby town of Nauplio. Midea township was ideal for my study because it relied heavily on agriculture, contained a number of villages in close proximity with contrasting subsistence strategies, and had a large number of immigrant agricultural laborers. Fieldwork began in 2003 and lasted for over fifteen months. A grant from the National Science Foundation and a sabbatical allowed me to spend two seven-month stretches in the villages in 2003 and 2004.

My first real introduction to the people of Midea township occurred on a cold night in February 2003 when I wandered into the men's coffee house in the mountain village of Gerbesi. The place was packed with men drinking, playing cards, and watching soccer on television. As I entered, one of the card players, who later was to become one of my closest informants and a friend, nonchalantly looked up and said "OK, what are you, CIA or Mossad?" Taken aback, I stammered something about being an anthropologist and after a few awkward moments was invited to sit down for a drink.

Although I didn't know it at the time, this initial meeting foreshadowed my position in village society and shaped much of my research. As is often the case in small communities, Greek villagers are suspicious of outsiders and reticent about divulging information. Toward the end of my fieldwork, when I finally felt that I had been accepted by the villagers, or at least tolerated, I realized that most of the initial interviews I had conducted were worthless. It took months of hanging around coffee shops, volunteering as free labor, and generally making a nuisance of myself before I felt that I was finally getting "inside" the three villages I chose to focus on. The opaqueness of village life to the outsider is partly a result of villagers' resistance to outsiders, a strategy that serves to both protect the village from outside surveillance and regulation and shield internal power relations.

As an outsider investigating village life, I had to constantly confront villagers' suspicions, perhaps justified, that the information would in some way be used against them. Among some of the villagers I became close with it became a running joke that I was "their" CIA agent sent to prepare files on the rebellious Greeks. As I came to realize, this joke reflects villagers' sense of resistance to outside forces, a resistance that in the contemporary situation has become increasingly complex and contradictory. In more serious conversations, villagers often pressed me to consider the outcome of my research with comments like, "Come on, in truth, who is going to read what you write? The CIA, to learn better ways to exploit us!" My feeble excuse that the CIA, preferring more heavy-handed approaches, was probably not interested in the subtleties of social relations was greeted with skepticism. It is a question I still wrestle with, especially given the recent push to harness academic research in social sciences to US government policy objectives.

My entry to village society through the coffee shop, so to speak, had other implications as well. Like all communities, Greek villages contain a dynamic and fluid array of social divisions. One of the most prominent concerns gender. In most cases the village coffee shop is still a male preserve in Greece, in essence a male clubhouse. One of my original research objectives was to correlate the incorporation of immigrant labor with the increasing social freedom of women. I quickly realized that the situation was much more complex than a simple correlation, and that although many women have entered the formal workforce and managed to evade some of the more onerous patriarchal restrictions, villages remain to a large extent gender-segregated. As a male I was rarely able to interview female villagers without a male relative present. Nor did I obtain as much access to female-dominated spaces as I did to male-dominated ones. Thus my analysis should be qualified by the fact that it relies more heavily on male informants than female.

The villages I studied are also deeply divided along ethnic lines. Immigrants, mostly Albanians but also Romanians and Bulgarians, are largely segregated, both spatially and socially, from native Greeks. As I explain later, this division is often conceptualized by Greeks in terms of "race" or genetics. In fact my own acceptance into village society was rationalized by some of the villagers with the explanation that my "Greek" genes outweighed my "American" genes. When I entered that first coffee shop I immediately noticed that the Albanian laborers were sitting together at their own table, segregated by an invisible social divide. Throughout my fieldwork, my position as a Greek-American placed me firmly on the Greek side of this division. I interviewed and worked alongside many immigrants, but the relationships I established were colored by the unequal nature of our respective statuses. Therefore, this ethnography should not be read as a study of immigrants or the experience of immigration but rather as a study of how immigrants have been incorporated into village society.

I offer these qualifications to make my analysis more transparent. Problems of positionality and perspective are inherent to participant-observation, the main methodology of this study. For the reader, understanding the social context of the research is important for evaluating the results. My main goal during fieldwork was to understand contemporary social relations from the perspective of Greek villagers. To this end I lived and worked among the villagers for an extended period of time. I also conducted formal and informal interviews with individuals across the social spectrum of village society. In the end, however, the analysis presented here is my own, colored by my own experiences as well as my theoretical training in social anthropology and political economy. It is offered as a contribution to our collective understanding of social relations in a world being transformed by new global networks of exchange as well as new transnational forms of social inequality.

INTRODUCTION: THE TRANSFORMATION OF RURAL GREECE

Since its accession to the European Union (EU) in the early 1980s, Greece has undergone dramatic changes in almost every aspect of social life. One of the most important changes has been an extensive reorganization of the social relations of production and consumption that shape the economy of Greece. These changes are perhaps most apparent in rural areas that, until recently, maintained a relatively "traditional" model of social relations. In stark contrast to the postwar era during which they exported labor to industrialized nations, Greek agricultural communities have become increasingly dependent on immigrant labor, mostly from Eastern Europe. Today immigrants, many of them illegal, make up an estimated 10 percent of the population of Greece. At the same time, rural Greeks have become increasingly integrated into European markets, both as agricultural producers and as "Europeanized" consumers. This ethnography documents the ways in which these developments are fundamentally linked in practice.

Under pressure exerted by declining prices in European markets and the rising consumption needs of a European lifestyle, Greek farmers face a crucial paradox provoked by the move toward market liberalization in Europe. As the value of family labor declines and consumption pressures rise, families have adapted by dramatically lowering their birthrates and diversifying household labor, creating in turn a crisis in agricultural labor. In short, while rural Greek families still depend on agriculture for survival, they can no longer afford to devote household labor to agricultural production. The same global pressures of market liberalization have created the solution to this problem: the dislocation and mobilization of large numbers of Eastern European laborers. Simultaneous "push" and "pull" factors have stimulated a massive, illegal immigration of low-cost and flexible labor into Greece. These developments have in turn given rise to several contradictory dynamics. Greeks have become economically dependent on immigrants, but the economic value of immigrants is based on their continued social and political exclusion. Because Greeks' survival hinges on the exploitation of immigrants, immigration has stimulated a resurgence of ethnic nationalism at the same time that EU integration has liberalized many aspects of Greek social relations.

Greek farmers have responded to the pressures of globalization by elaborating a discourse of racism and social exclusion directed at immigrant laborers. It has been widely noted that European society is experiencing a resurgence of racist discourse and xenophobic sentiment. In rural Greece immigrants are subject to social and political exclusion through a variety of means. They are subject to a popular discourse of racial and ethnic inferiority, exclusion from legal and political rights, and even physical beatings. In the following chapters I document contemporary methods of social and political exclusion, but also compare the contemporary situation with similar conditions in the early twentieth century. This comparison allows us to better understand contemporary European racism as well as the contours of contemporary globalization. From this understanding, I argue that rather than being simply a reaction to globalization, the social and political exclusion of immigrants serves to facilitate the spread of neoliberal markets by resolving some of the social contradictions they have spawned. Further, I argue that this arrangement between the globalized economy and localized production of inequality represents a novel political system that has re-articulated the relationship between nation and state in Europe in ways that are profound and probably enduring.

The Greek experience of immigration and Europeanization can only be fully understood from a historical perspective. Anthropological research has long pointed to the fluidity and historical specificity of cultural processes of identity formation. Greece is certainly no exception. What it is to be "Greek" and "not Greek" has shifted over time and place, reflecting political and economic conditions as well as history. The creation of "Albanians" (as immigrants are generically called) as a class of labor is a product of both the contemporary political economy and the historical peculiarities of the Greek nation. However, the particularities of the Greek experience also provide a platform for generalizing about global trends. After all, illegal immigration has become one of the hallmarks of what we call "globalization," and understanding the role of immigration is essential for analyzing contemporary shifts in the global economy of capitalism.

Since the early 1990s "globalization" has become an increasingly common focus of anthropological studies. Starting from diverse theoretical orientations, many theorists, as well as lay observers, have argued that during the last decades of the twentieth century profound social, political, and economic changes swept the planet. This transformation, which is still in progress, has left few people unaffected. Various models have been proposed to explain the engines driving globalization. Harvey (1990), Arrighi (1994), and others drawing from Marxist theory and variants on world-systems theory have explained it in terms of cycles of capitalist crisis and accumulation. Others, such as Appadurai (1990) and Castells (1996), have preferred a more culturalist approach emphasizing new technology, communication, and mobility. Few would argue, however, that the world today is not significantly different from the previous arrangement of nation-states that held sway for much of the twentieth century. More recently, however, the sheen of globalization theory has begun to fade, perhaps through overuse. As with many new paradigms, globalization was embraced with perhaps too much enthusiasm and too little skepticism. Much of early globalization theory necessarily took a macro approach, using the globe and global relations as its unit of analysis. This methodological shift of scale may have encouraged us to overlook or discount previous manifestations of what today we take to be elements of globalization, such as cultural hybridity and mobility (Mintz 1998). As anthropologists have returned their attention to particular locales, it has become clear that there are still many questions to answer. Like the morning after a wild party, the heady intoxication induced by postmodern and globalization theory has given way to the painful and mundane tasks of picking up the pieces and cataloging the damages. What exactly is different about the world today, and how different is it? As we look around, we see that globalization's effects have been uneven and contradictory. Most people, it turns out, are not significantly more mobile or hybrid, despite the fact that they increasingly participate in the same markets. For most people, capital mobility and global communications have increased global inequality and social distance rather than lessened it. And while the proportion of people involved in labor mobility and migration today still pales when compared to other historical eras, migrants are increasingly likely to have an illegal status.

This ethnography aspires to contribute to the debate on contemporary global changes. By documenting and analyzing the experiences of people in one locale I hope to provide a perspective from the "bottom-up." The area I selected, comprising several small villages in rural Greece, is remote from the global centers of power but has nevertheless been buffeted by the winds of change, as have most other corners of the globe. The people of this rural community have been engaged in processes of adaptation and accommodation that may be particular to their own history and location but also shed light on how global changes have been enacted in specific practices. The locale described in this ethnography, Midea township, relies primarily on agriculture for subsistence, a fact that has always influenced the forms and functions of social relations there. In recent years, since accession to the European Union, local social relations have been profoundly affected by developments tied to global political-economic changes.

Agricultural households in Greece have experienced economic globalization in several ways. Most importantly, as Greece has become integrated into the economy of the EU, households have become direct participants in the transnational markets for agricultural products. On the whole this has created downward pressure on prices for these products, a situation that has been somewhat mitigated by the expansion of subsidy programs. Yet although these programs have acted to insulate agriculturalists from the "shock" of conversion to transnational "free" markets, their ultimate purpose is to accomplish the gradual transition to capitalist agriculture through the regulation, attrition, and ultimate shrinking of the agricultural sector. At the same time that agricultural households have been integrated as producers for transnational markets, they have also been integrated as consumers. Subsistence production has declined, and households have become more dependent on transnational markets for commodity consumption. Indeed, the novelty of contemporary processes of globalization, from the perspective of the rural household, is the way that commodity consumption has come to define and condition the integration of the household into transnational markets.

The integration of Greek rural household production into global economies is nothing new. In the past however, peasant communities were integrated into the world system primarily as producers of both agricultural products and industrial labor (Wolf 1982: 317-318). Modern Greece had been successively integrated into several world economies before the advent of the EU, including the Ottoman, British, and American systems. Each of these earlier phases of world-systemic globalization was accompanied by particular sets of relations between external and internal forms of social domination that were mediated by the construction of national identity and the development of the nation-state. Each also gave rise to particular sets of contradictions that were often resolved by military force through a succession of political-military struggles. In the post-World War II period the Greek nation-state developed under conditions characterized by its semiperipheral relation to the US-dominated world system. Agricultural households developed internal relations of production that were characterized by a gendered division of labor consistent with a reliance on subsistence production as well as by an integration into systems of patronage that insured their domination by urban elites and, by extension, a national bourgeoisie. National identity acted both to condition the subordination of rural households and to provide an avenue of resistance to this same domination, as demonstrated by the series of nationalist struggles against foreign domination that characterized the postwar period. Both communist insurgents and right-wing military dictators claimed legitimacy and mobilized their supporters through a discourse of nationalism.

In contrast to earlier integrations, however, the current phase of integration has been accomplished not through military force but through the techniques of neoliberal governmentality that characterize the "globalized" capitalism of the EU, a process that has given rise to a distinctive set of contradictions. Some of these contradictions can be seen in the system of agricultural subsidies. Borrowing a page from Fordism,[1] subsidy programs use price supports in order to accomplish the transition to capitalist agriculture, but at the same time create an arena of autonomy and resistance for farmers. Fraud and political lobbying enable farmers to use the subsidy programs as a way of forestalling the transition to more cap-italist agriculture and mitigating the effects of free markets. That is, sub-sidies encourage the use of wage labor rather than family labor in agricul-tural production, but at the same time allow farmers to avoid, at least tem-porarily, other aspects of the shift to "modern" industrial agriculture such as the consolidation of landholdings and intensive capitalist investment that would more seriously threaten the social fabric of the villages. The effectiveness of the subsidy program for the EU, however, reflects not only its effectiveness in transforming agriculture but also its effectiveness in promoting the political legitimacy of the EU itself. That is, even as farmers use the subsidy programs as an arena of resistance, their depen-dence on subsidies has been an important element in their support for EU integration and therefore in the political legitimacy of the EU project. Despite their opposition to the goals of EU agricultural policy, rural households increasingly recognize the sovereignty of the EU by support-ing political parties that accept the EU political structure and abandoning those parties, such as the Communist Party of Greece (KKE), that have been most opposed to EU integration. Thus, despite their regulatory nature, subsidy programs can be seen as conducive to techniques of neoliberal governmentality through their role in the manufacturing of consent among the governed and the political legitimacy of the EU. An important effect of this process is the creation of an aura of inevitability to cloak the logic of capitalist markets. Resistance is deflected from opposi-tion to the capitalist basis of transnational markets to demands for gov-ernment protection from their effects.

The effects of the neoliberal production of governmentality can be seen in agriculturalist households in the widespread perception of a dramatic increase in "equality" and "freedom" among rural Greeks. Most Greeks feel that the "modernization" of the countryside has freed them from the fetters of gender, age, and class distinctions that characterized the post-war era. For example, women are perceived to exercise greater freedom of choice in marriages and careers, and children have been freed from the labor requirements of households. In practice, these freedoms are accom-plished through commodity consumption, primarily the exercise of pur-chasing power by women and children in the markets for consumer goods. Baudrillard was particularly prescient on this point when he argued that in contemporary consumer society, "the democratic principle is transferred from a real equality of capacities, of responsibilities, of social chances ... to an equality before the Object ... the democracy of social standing, the democracy of the TV, the car and the stereo" (1998: 50). The link between rising levels of consumption and perceptions of equality thus acts to veil emerging patterns of inequality engendered by the diffusion of neoliberal modes of governance and integration into global markets.

A dominant neoliberal ethos of the "marketing" of identities, and of the marking of identities through commodity consumption, provides a new basis for the exercise of social control. This can be seen most dramatically in new attitudes and practices of raising children. To be successful in job markets, children require capital investments in the form of commodities and education. These requirements place enormous burdens on households and stimulate their productivity, but at the same time have encouraged smaller family size. The success of children is seen as a reflection of the discipline of parents, but is also ultimately a product of the children's own participation in these forms of cultural capitalization, of their "desire" to succeed. In sum, households have come to see themselves as "petty-bourgeois," that is, as small capitalist enterprises.

The twin processes of economic integration into the EU markets and the infusion of neoliberal discipline have created a contradiction that is acutely experienced by agriculturalist households as a labor crisis. Even as declining market prices have increased agricultural labor needs, the access to surplus labor, in the form of the labor of women, children, and lower-class co-villagers, has been reduced. In the past all these sources of labor could be called upon to provide for the production necessary for subsistence. Today they have been curtailed precisely through the spread of neoliberal concepts of freedom and equality as well as neoliberal techniques for the expansion of markets through the discipline of consumerism. Part of the slack has been taken up by technological solutions, such as increased availability of machinery, fertilizers, deep-well technology, etc. Yet the labor shortage remains a serious problem, especially given the relatively small plots and labor-intensive crops on which villagers depend. For agricultural households, the effects of neoliberal capitalist globalization present a dilemma: if everyone has a choice, who will choose to be exploited? That is, given the neoliberal ideology of freedom, how are exploitable sources of labor to be reproduced?

Robert Miles (1987) has argued that capitalism, despite the processes of commodification of labor described by Marx, continues to be dependent on the reproduction of "unfree," fettered labor in order to sustain relations of production and the extraction of surplus. In Greece, we can see a clear demonstration of this process. As agricultural labor has been freed from the fetters of kinship, gender, and patronage that in the past organized and sustained rural relations of production, traditional forms of social hierarchy have disappeared. The simple and immediate effect is that Greeks no longer work in the fields, having been "freed" to participate in the labor markets of the service industry. This process has been represented as the "modernization" of the countryside. At the same time, given the conditions of agricultural production, there is still a demand among households, even an increased demand because of growing consumer needs, for access to forms of fettered labor that can be flexibly exploited to support rising standards of living. Subsidies, which help to ease the pressure on households, can never fully resolve the contradiction faced by rural households since their goal is to prod households toward transformation. The new fetters of agricultural labor are constructed through the exclusion from citizenship rights that characterizes the illegal market of immigrant labor.

Agricultural households in Greece have responded to this crisis of labor in a typically post-Fordist fashion by outsourcing the reproduction of exploitable labor to neighboring countries of Eastern Europe. This option is made possible by the same global forces that created the labor crisis in the first place, that is, by the global hegemony of capitalist markets. The global expansion of capitalism in the last several decades of the twentieth century brought with it the destruction of Eastern European economies and the proliferation of transnational social and cultural flows. The expansion of capitalist markets into Eastern Europe and the destruction of national economies there created a vast pool of surplus labor. Advances in information, communication, and transportation technologies increased the mobility of Eastern European labor. At the same time these advances made possible its diaspora character, whereby the social costs of the reproduction of labor exploited by Greek households can be displaced to Eastern European societies. In other words, what makes Albanian labor so cheap for Greeks is the fact that so many of the costs of sustaining and reproducing "Albanians" as a category of labor are absorbed by Albania and other Eastern European countries. As in the old transatlantic slave trade, Greeks mostly employ healthy male immigrants in their prime. The costs of raising children and caring for the old and infirm, many of whom are dependent on remittances, are absorbed by the sending countries, where they are lower. In addition, the dreams and hopes for the future that motivate immigrants to work are more cheaply realized in countries such as Albania. Thus immigrants in Greece can work for a lower wage and still support families and save money for future investments back home. The result is that the majority of agricultural households in Greece are now directly dependent on immigrant labor and, by extension, on the vulnerabilities of Eastern European economies wrought by new global processes of social inequality.

For rural Greek households, the alleviation of the labor crisis, and thus the resolution of the main contradiction arising from their incorporation into the new globalized capitalism, is dependent on the maintenance of the difference between "Greeks" and "Albanians." Eric Wolf (1999: 274-291) has argued that societies under the stress of transformation often respond by developing powerful ideologies that structure the differentiation, mobilization, and deployment of social labor. Such ideologies are often constructed, or naturalized, as a cosmological imperative. Shades of this process can be seen in the rise and spread of a neoracist ethnic nationalism among Greeks. For Albanians and other Eastern Europeans, the structural conditions of their integration into the Greek economy has precluded the development of nationalist ideologies, or at least deflected it to their home countries, making assimilation a more attractive goal than differentiation. Given the economic integration of immigrant labor into the household economies of rural Greece, their social and political marginalization presents an acute problem, one that is solved through the elaboration of a set of national identities that explains and naturalizes the difference between the two groups. The elaboration of difference entails a legitimation of Albanians' political exclusion and social subordination, the naturalization of their position at the bottom of the social hierarchy, and the appropriateness of Greek social and political supremacy.

All this suggests that the revitalization and spread of nationalist, racist, and xenophobic discourse has been instrumental in creating the social relations necessary for integration into the new political economy of Europe. While the type of neoracist nationalism pervasive in rural Greece may, on the surface, seem incompatible or contradictory with the neoliberal tendencies of the EU, in actuality it has served to subsidize political and economic integration through a resolution of the main contradiction facing Greek farmers. As Greeks have elaborated a complex ideology of the social marginalization of immigrant workers, even including demands for their expulsion, at the same time they have become almost completely dependent on their labor. Indeed, the expulsion of immigrant workers would undoubtedly require a fundamental restructuring of the Greek economy. Thus the vulnerability and exploitation of immigrant workers has been a key factor enabling the successful integration of rural Greece into the contemporary regime of the Greek state and the EU.

Looking back on the history of modern Greece, we can see that patterns of exploitation conditioned by nationalist ideologies have always been crucial to Greece's integration into world systems. Indeed, we can argue that the emergence and spread of Greek nationalism was what allowed the Greek Orthodox merchant class of the Ottoman Empire to assert itself as a national bourgeoisie with monopoly rights of exploitation of a diverse rural peasantry. On the semiperiphery of the British- and later American-dominated world capitalist systems, nationalism acted to organize an ethnicized and gendered system of class relations that facilitated Greece's exploitation by a national *comprador* bourgeoisie supported by the armed force of successive world powers. A somewhat different process has characterized Greece's incorporation into the current EU regime. For one thing, the old core-semiperiphery relationship that characterized Greece's relation to world systems no longer seems to hold. Instead, there has been a clear attempt by the EU to fully integrate southern European economies into the European core. The success of this attempt has yet to been seen, but it is no longer adequate to describe Greece in terms of the postwar twentieth century. What seems to be emerging is a kind of internalization of the semiperiphery. With the weakening of internal borders and widespread dependence on foreign immigrant labor in Europe there has developed a kind of internal core and semiperiphery defined by differentiated access to wealth, policed by strong ideologies of ethnic and national difference, and manifested in new strategies of labor mobilization and labor discipline.

Thus, nationalism in Greece is not the vestige of an earlier era but rather the product of changing political-economic conditions. Recent trends toward globalization of capitalist markets have produced both the need for a new source of exploitable labor and the technological means for the creation of a diaspora working class of immigrants with strong social ties to their home countries. As a result, nationalism works to promote a form of "hybridity" based on exclusion. Rural Greece is indeed becoming "multicultural," but cultural difference is being used to construct class distinctions and enforce vulnerabilities. Immigrants are actively pushed to maintain their interest in their home countries by their exclusion from Greek society on the one hand and the ease of movement and communication on the other. The effect is the creation of a particularly vulnerable workforce that is easily exploited by the host society. In this sense nationalism acts as a force of heterogeneity constructing and naturalizing national differences within the communities of Greece as opposed to a homogenizing force. Social classes are economically and politically integrated through the creation of difference rather than solidarity. This strategy of national differentiation rather than homogenization represents a significant change, for both the state and nation, in how the contradictions of capitalist development are resolved. The production of national identity, at least in rural Greece, has become primarily a strategy of exclusion rather than inclusion. Whereas formerly nationalism was primarily a force that sought to include classes, thereby legitimizing capitalist exploitation and stimulating the production of gender, age, and kinship stratification in rural households, the new nationalism defines class through exclusion, stimulating the production of ethnic and racial stratification in order to create exploitable labor.

Notes

1. The concept of "Fordism" has been used by numerous theorists (see Harvey 1990: 125-140 for a synopsis) as a model of a relatively stable regime of capitalist accumulation that held sway in the US and Western Europe between World War II and the 1970s. Briefly, it linked mass production to mass consumption in a system that provided benefits to a privileged sector of the working class in exchange for a stable rate of profit, labor peace, and expanded consumer markets. The agricultural subsidy programs of the EU continue that logic to the extent that they are intended to support consumption levels among the rural population, at the same time deflecting social discontent and buying the public support needed for the political legitimacy of the EU project. It should be noted, however, that unlike Fordist social welfare and entitlement programs, agricultural subsidies are conceived as temporary measures intended to ease the transition to "free" markets.

Chapter I

A BRIEF HISTORY OF CONFLICT AND ACCOMMODATION IN ARGOLIDA

℮ ∽

The township of Midea lies in the Argolid (*Argolida*) region of the north-east Peloponnesos, about 150 kilometers southwest of Athens. Argolida is a relatively rich agricultural region consisting of a wide plain opening onto the Gulf of Argos. Hemmed in by mountains on three sides, the Argolid valley enjoys abundant (for Greece) water as well as mild winters. The two main towns of the region are Argos, the inland commercial center of the Argolid valley, and the touristic port town of Nauplio. Roughly equidistant from both lies Midea township, which takes its name from the ancient Mycenaean site of Midea lying nearby. Today Midea township is a thriving slice of Argolida, stretching from the coast all the way up to Mt. Arachneo. The township, within its current boundaries,[1] consists of twelve villages and as of 2001 had a total population of 6,724. The largest of these villages is Agia Triada, the administrative and commercial center, with a population of 1,267.[2]

My research focuses on three villages of Midea township: Agia Triada, Manesi, and Gerbesi.[3] Agia Triada, the "head village" of the township, lies in the valley surrounded by orange groves. During the winter harvest season it bustles with trucks ferrying oranges and workers to and from the fields as well as people from the surrounding villages running errands. In contrast to the coastal villages it has no tourism to speak of, except for former residents returning for vacation, so the summers are relatively quiet. Manesi, with its co-village of Dendra, lies about 2 km outside Agia Triada and up the mountain. Its population of 622 is about half that of Agia Triada. Here the orange groves give way to olives, vegetable fields, and until recently, tobacco. While there are some orange groves in the village and other villagers own land down in the valley, Manesi lacks the abundant water of the valley villages and so has been limited agriculturally, missing out on the wealth that citrus brought over the last several decades. Past Manesi about 2 km farther up the mountain lies the village

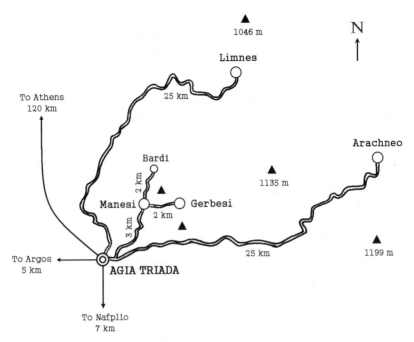

Figure 1. Villages of Midea township

of Gerbesi, with 454 residents. Gerbesi, being a "high village," also lacks the water necessary for large-scale citrus production and continues to subsist on tobacco, truck farming, and herding.

Together the three villages of Agia Triada, Manesi, and Gerbesi demonstrate a type of vertical differentiation common in rural Greece. The valley town of Agia Triada is the wealthiest, with a large part of its income deriving from citrus production, as well as the administrative and commercial jobs inherent in its position as the township center. As one moves up the mountain the villages become poorer, rely more on herding and tobacco, and are more dependent on agricultural subsidies and pensions. In the recent past, villagers from Manesi and Gerbesi supplied a significant labor pool for Agia Triada, working for day wages during the harvest. Politically, the villages formed a spectrum from the traditionally right-wing Agia Triada to the staunchly communist Gerbesi, with Manesi as a center-left, socialist stronghold. With notable exceptions, this pattern tends to hold throughout Argolida. Many of the mountain villages have a strong history of rebellion. During World War II and the subsequent civil war in Greece, mountain villages such as Gerbesi and nearby Limnes were local centers of the communist partisan resistance. The villages also differ ethnically. One of the first things that the villagers of Gerbesi will tell you about themselves is that they are *Arvanites*, descended from Albanian-speaking immigrants of the fourteenth and fifteenth centuries (Ouli 1965). While all three villages are considered to be historically

Arvanitika, Agia Triada is considered to be less pure and more Greek. Manesi falls somewhere in between. This spectrum of economic, political, and ethnic differentiation provides a framework for understanding the uneven historical development of the villages as well as points of comparison for analyzing contemporary social changes.

Like virtually all villages in Greece, since the early 1980s the villages in Midea township have also become home to a growing number of immigrants from Eastern Europe, particularly Albania. It is often assumed that the introduction of immigrants represents a radical change for a society that was previously culturally homogenous. However, a closer reading of local history, and Greek history in general, reveals successive waves of immigration over the centuries. In this chapter, I offer a brief history of Greece and Argolida, highlighting the influence of global markets and their effects on ethnic and class relations. This history is important for understanding contemporary problems because many of the same issues continue to resonate in the social relations between immigrant laborers and Greek farmers today.

Early History

Argolida has been continuously settled since ancient times. Since the Mycenaean era, it has been under the continual occupation of successive empires and states, from the city-states of ancient Greece through Rome and Byzantium, the Venetians, Ottomans, and finally the modern Greek state. Successive waves of conquerors and immigrants have all left their mark. Today the area is widely considered to be the heartland of modern Greece. The revolution that led to the founding of the modern Greek state in 1821 was centered in the Peloponnesos, and Nauplio became its first capital. Since then, the construction of Greek national identity has tended to efface processes of social differentiation. The institutions and ideology of the Greek nation-state have sought to project an unproblematic narrative of Greek history stretching back to ancient times (Herzfeld 1982). Despite these efforts, however, it is difficult to document a continuous lineage of "Greek" identity. Instead what we find is a long history of confrontation, contradiction, and assimilation among contentious social groups and ethnic identities.

The notion of a "Greek" identity in the modern sense is itself in large part the creation of the movement toward statehood. It was not until the nineteenth century that the term came to describe a homogeneous ethnic group in the modern sense. Instead, the peoples of the Peloponnesos, including Argolida, made up an intricate mosaic of ethnicities and languages. In Argolida, dialects of Albanian, Greek, Turkish, and other local languages were spoken (Andromedas 1976). From the Byzantine Empire and onward, religion was an important marker of social identity. The Byzantines were Greek speakers, but they associated the Greek language with Christianity rather than ancient Greece, and in fact ethnically defined themselves as "Romans," a term carried over into the Ottoman Empire as "Rum," meaning Orthodox Christian.

Argolida, like the coastal areas of the Peloponnesos in general, has a long history of invasion and immigration due to the economic significance of the area and its location along the eastern Mediterranean trade routes. The three villages of Agia Triada, Manesi, and Gerbesi all trace their history back to the decline of the Byzantine Empire. The original name of Agia Triada was Merbeka, probably derived from the surname of the Catholic bishop of Corinth during the Frankish crusader state, Wilhelm von Moerbeke, who established the diocesan seat there in 1277 (Salapatas 2000). It is mentioned in a census of 1700 as containing thirty families and 157 residents. It 1817 it is listed as having 160 residents. In 1834, Merbeka was incorporated as a town (*dimos*) with a population of 320 (Skiadas 1993). Gerbesi and Manesi both seem to have been founded in the sixteenth century when the area was under Venetian control. Both names apparently refer to the names of immigrant Albanian soldiers working for the Venetians that also appear as names of villages in what is today southern Albania (Mauros 1980). Albanian speakers moved into Argolida in several waves over the next centuries, creating differences that are still perceived today. Residents of Gerbesi are thought to share lineage with the people of Limnes, a village some 20 km away, while the villages of Prosimni and Arachneo are thought to represent a later immigration. Residents of Gerbesi often cite this history in explaining intervillage difference and conflicts. In the early 1950s the names of Merbeka and Gerbesi were changed to the more "Greek sounding" Agia Triada (meaning *Holy Trinity*) and Midea (from the Mycenaean site), the culmination of a long process of cultural homogenization initiated by the emergence of the modern Greek state in 1821. Manesi, for unexplained reasons, was allowed to keep its Arvanitiko name.

The Greek Revolution and National Project

In the early 1800s, Argolida was a relative backwater of the declining Ottoman Empire. It was an unlikely location for a Greek revolution given the diversity of linguistic, religious, and political identities. Relatively few people identified as Greeks at the time. However, following a historic alliance between the Greek-speaking mercantile class of the Ottoman Empire and the mostly Albanian-speaking "bandits" (*kleftes*)[4] of the Peloponnesos, it was here that the fledgling Greek state began its contest for the hearts and minds of the Balkan peasantry. The alliance between Greek-speaking merchants and Albanian-speaking bandits, first engendered by a common religion and later enshrined in nationalist ideology, proved tenuous. The inherent tensions within the alliance have, at various times, broken out into violence and civil war. As a metaphor for the nation itself, the Revolution helped to forge a national identity but also continues to provide the symbolism of social division and class conflict.

The Greek Revolution grew from the decline and collapse of the Ottoman Empire and was conditioned by the Ottoman *millet* system of governance. When the Ottoman Turks conquered the Byzantine Empire in the fifteenth century they effectively absorbed its population and many of its institutions. Byzantine Orthodox Christians, known as *Rum* (Romans) to the Ottoman Turks, were deprived of their state, but the church was absorbed into the new Ottoman state. Under the Ottoman state, subjects were divided by religion into millets, administrative units with their own civil law, tax collection, and social institutions. The "Rum millet" of Orthodox Christians used the liturgical language of Greek to administer ethnically and linguistically diverse communities under the leadership of the Orthodox Patriarchate in Istanbul. Millet affiliation was assigned and registered at birth. Millets were also largely endogamous, and proselytism and conversion were actively discouraged.

As the Ottoman Empire weakened, the millets began to take on national characteristics, becoming incubators for the nation-state successors to the empire (Karpat 1973). But while millet divisions were convenient points of fracture for emerging national identities, the lack of geographical separation meant that state formation was a long and bloody process. In addition, the millets were themselves riddled with various ethnic and class divisions. Thus the transformation from millet to nation was not even or smooth (Augustinos 1992).

Under Ottoman rule a Greek-speaking commercial class was able to develop and prosper. While the rural Orthodox Christian peasantry in many areas, particularly the interior of Asia Minor, was marginalized and declined through conversion to Islam (Vryonis 1971), in urban areas Christians thrived and established strong niches in the merchant and artisan classes. By the eighteenth century, Greek-speaking Orthodox merchants controlled the increasingly important trade between the Ottoman Empire and Europe. This new commercial class drew from various ethnic and linguistic groups (Greek, Slav, Vlach, Albanian, etc.) but the liturgical language of the millet also became the language of business, and all Orthodox merchants gradually came to be identified as Greek, regardless of their background (Stoianovich 1960: 291). As the military expansion of the Ottoman Empire stalled, the religious hierarchy of the Orthodox millet formed a political elite, providing important technical and economic advisors to the sultanate.

By the early nineteenth century much of the Greek-speaking merchant class, especially on the periphery of the Ottoman Empire, had fallen under the sway of the European Enlightenment and were quickly reconstructing their Hellenic roots. Nationalist ideas spread through secret organizations such as the Filiki Etairia (Friendly Association) and the neoclassicism of European universities where merchant sons were sent to study. In many ways, though, they were an elite in search of a nation. The first Greek revolution, attempted in what is now Romania, failed largely through lack of support among the peasantry, among other reasons. However, the mostly

Albanian-speaking Orthodox peasantry in the western regions of the empire, what is today Greece, were more receptive. As the Ottoman Empire weakened, the impoverished peasantry turned increasingly to piracy and brigandage, taking advantage of their position along important trade routes between Europe and the East (Stoianovich 1960). They slowly came to dominate these trade routes through violence and extortion, and their battles with Ottoman authorities became, under the tutelage of the nationalist Orthodox merchant elite, revolutionary acts.

Though the Peloponnesos was a peripheral region of the Ottoman Empire, it was heavily dependent on world markets. At the time of the revolution, Argolida was producing currants, wheat, tobacco, and cotton for export (Lamprinidou 1950), mainly to European markets. In fact, it was the economic and political position of Peloponnesian society rather than its ethnic makeup that made the area ripe for rebellion. Unlike other areas of the Ottoman Empire, the Peloponnesos did not have a well-developed *tsiflik* system. A few large Ottoman plantations, or *tsiflik*, controlled by the Muslim elite, were counterbalanced by a tradition of smallholders. These smallholders, Orthodox Christian for the most part, were heavily taxed by Muslim authorities. As European markets became more lucrative during the eighteenth century and indigenous, illegal trade networks flourished, resentment of Ottoman authorities and taxation increased, providing fertile ground for revolutionary activity.

The Greek Revolution of 1821, largely a product of the alliance between a nationalist commercial elite and a rebellious peasantry, succeeded only with the direct intervention of Britain, France, and Russia, who each had an interest in weakening the Ottoman Empire and whose price was the imposition of an imported European monarch, Otto I. The fledgling Greek state, established in 1831 with its capital at Nauplio, set about building the Greek nation with several important social contradictions providing the dynamic for its development. There was the tension between the European-oriented commercial class and the Balkan peasantry, a class division partly pacified by nationalist ideology. There was also conflict between the commercial class and the religious hierarchy, which was skeptical of European intentions and had remained mostly loyal to the Ottoman Sultanate. This conflict was manifested in the struggle between a Greek identity as marked by language and classical heritage and one defined by Orthodox Christianity. In addition, Greece's semiperipheral status and the competing interests of the European powers led to domestic discord as separate political parties with distinct patronage networks were established.

The formal establishment of the Greek state in 1831, under the continuing protection of the European powers, was a major step in the consolidation of a Greek nation. The "imagining" of the Greek nation was a long and tortuous process, and was not to be fully realized until ninety years later. Through the institutions of the Greek state, the educational system with its new university, the press, neoclassical architecture, and the formalization of a modernized Greek language, a Hellenized Greek national identity gradually spread from a small core in the merchant class to the linguistically and ethnically diverse population.

The Consolidation of the Greek Nation-State

Until the end of World War I, Greece continued to acquire new territory and population at the expense of the declining Ottoman Empire with sporadic help from the British and other powers when their interests coincided. In 1909, a charismatic and dynamic nationalist leader, Eleftherios Venizelos, came to power. Venizelos led Greece through a thirty-year period of intermittent warfare resulting in the dramatic expansion of the Greek state. In the Balkan Wars of 1912-1913, in which Greece allied itself first with Serbia and Bulgaria against Turkey and then with Serbia and Turkey against Bulgaria, Greece increased its territory by 70 percent and doubled its population.

The conclusion of the Balkan Wars in 1913, which was formalized in 1919 by the Treaty of Neuilly, brought about the first attempt by states to stabilize and consolidate national identities in the Southern Balkans through population exchange. Under the Treaty of Neuilly provisions were established for the voluntary exchange of populations between Greece and Bulgaria. The goal of the exchange was to secure a permanent border between Greece and Bulgaria and eliminate irredentist claims by separating the "two racial elements" (Ladas 1932: 77). Despite the commitment by the two states to provide equivalent properties to incoming refugees, the exchange was at first unsuccessful. By 1923 fewer than 400 people had applied for exchange. In addition, the cross-cutting linguistic, religious, kin, and community affiliations of local groups presented problems for the exchange commission in determining "national identity." National identity could be ascribed on the basis of race, language, or religion, any of which could be used to demonstrate a "Greek" consciousness. However, the number of exchange applications increased dramatically after 1923 as incoming Greek refugees from Asia Minor in search of land and housing put increasing pressure on Bulgarian speakers in Eastern Macedonia. By 1928 over 50,000 had emigrated. These Bulgarian refugees from Greece then targeted Greek-speakers in Bulgaria in order to get land, pushing 30,000 back to Greece.

The end of World War I brought the last major attempt at Greek expansionism. During most of World War I Greece was immobilized by a political schism between the nationalists, led by Eleftherios Venizelos, and pro-German monarchists. Venizelos prevailed with Allied support and brought Greece into World War I in 1917, just in time to make territorial demands at the Versailles Conference. As a reward, Greece gained Western Thrace and a foothold in Asia Minor around the city of Smyrni (today Izmir), a center of Greek commercial interests, from the crumbling Ottoman Empire. Ironically, Venizelos was defeated in elections soon after, the voters apparently exhausted by the long wars of expansion. The royalists who replaced him, however, could not resist the temptation to empire offered by the final disintegration of the Ottoman state and launched an offensive deep into Asia Minor. After a series of military blunders, the withdrawal of British support, and the reorganization of Turkish nationalist forces under Kemal Ataturk, the Greek army was defeated and forced into a disastrous withdrawal from Asia Minor.

As the Greek army fled Asia Minor in disarray they were followed by tens of thousands of panic-stricken, destitute refugees seeking protection in Greece. In the peace negotiations that followed, under the auspices of the League of Nations, both sides quickly agreed to the compulsory exchange of populations. Greece already faced a severe refugee crisis and was enticed by the possibility of expropriating the homes and property of 400,000 Muslims in Greece. In Turkey, much of the property of fleeing Greeks had already been seized.

The failure of the Neuilly exchange and the definite lack of enthusiasm among the target populations made a compulsory exchange necessary. But it also required a more objective marker of identity than the subjective definitions used in the Neuilly exchange. Religion became the sole determinant of nationality, overriding language or other cultural affiliations. A majority of the Greek Muslims subject to exchange spoke Greek and had virtually no ties to Turkish nationalists (Ladas 1932: 378). Similarly, many of the Orthodox refugees, particularly the "*karamanli*" Christians from the interior of Asia Minor, were Turkish speakers with virtually no cultural affinities with Hellenic Greeks of the coast. Others, such as the Pontic Orthodox from the Black Sea region, spoke a dialect unintelligible to other Greeks.

If many of the Greek Orthodox of Asia Minor were ambivalent about national identity, this was only reinforced by their reception in their new country. With the exception of some of the upper class who managed to escape with their wealth, Greek refugees experienced extreme hardship. In the overcrowded refugee camps and embarkation points food was scarce and disease rampant. Refugees were often mistreated and exploited by native Greeks, a problem exacerbated by the gender imbalance in groups from areas where many Greek males had been killed or imprisoned by the Turks (Giannuli 1995). In contrast to the ideology of inclusion inherent in national expansion, the arrival of refugees in Greece heightened the distinctions between Hellenic and Ottoman Greeks. Dissimilarities between the two groups were increasingly conceptualized as racial in nature, that is, as differences in physical appearance and mental capabilities arising from heredity as well as language and cultural characteristics. Refugees were often described as either sly, lazy and immoral, or as "Asiatic, dull-witted, backward and submissive" (Pentzopoulos 1962: 101).

The refugees increased the population of Greece by about 20 percent. About half the refugees, approximately 600,000 people, were eventually settled in rural areas, in particular Macedonia where the government hoped to consolidate a Greek majority. Most of the rest settled in urban shantytowns. Many natives perceived the refugees as a serious economic threat to their already scarce resources, competitors for land in rural areas and jobs in the cities. Argolida had a relatively small influx of refugees. They were settled in a swamp area along the coast that eventually became the town of Neo Kios and in a shantytown outside Nauplio called Pronoia.

The refugees had a profound effect on rural Greece by spearheading the national homogenization of Northern Greece and provoking fundamental changes in rural social relations. Almost half the refugees were directed to the northern province of Macedonia, which in the 1920s had a high proportion of Muslims and Bulgarian speakers and a low overall population density. During the Balkan Wars Macedonia had been the scene of violent intercommunal conflicts between Greek, Bulgarian, and Macedonian paramilitaries representing conflicting national interests. The Greek state used the refugees to consolidate its control over the newly acquired region and hasten the departure of the non-Greek population (Ladas 1932: 105).

To facilitate the resettling of the refugees, the Greek government also passed a general land reform that expropriated many large and unproductive landholdings as well as land left behind by departing Muslims. In the north much of this land consisted of the *tsiflik*, large plantations owned by Muslim landowners under authority of the Ottoman sultan. In the south, where tsiflik were rare, much of the seized land belonged to the Church. The land reform measures ultimately affected almost 50 percent of all landholdings (Pentzopoulos 1962: 155). However, the lack of surveys and titles made expropriation chaotic and in some places led to violent conflicts.

The process of land reform in Argolida differed somewhat in comparison with Northern Greece.[5] Argolida had no history of large tsiflik; neither did it have the pressures of large numbers of refugees. Smallholders dominated most villages. The main exceptions to this were areas where the Church controlled large parcels, either renting to locals or farming through monastic labor. In Agios Andrianos, a neighboring village to Agia Triada, much of the land was controlled by the monastery of Agios Dimitrios Karakala. Here, according to informants, there were three large landowners. The rest of the village either rented land or worked as laborers. The land-poor residents rented land from the monastery, and under the land reform these lands were distributed to village residents. In Manesi and Gerbesi both state and church lands, mainly pasturage, were distributed to local residents, each family receiving between 5 and 15 hectares, depending on family size and land quality. Much of this land had been used by transhumant pastoralists from Arcadia in Central Peloponnesos for winter pasturage. Technically they were entitled to receive shares but the villagers excluded them by drawing up titles during the summer. The land seizures from the monasteries were stopped after six months when a new government bowed to pressure from the Church. Thus in Midea township land reform tended to benefit local smallholders at the expense of the Church and alleviated local class tensions while excluding outsiders.

Urban refugee settlements exhibited similar processes of ghettoization and discrimination. Refugees were concentrated in urban shantytowns, providing the cheap labor that facilitated the industrialization of Greece after 1925. Between 1923 and 1930 the number of industrial workers quadrupled, although unemployment remained high. To encourage businesses to provide jobs, wages were kept low and labor laws were "tacitly abrogated," especially in regard to female and child labor (Pentzopoulos 1962: 161-162). The urban refugee ghettos also gave rise to an extensive criminal underground that frightened the native middle class and provoked severe police repression. Nattily dressed dudes, or *manges*, who made their living from drug-dealing, pimping, or theft became legendary figures. A new style of music called *rembetika* (Holst 1975) also evolved, based on the Anatolian scales and melodies favored by refugees from Asia Minor. Rembetika bears an uncanny aesthetic similarity to American blues and was banned from radio play for many years due to its risqué lyrics and drug references. Refugee women became stereotyped as loose and immoral, and prone to prostitution. Dominant cultural discourse of the time attributed these behaviors to the "mentality" of the refugees and what one observer termed a "masochistic complacency for being utterly destitute" (quoted in Pentzopoulos 1962: 201). This Greek version of the culture of poverty thesis attributed the extreme poverty of the refugees to both their racial characteristics and cultural inadequacies. Refugees were also commonly accused of exaggerating the discrimination they faced in order to exploit and manipulate government assistance.

In Argolida the refugees had a similar impact, although their numbers were relatively small. Refugees settled in three main areas in the period from 1923 to 1930. A small group from Asia Minor settled in the coastal swamplands forming the village of Neo Kios. Other refugees settled in shantytowns in the towns of Nauplio and Argos. Many of the initial settlers of Neo Kios were from the town of Kios (Gemlek) in Asia Minor. Their numbers were slowly increased as refugees who had settled in other areas moved there, encouraged by the availability of land. During 1929-1930 the Greek government dredged the Inachos River, which runs through the town, and built levies to alleviate flooding. The government also built primitive housing and offered incentives to attract refugees from crowded urban areas like Corinth. Each family in Neo Kios was given 10 hectares and a small house. The houses were built on pilings surrounded by mud and standing water. Today Neo Kios is a large village of 3,600 residents. Many are descended from the original refugees, although others have moved in through marriage. Today the village is relatively prosperous, and few physical manifestations of its past history distinguish it from the surrounding villages of Argolida. After 1965 the villagers began to produce citrus as well as vegetables for the Athens market and ceased working for surrounding villages. There are now approximately

150 foreigners living in the village, doing most of the agricultural and manual labor.

I interviewed several older residents of Neo Kios, all of whom were in their seventies and had been born in Greece shortly after their parents fled Asia Minor. One older resident recounted his family's experiences in terms strikingly similar to those recounted by more recent Albanian immigrants:

> My family came from Kios. They left there in 1924 when the Turks came and kicked them out. That was a Greek village, we had a few Turks there, but we got along well. When my parents came here they had a difficult time, they were hungry and had no work. First they were sent to a village in Macedonia where they were given forty stremmata. But they didn't like it there and had some problems with the locals. Then they heard from other villagers about this village and they came here. Things were hard in the early years. We had to eat wild greens. There was great hunger. You couldn't grow anything here, it was all swampland. Mud everywhere. All we had was a few fishing boats. That's what they used to do in Kios, fishing. That's the way we survived. In the summers we had to walk hours for work, sometimes all the way to Corinth. We worked from sunrise to sunset for a little bit of money or a little oil. Later we were able to plant our own fields. The other villages around here didn't want us. They were angry because we got some of their fields. They used to come around and make trouble. Big trouble! Fights and beatings, it was mostly about girls you know. We were like cats and dogs. They called us Turks and wanted us to leave, but we were stuck here. Where could we go?

Another older resident told me his parents, from different towns in Asia Minor, had met and married in the refugee camp in Corinth. They came to Neo Kios in 1929 after being offered 200 drachmas to move. The money was given by refugee leaders in Neo Kios, who were said to have skimmed 200-300 drachmas from the original sums given by the government. He said that the social structure in the early village tended to reproduce that of the Asia Minor communities. Those who had been merchants received better lands and buildings for stores in the center, while peasants were given less desirable land on the periphery.

Near the town of Nauplio, refugees lived along the beach in huts made from salvaged wood. In one local oral history collection an older resident recounted the hardships of this period: "No party, neither the *Laiki* [right-wing populist] nor the *Venizeliko* [liberal] helped us. They made many promises but they were all broken. They called us *Turkospori* [lit. Turkish seeds] and gangs used to roam the neighborhood at election time and threaten us" (N.A. 1992). Many refugees worked in the local canning factories at low wages. In 1927 the government built and distributed housing on the edge of town for refugee families. Politically and socially, however, the refugees remained marginalized. It was not until 1964 that the first councilman of refugee descent was elected to the local council. As difficult as the early years were for Asia Minor refugees, their rights to Greek citizenship and their settlement into corporate communities enabled them to both resist exploitation at the hands of native Greeks and slowly assimilate into Greek society. In contrast, as we shall see, the comparably massive numbers of immigrants from Albania and other Eastern European countries of the last several decades enjoy neither of these advantages.

Early in my research a man in Gerbesi, explaining the presence of both Arvanites and Albanians in the area, remarked that "every 100 or 150 years there is a wave of immigrants into Greece." The Asia Minor refugees were one such wave. Understanding this history helps to dispel the assumption that the Greek countryside existed as a historically stable and homogeneous society. As we will see, the end of the twentieth century has brought another wave of immigration that is in many ways comparable with that of the 1920s. In both cases the population of Greece swelled by around 10-20 percent and acquired a labor force that was used to transform the Greek economy. Also, in both cases the immigrants composed an ambivalent ethnic category, socially marginalized but with historic and economic claims to inclusion. The position of the state, however, is radically different in the two cases. In the case of the Asia Minor refugees, the state guaranteed their legality. In the case of the recent Albanian immigrants, the state guarantees their illegality.

Peasant Uprisings of the 1940s

During the first 100 years of the modern Greek state, constructions of national and religious identity subsumed ethnic and class divisions. After World War II, however, political affiliation came to the fore. The invasion and occupation of Greece by Axis forces in 1941 helped to solidify national identity, but at the same time created a polarization of political factions that was to dominate Greek society for the next fifty years. The liberation of Greece from Nazi occupation brought with it a political crisis that was only resolved after years of civil war. The contest between left and right was devastating, but in the end a form of right-wing state capitalism closely aligned with the political and economic interests of the United States emerged. The civil war and ensuing political struggles that continued until the end of the century are still fresh in people's minds, and narratives of partisan conflict are often used to explain the contemporary social situation.

The main resistance to the Axis occupation of Greece was organized by EAM (National Liberation Front), a communist-dominated popular front group that by the end of the occupation controlled most of Greece and numbered around 2 million members (30 percent of the population) (Vlavianos 1992: 24). From the mountains, ELAS (Greek Liberation Army, the military wing of EAM) launched raids on German troops stationed in the valley towns and battled rival Greek groups like the Security Battalions, a fiercely anticommunist militia organized by the Greek occupation government and equipped by the Germans. In the political vacuum created by the German invasion, mountainous areas were left largely to their own devices, except for having to endure occasional punitive raids by occupying forces. In many ways, EAM/ELAS was a throwback to the peasant movements of the Greek Revolution. Ad hoc groups assembled from particular villages and regions gathered around charismatic military chieftains, or kapetanoi[6], and operated in a semi-autonomous way under only nominal control of the urban political leadership (Eudes 1972). Kapetanoi were thus able to effectively control large areas and clandestine smuggling routes in mountainous areas, as well as administer crude systems of taxation and justice. Most of these leaders, well as their followers, were drawn from the peasantry. For some, the EAM represented an attempt at social transformation, foreshadowing a modern Greek society (Hart 1996). For others it was an attempt to grasp political power and settle old feuds.

In Argolida, as in the rest of rural Greece, resistance was centered in the mountains. Axis forces, first Italian and then German, occupied the main towns of Nauplio and Argos and established garrisons in the larger valley villages, like Agia Triada. These villages and towns coexisted with occupation forces peacefully, for the most part. Although many young men from the valley came to the mountains to fight against the occupation, the bulk of EAM/ELAS in Argolida came from the Arvanitiko villages of the mountains. One effect of this was a confirmation of the Arvanitiko Greek identity through a fervent and costly display of nationalism. The Arvanites became more "Greek" than their Greek neighbors in the valley by virtue of their activism and sacrifice. In Gerbesi, one older man remarked, "They're all ass-kissers down there. Our village here lost our young men fighting the occupation. They [in the valley] arranged themselves well and even profited." In fact, the EAM resistance drew heavily from ethnic minorities of the mountainous interior. In the south and west Arvanites were heavily represented while in the north many slavophone units were established.

Fighting in Argolida was sporadic and episodic. EAM/ELAS operated unhindered for the most part in the mountains, with occasional forays into the valley for ambushes and attacks on garrison towns. Most of the guerilla fighters were residents of local villages organized on an ad hoc basis, and the number of ELAS regular troops probably never amounted to more than a few hundred. Toward the end of the occupation fighting became more intense, and the Germans retaliated by burning the village of Prosimni and massacring civilians in Limnes and other villages (Zegkini 1968: 347-348). Both Prosimni and Limnes are large Arvanitiko villages near Gerbesi. Much of the violence during the occupation occurred between Greek groups. A unit of OPLA (Units for the Protection of the Popular Struggle), the ELAS internal security force, was formed in the village of Gerbesi during the occupation. OPLA conducted trials and sometimes executions of suspected collaborators at the church of St. John above the village. There were also conflicts between Arvanitiko villages. The nearby village of Arachneo (Hieli) was, and still is, the only Arvanitiko village in the area that is heavily right-wing. During the occupation townspeople captured and turned over to the Germans two suspected guerillas, who were executed. In retaliation ELAS burned Arachneo.

In Argolida, violence during the resistance and civil war was primarily used by particular political groups as a tool for enforcing dominance within and between villages. Much of the violence was used as retaliation or to demonstrate power and intimidate other residents, particularly in areas where neither EAM nor the German occupiers held clear authority. Data collected by Stathis Kalivas (2002) show that the largest number of killings happened in the "mid-elevation" villages that were a no-man's land between the German-controlled valley and the EAM-controlled mountains. For Argolida as a whole, 55 percent of victims were killed by EAM or EAM-affiliated individuals. Most of these were in the high and mid-elevation villages. In Gerbesi, for example, in 1944 twenty villagers were arrested and executed by their fellow villagers. The group included five women and five children, the youngest three years old. While the executed were accused of being rightists, they also had the misfortune of being the objects of a prewar vendetta conducted by several persons associated with the local EAM and OPLA.

Following the defeat of Axis forces in 1945, Greece faced a period of political instability. EAM controlled much of the country, but the possibility of a communist-dominated government receded quickly after the Yalta agreement between the USSR, Britain, and the US. The postwar conflicts of 1945-1949 began when a significant number of kapetanoi, reluctantly supported by the Communist Party leadership, resisted British attempts to impose a right-wing government on Greece. With the arrival of the British forces in 1945, ELAS units evaporated back into the mountains. Most of the fighters went home, retreating into the mountains with their weapons. A period of repression followed, and many former partisans were arrested and imprisoned (Iatrides 1972). A number of men from Midea were exiled or imprisoned in Nauplio, and several were executed for communist activities. By October 1947, however, many ELAS units were back under the command of the Democratic Army (DA), formed as the military wing of the Communist Party of Greece. As Greece slid into civil war following the exclusion of the communists from the postwar government and the severe repression of leftists, the mountain villages once again took up arms. The DA operated mostly out of former EAM villages like Gerbesi, Prosimni, and Limnes. In December of 1947, the DA attacked the village of Lirkeia, battling the local government-organized village self-defense units, and in January of 1948 attacked the railway junction at Koutsopodi. The biggest battle of the civil war in Argolida occurred in October 1948 when over 400 DA fighters unsuccessfully attacked the town of Argos. By January of 1949, the DA had been defeated.

In many ways the geopolitical and class divisions that broke out in open conflict during the chaotic political vacuum created by the occupation represented a return to the unfinished business of the Greek Revolution. The partisan struggles of the occupation and civil war operated on three different levels. First was the geopolitical contest between patron states with their corresponding local factions. The right-wing monarchists were supported by the patronage of Britain and the US, while the communists looked to the Soviet Union for support. Factional divisions linked to national political parties and their incumbent patronage networks have traditionally divided rural communities in Greece. During the occupation and civil war violence erupted in, and between, many villages as factions jockeyed for position within the power vacuum left by the occupation (Aschenbrenner 1987). Second was the class conflict, which in Argolida primarily took the form of an attempt by mountain agriculturalists and herders to overthrow the dominance of valley mercantile networks and establish independence. Finally, the civil conflict also contained an ethnic element manifested through a struggle over national identity between a Balkanized peasantry and a Westernized mercantile class.

Postwar State Capitalism

At the end of World War II Britain, exhausted from the war and unable to maintain its hegemonic position in the world economy, transferred its controlling interest in Greece to the United States.[7] The victory of the right-wing, US-supported government in the civil war ushered in a period of national consolidation. Minorities, Arvanites in the south and slavophones in the north, were actively repressed. Place names were Hellenized and minority languages were discouraged.[8]

In the postwar period the Greek economy continued to follow the distinctive semiperipheral structure of Mediterranean Europe. The economy was heavily dependent on American aid and emigrant remittances. Internally, the agricultural sector predominated, with a large peasantry still bound by precapitalist relations of production (Campbell 1964; Friedl 1962). The rural population was only partially integrated into market economies and served as a surplus pool of labor for international labor markets in developed countries and the uneven and unsteady urban industrial development of Greece itself. Domestic industry was dominated by small producers who made up the middle class together with a relatively large number of public employees, the result of the strongly clientelistic political structure.

Labor emigration continued to be an important economic activity until the 1970s. Greek workers have a long history of emigration. In the first two decades of the twentieth century, it is estimated that up to 25 percent of all young men aged 15-40 emigrated, mainly to the United States, but also to many other countries as far away as Australia (Clogg 1992: 71). Remittances from emigrants had a significant impact on Greece's balance of payments. At their peak in the 1920s, remittances covered more than half of Greece's trade deficit (Sweet-Escot 1954: 10). Emigration resumed after the disruptions of World War II, but with the imposition of quotas by the United States the main destinations became Australia, Canada, and Germany. Between 1951 and 1980 almost 12 percent of the population left (Clogg 1992: 149).

Besides providing remittances, emigration has been important for absorbing the vast rural labor surplus in Greece and has declined as birthrates have fallen in the postwar period. Most of those who emigrated never returned home, although a substantial number used emigration to acquire capital for investment upon their return. In Agia Triada, for example, I found three small business owners who had worked in Germany, or had relatives who worked in Germany, before returning home and opening small shops. In Gerbesi several men of one lineage had emigrated to Oregon, and their remittances had greatly increased the stature and wealth of the family.

The postwar period in Midea township was characterized by both the slow but steady expansion of commodity markets and state services and the maintenance of political repression. Political parties were important mechanisms of patronage and power. Valley villages like Agia Triada were relatively well connected with urban centers, both because of access to transportation routes and through allegiance to right-wing political parties. State-financed irrigation projects and other development schemes were often used to reward villages that voted for right-wing candidates. The local canning industry expanded, providing valuable jobs. Communist villages like Gerbesi could count on little in the way of state aid and villagers were often excluded from jobs in local industries and government because of their political affiliation. Still, people remember the 1950s as a period when relative equality between the villages was maintained. The residents of Gerbesi were able to make a good living off tobacco, as the prices then were relatively high. The valley produced mainly cotton and tobacco, but prices were low for cotton and the quality of their tobacco was inferior, bringing a lower price. During the 1950s, no villagers from Gerbesi or any of the surrounding villages reported working on the cotton harvests. Cotton was harvested in the valley by family members, local poor, and migrants from interior Peloponnesos.

The situation changed in the 1960s. Starting in the mid 1950s, citrus began to take over as the dominant crop in the valley, aided by expanded irrigation networks and high prices. Then, in the early 1960s, tobacco production was limited to 300 kg per family. The effect was the relative impoverishment of Gerbesi. A truck driver in Gerbesi remembers growing up in the 1960s:

> Towards the end of the 50s the valley people began to do better. They were all right-wing and besides, the oranges were selling better. In Midea there was great repression. The police used to beat us, send us to jail because we were

leftists. A lot of people suffered. When we were young [in the 1960s] and we went to the high school in Agia Triada we had nothing. The valley kids had new jeans, new bicycles, even a few motorbikes and we were jealous. They used to make fun of us and exclude us. We could never get girls. But we were tougher and more sly. I quit school early, I was bored and wanted to work. We used to do everything, whatever we could for a day wage. We worked in the canning factories, worked the harvest, construction, whatever. We worked hard. And you know what we did with the money? We blew it going out and buying things. I remember working all week to buy a pair of Levi's. Those were the big thing then. We would go all around, Argos, Nauplio. We were cool. I remember we all got into rock music in the 60s. Mitso had the pirate radio station, he always had the new music and we were like, what is this? We heard it all, Doors, Pink Floyd. We were in love with that stuff.

In the 1960s many villagers from Gerbesi worked as day laborers during the orange harvest. Villagers describe how trucks would come up from the valley before dawn to collect workers. This situation continued until the 1970s, when electricity and deep-well technology enabled villagers of Gerbesi to irrigate their lands and increase production, thus mitigating the economic disadvantages of the upper villages.

The US had a strong military interest in Greece during the Cold War and maintained tight control over the Greek military and government, which extended even to engineering electoral systems to favor US-backed candidates (Clogg 1992: 147). Opposition to US domination was regularly fueled by recurrent crises in Cyprus and in Greek-Turkish relations in general during which the Greek government was forced to follow US interests. In 1964, a center-left party took power, led by Georgios Papandreou—who, to the displeasure of American authorities, initiated a more independent foreign policy. The US subsequently helped to engineer his downfall, and the ensuing political crisis was only resolved through the imposition of a military coup in 1967 by officers with strong ties to the CIA (Couloumbis et al 1976). The Greek junta in many ways resembled the military dictatorships in Portugal and Spain (Poulantzas 1976). Within the context of the semiperipheral status of Southern Europe in the postwar period, military dictatorships facilitated the penetration of foreign capital into a relatively undeveloped economy. The ultranationalistic military junta ushered in a period of severe political repression in which thousands of communist activists were arrested and imprisoned, including about fifteen men from Gerbesi. The political repression of the military junta served US interests but also gave rise to strong popular opposition. After a bloody student uprising in Athens in 1973 and another crisis with Turkey following the invasion of Cyprus in 1974, which was partially provoked by the inept adventurism of the Greek leaders, the junta was forced to resign and a new government was formed under center-right politician Konstandinos Karamanlis.

The Karamanlis government ushered in a modest liberalization of Greek politics. The US, preoccupied with its own economic and political crisis, was less concerned with Greece, particularly after the détente of the Nixon years. Karamanlis negotiated the entry of Greece into the European Community in 1979 and normalized relations with its Balkan neighbors. During this period, however, the socialist party PASOK (Panhellenic Socialist Movement) under the leadership of Andreas Papandreou[9] steadily gained support, finally winning power in 1981. PASOK remained in power until 2004, with the exception of a short period in the early 1990s, and oversaw the incorporation of Greece into the European Community.

The EU Regime in Greece

The historical development of the Greek nation-state has been shaped by its semiperipheral position vis-à-vis successive capitalist world economies. Transnational or global forces have molded the development of state practices and national identity since its beginnings in the disintegration of the Ottoman Empire. The Greek nation-state, then, cannot be seen as a purely autochthonous development, but rather is the product of a particular geopolitical context. In addition, the history of the nation-state, and of Greek society in general, is also the product of contradiction between social groups, organized along ethnic, class, geographic, and gender divisions, in the struggle for social dominance. The current conflict over immigration is the latest manifestation of discord that dates back to the earliest days of the Greek nation-state. The "imaginings" of Greek nationalism have not only been a force of solidarity, but have also and perhaps more importantly been techniques in the reproduction of social inequality necessary for Greece's incorporation into the capitalist world economy.

The latest stage in this history has come about with Greece's entry into the European Union, a peculiar and innovative transnational form of political, economic, and social integration that has sought to project European power in the twenty-first century era of globalized capitalism. The EU operates as a sort of "supranational" state that is constituted as an integrated set of treaties, institutions, and policies among member states. In this sense it is a transnational form of governance relatively closed to the outside world. It also, however, conditions European participation in global economic networks, centralizing European capital and structuring its flow.

The context of globalized capital flows and the reorganization of capitalist economies since the 1970s is crucial to understanding the development of the European Union. From its postwar origins as the European Coal and Steel Community to the present day, the EU has promoted the development of transnational flows of capital, labor, and goods in Europe as a way of solving the problem of violent competition between national economies. Early economic successes prompted more ambitious plans for

integration. In 1970, the Werner Plan proposed complete economic unification, including a single currency, but failed amidst the disorganized
response to the global economic crisis of the 1970s. In the early 1990s the
plan was proposed again, this time more successfully. Throughout the
1990s, economic and monetary unification was strongly backed by the
business community "as a strategy to deal with the increasing lack of
competitiveness and the perceived decline of the economic power of
Europe vis-à-vis the United States and the Pacific Basin" (Verdun 2002: 4).

With the introduction of a single currency, the euro, and the elimination
of internal customs barriers, the EU has provided for the more or less
seamless circulation of capital within Europe while continuing a limited
amount of protection from external competition. For Greece and other
areas of what was traditionally the semiperiphery of Europe, membership
in the EU has facilitated the increased intrusion of European capital into
local economies as well as the "rationalization" of the industrial base and
the restructuring of many state-supported industries. In return, the EU
offers Greece the chance to develop economically through access to
expanded trade networks (Damianos and Hassapoyannes 1997). For these
reasons the left-wing political parties and trade unions vehemently
opposed entry in the early 1980s. In fact, the socialist party PASOK under
the leadership of Andreas Papandreou, which oversaw Greece's entry to
the EU in 1981, was initially elected with strong support from urban
workers and trade unions on an anti-EU platform. Later Papandreou
managed to retain power through the increased support of the rural population after EU subsidies and development programs began to flow to
rural areas (Louloudis and Maraveyas 1997).

Perhaps the most important aspect of the EU for Greece has been the
set of institutions and policies related to the Common Agricultural Policy
(CAP). First envisioned in the Treaty of Rome and instituted as a
European Community policy in 1958, the goals of the CAP are to increase
agricultural productivity, ensure a fair standard of living for producers,
stabilize agricultural markets, and provide low-priced food for urban
markets (Molle 1994). These somewhat contradictory goals, intended to
benefit producers and consumers simultaneously, have been pursued
with a high degree of market regulation and subsidies, making the CAP
one of the most expensive EU programs and accounting for almost half
of EU expenditures. The two main types of market controls that have
been employed are price supports, where minimum prices are guaranteed by various mechanisms and world prices are screened off, and producer bonuses, where producers are directly subsidized while prices
remain low. The persistence of this type of market regulation in the face
of global trends toward market liberalization is a testament to the political sensitivity of agricultural commodity prices for both urban consumers and rural producers.

For rural Greeks the rapid and direct infusion of EU cash into the countryside has had far-reaching effects. Greek farmers receive many subsidies

directly from EU institutions, largely bypassing the elaborate labyrinth of patronage systems that previously held sway in rural Greece. Farmers in Midea still remember the golden days of the early 1980s, when high prices for oranges were virtually guaranteed by the EU and excess production was bought and destroyed. In the early days, that is, until around the mid 1980s, CAP policies were mainly focused on various kinds of price supports meant to maintain farmers' incomes and promote stable production. More recently, the CAP has shifted toward direct producer subsidies rather than price supports. Overall, the CAP has had little success in reforming Greek agriculture. The volume of production has remained flat with only a slight increase in productivity. "Traditional" Mediterranean products have strengthened, but in general there has been a decrease in agricultural investment. Farmers' incomes have increased significantly, but this is almost totally due to direct and indirect subsidies, which now make up over 40 percent of farmers' incomes on average (Maraveyas 1994).

In time however, serious problems have arisen with the CAP. CAP policies have resulted in overproduction in many areas. Agriculture, which makes up a relatively low proportion of EU GDP, continues to be a major part of the EU budget and requires a high level of taxation. Prices for consumers remain relatively high. In addition, producer countries outside the EU have been hurt by both European protectionism and Europe's dumping of excess production on world markets. In the last several years moves to reform the CAP have been initiated, including decreasing price supports, increasing limits on production, and "buying out" farmers in unproductive sectors. Within the debate on reforming the CAP a new approach to the "rural problem" became dominant (Gray 2000). Agriculture became somewhat marginalized from EU policies and more attention was given to nonagricultural aspects of rural life, such as education, leisure activities, transportation, and small businesses. This has led to an increasing focus on rural areas as locations of consumption rather than production that has radically changed the way EU policy makers see social processes in rural Europe (Marsden 1999).

The economic unification of the EU has been accomplished by the development of a suprastate apparatus that is technocratic in character. The development and administration of policy, including the CAP, is largely carried out by the European Commission, an appointed body ostensibly working under the direction of the European Council but in reality a relatively autonomous bureaucracy. Thus, despite a commitment to "European" ideals of democracy, much of EU policy making is opaque, carried out by a mandarin-type class of appointed officials in consultation with various "interests," both national and Europe-wide (Bellier 2000). This "democratic deficit" insures a regime that "puts the emphasis on the technical at the expense of the political" (Tsoukalis 1997: 272), empowering technical experts and leading to a growing gap between economic and political integration. The European parliament is relatively weak and peripheral to policymaking, a fact reflected in low voter turnouts and the undeveloped international party structures in European elections (Smith 2003). Electoral politics continue to be the domain of increasingly hamstrung national governments, a result of the EU principle of "subsidiarity" or selective centralization by which state functions are relegated to different economies of scale (Holmes 2000). National states continue to be important sites for both implementing and resisting EU economic policies.

The expansion of the EU as a political and economic entity presents a stark contrast to previous attempts to unify Europe under a single system. Instead of force, the EU relies on the political consent of local populations. Social cohesion and stability are thus important goals of the EU not just in a moral sense springing from liberal ideals of democracy and equality, but also in order to facilitate the smooth expansion and functioning of markets and legitimize EU political institutions. There are three specific areas in which EU institutions focus their efforts to promote social cohesion, all of which can be seen as facets of "development." First, there is the definition and regularization of issues of citizenship, with the attendant rights to social services, between and within member states. Second, there is the promotion and facilitation of increased commodity consumption through the free flow of capital and goods. The third and perhaps most ephemeral area is the promotion of a "European" identity. This is sometimes conceptualized as "Europeanization" (Borneman and Fowler 1997; Featherstone 2003), a deliberately vague concept that nevertheless highlights the effects of contemporary European-wide policies and governance. However, questions remain concerning the extent and nature of Europeanization, especially given the resurgence of nationalism and neoracism throughout Europe.

From the beginning, the integration of Greece into the EU has been marked by ambivalence and alternating periods of enthusiasm and skepticism on the part of the Greek government and people (Frangakis and Papayannides 2003). The rapid accession of Greece in 1981, engineered by the conservative politician Karamanlis, was motivated mainly by political concerns. Karamanlis saw EU membership as a way to stabilize Greek politics, cement Greece's ties to Europe, and end Greece's dependency on an increasingly undependable US, particularly in light of the growing US tilt toward Turkey in foreign affairs (Kazakos and Ioakimidis 1994). On the economic side, the benefits were less clear, given the weak and underdeveloped position of Greek industry. Throughout the 1980s the PASOK government worked against international neoliberal trends by expanding the public sector, legislating wage increases, and in general following Keynesian methods of economic regulation (Fouskas 1997: 69). Among Europeans, Greece became "notorious for squandering its share of the structural funds" (Dinan 2004: 311). For many Greeks, however, Papandreou was admired for his ability to manipulate and exploit European interests. The election of Kostas Simitis to replace Papandreou as party leader in 1996 marked a shift away from populist and clientelistic politics toward a modernization of the state and party more in line with a European, technocratic model. Despite the continued language of social democracy employed by PASOK, during his tenure Simitis oversaw the spread of neoliberal economic policies, particularly through Greece's inclusion into the European Monetary Union (EMU), which is characteristic of the growing convergence of social democratic and conservative party programs in Greece (Tsakalotos 2001: 170).[10]

Despite the uneven and unsteady development of economic integration, the general trend in Greece has been toward the liberalization of markets, especially following the implementation of the EMU. EU integration has brought a dramatically increased market penetration of foreign products, mainly consumer goods, while domestic firms have been culled by squeezed profit margins (Giannitsis 1994). Since the mid 1990s both major political parties have tended to reflect an emerging consensus on the need to shift from a statist economic policy focused on employment and social services to one more in tune with a European liberal model emphasizing controls on inflation and deficit spending as well as the privatization and deregulation of industries (Kazakos 2004). This process has been uneven, however, and the state continues to support a large public sector. The state has followed a "twin-track strategy" by which formal changes in line with EU requirements are made but real structural reform is often blocked or diluted (Kazakos 2004: 915). The result so far has been that Greece continues to have a high unemployment rate (hovering around 10 percent) and consistently ranks near or at the bottom of the EU for most economic indicators.

At the beginning of the twenty-first century, new challenges are arising as a result of the impending expansion of the EU into Eastern Europe. With the collapse of Eastern European socialism after the Cold War, the EU has been inevitably pushed to incorporate Eastern states by both its claims to a pan-European unity and the need for new markets, as well as the Eastern states' aspirations for stability and prosperity. The outcome of this process has yet to be determined. One result of the enlargement process has been the continued and intensifying pressure to reform the CAP and the administration of structural funds, which are intended mainly for social stability and development. Because the Eastern European states are heavily agricultural, integration is certain to bring with it major cuts in EU agricultural price supports and subsidies (Dinan 1999: 347). Enlargement will also almost certainly affect the political and decision-making processes of the EU, making the current system of national vetoes and negotiation even more unwieldy. This could perhaps lead to a greater degree of political centralization, or alternately, to a dilution of political cohesion.

The enthusiasm for enlargement has varied among EU member states. Some countries, such as Germany, clearly stand to benefit, while others, such as France, fear marginalization. The Greek government has generally been supportive of enlargement. Enlargement would tend to decenter the

EU from its Western European core and strengthen Greece's traditional ties to Eastern Europe (Frangakis and Papayannides 2003: 175-176). However, there are also dangers for Greece, particularly concerning the potential accession of Turkey, a historic rival, and the threat to Greece's share of EU CAP and structural funds, which would surely be decreased.

The villagers of Midea see the EU as a faraway power with significant influence over their daily lives. The EU for them is a faceless institution that offers considerable benefits but also dangers, and their relationship with it must be constantly negotiated so that they can take advantage of the benefits while resisting the dangers. In this negotiation, villagers see the Greek state as a mediator. Villagers constantly call on the state and its officials to represent their interests vis-à-vis the EU, meanwhile also blaming them for their vulnerabilities. As villagers have adapted to the political-economic changes of the last quarter-century, of which the EU is a significant part, village life has changed considerably. Social differentiation among villagers, both in terms of class and gender, has narrowed due to demographic changes, greater rural-urban mobility, and an infusion of cash through price supports and development schemes. At the same time, villagers have become entangled in a new set of market relations as both producers and consumers. As we shall see in the following chapters, pressures from these markets have stimulated a new process of social differentiation through the increasing dependence on immigrant labor.

Notes

1. Township boundaries have shifted fairly frequently. The latest configuration dates from the early 1990s, when it was expanded to include the community (*koinotita*) of Arachneo.
2. All population figures are from the 2001 census (Greek Statistical Services).
3. The official name of the village of Gerbesi is "Midea." The name Midea derives from the ancient Mycenaean site adjacent to the village. "Gerbesi," the Arvaniti name, was replaced after World War II in an effort to Hellenize place names. Locals still refer to it as Gerbesi, however, and I have followed their terminology to avoid confusion with the township as a whole, which is also called "Midea township" (*Dimos Midea*). Manesi is also an Arvaniti name, but for unknown reasons was not Hellenized.
4. *Kleftes* (lit. "thieves") operated mainly in mountainous areas. They were charismatic local military leaders who worked sometimes for local merchants and landowners and sometimes on their own account. They often controlled overland trade routes and frequently came into conflict with Ottoman authorities. In some ways they were comparable to the early "mafia" or "violent peasant entrepreneurs" of Sicily (Blok 1974), but they developed under different circumstances, most notably the absence of a powerful landowning class. During the Revolution many were recruited to support the uprising against the Ottoman Empire.
5. For a description of immigration of Asia Minor refugees and land reform in Northern Greece, see Karakasidou (1997).

6. The *kapetanoi* in many ways resembled the *kleftes* of the revolutionary period (see p. 13). Like the *kleftes*, *kapetanoi* were charismatic leaders of ad hoc rural guerrilla groups and operated in semi-automony from the intellectual, and mostly urban, political leaders of the movements they represented. Both have became symbols of national resistance to foreign oppression.

7. The departure of Britain and arrival of the US as the dominant force in Greek politics and economy corresponds with the decline of what Arrighi (1994) calls the third systemic cycle of capitalist accumulation and rise of the fourth (US) cycle.

8. As noted before, village names were changed during this period in Argolida. Schoolchildren were also actively discouraged from using the Arvanitiko Albanian dialect. For the analogous situation in Northern Greece, see Karakasidou (1993).

9. Andreas Papandreou was the son of Georgios Papandreou, the former leader of the Center Union party and prime minister during the period leading up to the military coup of 1967.

10. In general elections in the fall of 2004, PASOK was replaced by the conservative New Democracy Party as the governing party, and Kostas Karamanlis, nephew of Konstandinos Karamanlis, became the prime minister.

Chapter II

AGRICULTURAL PRODUCTION AND
HOUSEHOLD ECONOMIES

Agriculture still provides the foundation for the local economy in Argolida, although in some areas other industries play important roles. The coastal villages from Epidavros to Asini have a significant tourist industry, and the towns of Nauplio and Argos rely mainly on service industries, commerce, and small manufacturing. For the interior towns and villages, however, agriculture remains the main productive activity. In Midea township, 57 percent of employed persons claim agriculture as their main source of income.[1] For many others, agriculture is a secondary income. While there is significant production of other crops, such as apricots, olives, grapes, vegetables, and others, the dominant crop in Argolida is citrus, mainly Merlin oranges. Virtually all agricultural production is carried out on small family-owned plots. As in the rest of Greece, landholdings tend to be small. The average plot size in Midea township is 6.4 *stremmata* (one *stremma* = 1,000 sq. meters, or one quarter of a hectare), but farming families tend to have multiple plots, a result of the trajectories of inheritance. In the citrus growing valley of Midea township the largest landholding is 60 stremmata. However, a few families actually control more, since ownership is often spread out among household members. For example, one wealthy family in Agia Triada works 150 stremmata. Many families produce on less than 10 stremmata.

While land ownership is relatively egalitarian in Argolida, the quality of land, as well as the ability of families to work it, varies greatly. In general, valley plots are more productive, having richer soil and easier access to water. As one moves into the upper elevations, land is less productive and has poorer access to water. In addition, households vary in their ability to work the land through the amount of labor they can muster. These differences affect the agricultural strategies of landowners and thus condition their interaction with global markets. In the upper-elevation villages, for example, citrus production is difficult or impossible, so farmers turn to other crops that are less lucrative, more labor intensive, and often more directly dependent on EU subsidy programs. Differences in production and labor among households also influence the nature of their interaction with immigrant workers. Citrus producers, for example, who subcontract harvesting to labor crews, deal with immigrant laborers differently than truck farmers who employ individual workers on a regular basis. Taking these variations into account is important for understanding how communities have adapted to both EU markets and transnational patterns of labor migration.

Historically, the dominance of particular crops has waxed and waned with both global and national market conditions. Local production of wheat, cotton, currants, tomatoes for paste, and tobacco, each once an important crop in Argolida, emerged, declined, and eventually disappeared under pressure from international markets. Today's crops are no different. Citrus began to spread in Argolida in the 1950s, replacing olives, cotton, and tobacco and raising the standard of living "like a blessing," as one local history puts it (Antonakatou 1973: 73). Citrus spread through the valley following irrigation projects from the late 1950s on, bringing wealth to many villages. The ascendancy of the citrus monoculture in many areas of Argolida can be attributed to the postwar expansion of European consumer markets and improvements in transportation that made those markets accessible to Greek farmers. Citrus was further stimulated in the 1980s as Eastern European markets were opened with the easing of the Cold War and the granting of trade credits. In the last decade, however, Greek citrus production has been under intense pressure from foreign producers, both inside the EU (Spain) and outside (Israel, Turkey). Both the Greek government and the EU have sought to promote crop diversification in Argolida, but so far with little success.

The dependency of the local economy on citrus has had a tremendous impact on social relations in Argolida. Citrus is the main export crop and thus the mainstay of the local economy. It is also the crop that, in keeping with the liberalization of global trade, is regulated the least. But the "deregulation" of the citrus industry does not mean there is a lack of regulation, but rather that there has been a shift in the forms and agents of regulation, from the state and farmers' cooperatives to the multinational companies that buy and market the fruit to consumers. The transnational "free" market of citrus has squeezed farmers financially and contributed to the growing marginalization of agricultural labor.[2]

Today the yearly Merlin orange production in Argolida ranges from 300,000 to 400,000 metric tons[3] (1 metric ton = 1.1 US ton). Other types of oranges, tangerines, and lemons make up another 50,000 tons of production. Midea township produces about 60,000 tons of oranges on 17,000 stremmata of groves. Production has been steady over the last several decades, rising slightly as the average age of the trees has increased. In the 2003 season Argolida produced around 400,000 tons of Merlin oranges. Merlin oranges must be consumed within two months, so while the bulk of the crop is shipped north to both Western and Eastern Europe, a large portion also goes to the domestic market. Whatever is not absorbed by fresh fruit markets is sold for juice to local factories under government subsidy. In 2003, 150,000 tons were exported, 40,000 tons went to the domestic market, and 100,000 tons were sold for juice. The remainder was spoiled by bad weather, purchased by the Greek government under a special subsidy program, and buried in landfills.

Variations in environmental conditions, such as water, soil condition, and winter temperatures, within both Argolida as a whole and the township of Midea, have contributed to significant differences in production from village to village. Citrus is the most important and, in recent times, the most lucrative crop, but not all villages can produce citrus. For example, in the village of Agia Triada 71 percent of village lands are planted with citrus, and in Manesi 14 percent, while in the village of Gerbesi, where water is less available, there is very little. Even within citrus growing areas there is great variation in the quality and quantity that can be produced on a given plot of land. Thus villages tend to produce different combinations and relative quantities of crops, contributing to the competitive and antagonistic nature of the social relations between them. While the valley villages tend to concentrate on citrus, the higher villages tend toward herding, olives, truck farming, and until recently, tobacco.

The dominance of particular crops has significant implications for social relations between villages. Historically, relations between villages have been strongly influenced by their relative access to land, water, and markets. Older residents of the higher villages remember the pre-citrus days as a time when the mountain villages were relatively well off thanks to their herds and superior tobacco.[4] As citrus production increased, residents of the higher villages began to work as day laborers for their richer neighbors in the valley. In general, valley villages, with their more bountiful water supplies, fertile land, and access to transportation, have been more successful and wealthy during periods of stability in world markets. There are some exceptions to this. In the early twentieth century the higher villages were able to enrich themselves by producing a higher-priced type of tobacco that did not do well in the valley. During periods of instability, mountain villages were wealthier than the valley due to their control of smuggling routes and their ability to produce for local markets. These differing economic strategies have contributed to the historical antagonism between villages that is often expressed in terms of ethnicity or political affiliation, with the valley being "Greek" and right-wing and the mountains being "Arvanitiko" and left-wing. More recently these antagonisms have been somewhat defused through the effects of subsidies and the availability of cheap immigrant labor.

Changing crop regimes have affected not only local society but the environment as well. Citrus crops need more water and fertilizer than other traditional crops, such as olives. Citrus trees must be watered at least every twenty days during the dry period from May to October and as a result have brought greater humidity to the valley and have severely taxed local water resources. Despite the expansion of the irrigation system over the last half-century, in many areas farmers still depend on electric-powered wells to water their trees. As a result the water table has steadily fallen and its salinity has increased as the aquifer is depleted. In addition, the regular and heavy use of fertilizers to maximize crop yields has polluted the ground water. Valley residents can no longer drink local water and now depend on bottled water, which is a considerable expense and requires disposing of massive amounts of plastic bottles, or they must drive to one of the few public fountains in the area that are still potable and fill containers.

Farmers in Midea township, as in other areas of Greece, are organized into local cooperatives. Each village has its own farmer's cooperative, and the larger villages often have several that are divided by political affiliation or produce. Up until the 1980s farmer's cooperatives were usually associated with political parties, and many villages had two: one associated with the right-wing party *Nea Democratia* (New Democracy) and another associated with the socialist party PASOK (Panhellenic Socialist Movement). Agia Triada has only one cooperative, started in 1937, that was historically associated with conservative parties. The cooperative of Gerbesi, on the other hand, was controlled by communists. The role of cooperatives has changed somewhat in the past several decades. They were originally used for political lobbying, bulk purchasing of supplies, and organizing local production. Since the early 1980s, however, cooperatives have taken on an increasingly bureaucratic role. Cooperatives often maintain weigh stations where weights are certified, and payments, taxes, and subsidies are usually channeled through local cooperatives. Part of the "pro-farmer" policy

Figure 2. View of the Argolid valley

of the socialist government when Greece entered the EU was a bureaucratic decentralization that put much of the control over subsidy distributions in the hands of cooperatives. At the same time there was lax oversight of the large amounts of money that began to move through cooperatives. The result was a series of scandals, many real but at least some exaggerated by media coverage that tended to discredit farmer's cooperatives in general. Today the independence of cooperatives seems to be in decline, as they have become mostly institutions for the certification and distribution of subsidies. Other tasks like product marketing, bulk buying of fertilizers, and political lobbying have become less and less common.

Valley Agriculture

In the valley village of Agia Triada 3,450 out of 3,950 cultivated stremmata produce citrus, almost entirely Merlin orange. In 2003 the village produced approximately 15,000 tons of citrus. There are 265 citrus producers (out of a total population of 1,267) registered with the local cooperative, who each produce an average of around 50 tons although individual amounts vary widely between one and 300 tons. Most of the registered producers are elderly, a reflection of both the aging of the farming population and the tendency of Greek farmers to hold on to ownership of landholdings even while sons are doing most of the labor. Land is rarely rented, although it is common for farmers to manage and work groves for relatives who have moved away to cities.

Citrus prices have been falling since their peak in the mid 1990s.[5] The peak-season price in 2003 was around €0.16 per kilo, going up to around €0.32 per kilo by the late season.[6] Costs of inputs, such as fertilizer, gasoline, and labor, have increased significantly, squeezing the profit margins of farmers. Prices are set by merchants and middlemen, who will quote prices that vary by the quantity and quality of each farmer's crop as well as the market. The size and quality of a farmer's crop can move the price paid up or down by several cents. A floor price for oranges is set by juice factories, which are subsidized by the government to maintain a minimum price for the protection of the farmers.

Production is greatly affected by soil condition, age of trees, and other factors but averages around 4 metric tons (4,000 kilos) per stremma. The actual amount can vary from around 3 tons to a high of 10 tons. There are 40-60 trees per stremma, and each produces from 60 to 200 kilos. The amount of care provided by the farmer is another important variable: careful pruning and fertilizing can increase yields, and conversely, poor care can decrease yields. Local farmers estimate that 30 stremmata (approximately 8 acres) are needed to provide minimum support for a family in the area. In 2003, information I collected from informants suggests that net income in the area averaged around €700 per stremma (€2,800 per acre). In practice, however, it is rare to find a family surviving solely on 30 stremmata. The vast majority of farmers at this level of land ownership also receive some other income through other work, pensions or rents.

Orange production has a seasonal rhythm that influences the social and economic life of the township. The heaviest labor occurs at harvest time. Merlin is harvested from February to April, and during this period Agia Triada is crowded with tractor-trailers hauling oranges to market and smaller trucks ferrying workers to and from the fields. Depending on field conditions, one person can harvest around 1,000-1,500 kilos per day; 30 stremmata take around 90 labor-days to harvest. Harvest labor can be mobilized in several different ways. Merchants will often provide labor crews and deduct €0.03 per kilo. Farmers can also opt to hire labor crews themselves. In addition farmers can harvest the crop themselves with their families and friends,[7] supplemented with day laborers as needed. The months following the harvest are devoted to pruning and fertilizing the trees and plowing the ground. This is less intensive work, and the pruning can be skipped some years. More farmers elect to do this work themselves, or to work only with trusted laborers, as pruning is something of an art and requires more skill and care than harvesting.

Citrus farmers are well aware that their production is inefficient. However, relatively few choose to take steps to improve production. Most

Figure 3. Laborer harvesting oranges

ways of improving production require more labor or involve taking risks in the market. One way to do this is to take particular care with pruning and fertilizing. One farmer told me he is experimenting with pruning and fertilizing techniques that would result in a stronger crop that could be harvested later in the season, when prices are higher. Another option is to change to another type of orange, one that might bring a higher price. Orange trees can be cut and new species grafted on to the stump. Planting a new species is risky for the farmer. Less common species can bring higher prices on the market, but may also be more difficult to sell, or may not do well in that location. New trees also take several years to begin producing fruit, which means a loss of income for the farmer. A new planting or grafting needs three years to start producing fruit, and then produces only around five kilos per tree. A tree takes around ten years to reach maturity and full production.

Some farmers are turning to organic farming methods, and many more think about it as a future possibility. Organic crops require more labor and must be certified over a three-year period. The crop is then sold to specialized merchants who market the organic produce in Europe. The organic farmers I spoke with complained that the market was disorganized and merchants unreliable, often going bankrupt. One farmer I spoke with had started the certification process but abandoned it after two years of low yields because he deemed the price premium inadequate. Given the widespread perception of declining prices together with the availability of low-cost immigrant labor, most citrus farmers choose to accept lower incomes rather than intensify or alter production. The benefit of this strategy is to free up family labor for potentially more lucrative endeavors.

There are several different strategies that households can adopt in citrus growing. Generally, given the seasonal rhythm of labor requirements, the small plot sizes, and the low returns, farming is a part-time occupation. In most households—about half by my estimates—the citrus crop is managed by elderly males while other household members, such as grown children and their spouses, are engaged in other occupations. The elderly male manages the groves, overseeing irrigation, pruning, and fertilizing. At harvest time the crop is sold to a merchant who brings in a work crew of immigrants to collect the fruit. Thus, farming provides an important but supplemental part of the household income, in combination with pensions and the income of other household members, often wages from labor in the nearby towns of Argos or Nauplio. Younger farmers combine farming with other occupations that are flexible enough to allow them to do both. An example of this strategy is two brothers who owned a small café and together worked their landholdings, totaling 60 stremmata. By taking turns at the café they could also manage the groves. Another example is a young farmer who managed 40 stremmata while holding a civil service position. In both cases harvesting was done by work crews sent by the merchant purchasing the crop. In these cases the farmer only carries out the less intensive and more flexible tasks of pruning, irrigating, fertilizing, etc.

It is uncommon for young farmers in Agia Triada to work exclusively in agriculture. Those who do have usually made a conscious decision to forgo a higher income in favor of a flexible work schedule with long periods of free time. However, these farmers can usually make more money per stremma because they can devote more time to care of the trees and can be more flexible with the timing of the harvest. One such farmer I interviewed supports a family of four on 25 stremmata. He has converted 8 stremmata to clementines, which he can harvest with family members and sell for up to €1 per kilo. Because he works full-time in the groves he can raise productivity through careful pruning and fertilizing. He also watches the weather and markets carefully in order to harvest at the maximum price. In 2003 he was able to wait until late in the season and received double the peak-season price of €0.16. At harvest time he employs as much family labor as possible by spreading the harvest out and selling to merchants in smaller quantities, hiring day labor only when necessary.

Hill Agriculture

As one moves up the mountain, citrus groves give way to fields of vegetables, olives, tobacco, and animal fodder. Landholdings are larger, but the lack of water reduces the productive potential. In the past, the lack of water in the higher villages of Manesi and Gerbesi limited agricultural production to herding and "dry" tobacco, enforcing social subordination to the wealthier valley. With the arrival of electricity in the late 1960s followed soon after by deep-well technology, the higher villages have attained a certain amount of economic autonomy. Wells are expensive, sometimes going down more than 300 meters, but they have been used to irrigate large areas of the upper elevations. They are usually cooperatively owned and operated by four or five neighboring landholders.

The most dynamic agricultural sector in the upper villages, and the only one not directly dependent on state and EU subsidies, is the truck farming of vegetables. In Agia Triada only 4 percent of cultivated land produces vegetables, while this figure goes up to 67 percent in Gerbesi.[8] Truck farming has become more common in Argolida over the last decade as new road construction has provided faster links to the urban areas of Corinth and Athens, now reachable in less than two hours. Local farmers produce a variety of seasonal vegetables and fruits, such as spinach and other greens, artichokes, okra, tomatoes, apricots, and others, to sell in the weekly neighborhood farmers' markets (*laikes*) of Athens and Corinth. In Manesi, some of this production occurs in hothouses. Full-time truck farmers usually make two or three trips to markets a week. In Gerbesi and Manesi there are approximately thirty full-time truck farmers, plus another thirty or so who do one or fewer runs per week.

Figure 4. Truck farmer in his field of artichokes

Truck farming is a labor-intensive activity. On the days when farmers are not traveling to markets they are usually busy caring for their fields. Almost all employ family labor, usually a husband and wife team supplemented by elderly parents and unmarried children. In addition most employ immigrant laborers on a regular basis. Usually they hire one or two immigrants for ongoing work, often housing them in older houses or outbuildings. Others hire immigrants for day labor as needed. As one truck farmer explained, "With a [immigrant] worker you can make a third trip to the market."

Until recently, tobacco was still a main crop in the mountain villages. In the early 1980s tobacco was the major crop of Gerbesi and Manesi. At that time a combination of heavy subsidies from the EU and the lifting of production quotas by the socialist government of PASOK, together with lax regulation that enabled farmers to over-report production, enabled mountain villages to make huge sums of money, leading to a frenzy of new home construction and providing political support for Greece's entry into the EU. Since 1993, however, tobacco production has been limited, and it is now being slowly eliminated by the state. In 1993 licenses were issued to tobacco farmers and production was frozen. Licenses are nontransferable, so production has dropped partly through attrition. In addition, the government and EU have been providing incentives for farmers to give up their licenses. The result is that tobacco, once a major crop, is being grown on only 1,000 stremmata in Midea township, producing 300-500 tons. What tobacco remains is produced in the higher villages, where other possible crops are limited. Tobacco is a labor-intensive crop that is generally grown and harvested by family labor with additional labor provided by immigrant workers as needed. The rhythm of planting, harvesting, threading,[9] and drying tobacco once defined village life the way citrus does in the valley (Athanasopoulou 2002). Few families survive solely on tobacco any more, but many in Gerbesi still receive some tobacco income and hold on to their production quotas in order to collect the subsidies.

Olive groves also increase as one moves further up the mountain. In Agia Triada 14 percent of the land is in olive cultivation, while in Manesi and Gerbesi the amount is 24 percent. In the valley many olive groves were replaced with citrus, but the higher elevations, and areas of the valley without adequate water, continue to produce olives. Most olive species do not require irrigation in Argolida, and many families with enough land maintain small groves for their own consumption. Olives require intensive labor at harvest during the late fall, but little labor at other times. Virtually all olives are harvested with migrant labor. However, prices are low and few people make a living producing olives. Olive oil production is subsidized at one euro per kilo, regardless of the amount, providing many residents with a little extra income. Recently the EU has moved to regulate olive oil production. Owners are being required to register their groves in order to receive the subsidy, a first step toward production limits.

At the higher elevations, agriculture gives way to herding of sheep and goats. In Gerbesi many families keep small numbers of sheep or goats for home consumption, and between fifteen and twenty families keep larger herds of over twenty head. Five families survive solely on herding, with over 200 head each. Milk is either sold to merchants, who come to the village in trucks each day to collect the day's production, or taken to local collection stations. Many families sell as little as 20 liters of milk a day. In 2003 milk prices were just over one euro per kilo, with goat milk receiving less due to its lower fat content. A prime ewe can produce two kilos a day for much of the year. Meat is sold to merchants or to local butchers, or used for home consumption. In addition to income from the milk and meat, there is a yearly per head subsidy from the EU of approximately €30 per head, which herders depend on. The number of animals a farmer can claim is fixed at the size of their 1991 herd. The only exceptions are young herders, who can increase their herds by enrolling in the New Farmers program—or by certifying organic production, in which case a herder can have up to 750 head.

Like citrus farmers, herders have been squeezed between flat prices and rising expenses over the last twenty years. The costs of medicine, feed, and fuel have risen much more quickly than milk and meat prices. In order to boost production by supplementing grazing, animals are given industrial feed, which is a major expense at around €0.10 per kilo. Herders, unless they own their own grazing lands, must also rent land on which to grow fodder and graze their livestock. Full-time herders tend to be the poorer residents of the village, and herding is the only activity that does not employ migrants as day labor. Because herding involves a steady, daily work routine, hiring non-family labor, even at the low rates paid to immigrants, would seriously decrease earnings.

Thus herding is still mostly a family occupation. The daily milking and grazing requires the steady and heavy labor of several individuals. However, few young men are becoming herders. For one thing, herding is considered an undesirable occupation due to the low income and steady routine of work. As one herder explained, "There are no holidays for shepherds; Easter, Christmas, whatever, you must go to the sheep." For another, it is considered dirty, smelly work, and young herders have a notoriously difficult time finding brides. Some herders have married immigrant Albanian women, who are said to be less averse to hard work.

The Role of EU Subsidies in Local Agriculture

Farmers in Argolida experience EU policies most directly through the various subsidy and price support programs of the CAP. These programs work in various ways for different crops and are supplemented by various Greek government programs. For oranges, price support is provided through subsidies to juice producers, who are able to absorb excess production and effectively set floor prices. Juice factories absorbed about one quarter of the 2003 production, around 100,000 kilos. Oranges sold for juice are usually inferior in quality to those sold as fruit, and factories pay the farmer about €0.10. Of this sum around €0.08 is subsidized. The other form of support is payment for oranges destroyed by bad weather. In the winter of 2003 heavy rains destroyed about 100,000 tons of oranges. The spoiled oranges were purchased by the state-run ELGA (Greek Agricultural Compensation) fund at a price of €0.13 per kilo, which was about 20 percent less than the peak-season market price.

The collection, certification, and disposal of spoiled oranges in 2003 were organized through the local farmer's cooperatives in each community. Farmers collected their spoiled fruit off the ground and once a week took them to the local cooperative to be weighed and loaded on trucks. The oranges were then transported to landfills for burial. The program was available to all communities even though the destruction had been centered in a few areas that suffered most from excessive rainfall and frost. This meant that in many areas farmers collected and took in fruit that had fallen off the trees in the course of normal spoilage, which enabled them to collect a little extra money. In addition, the compensation guarantee encouraged some farmers to risk frosts and wait for market prices to go up, since they felt they had a guaranteed price to fall back on if their strategy failed and their crop was destroyed.

Other crops, like tobacco and olive oil, are protected by direct subsidies that guarantee minimum prices to the farmer in excess of the market price. These subsidies are given on a per kilo basis after certification of weight by local farmer's cooperatives. Tobacco subsidy policy has had an important impact on the higher villages, and its history is a good illustration of how EU policies have affected Midea township. Tobacco was a source of wealth for the upper villages, and for the first half of the twentieth century insured their high socioeconomic status within Argolida. Beginning in 1960, the government began to restrict production, limiting it to 300 kilos per family. The mountain villages became impoverished compared to the valley, and their residents began to work as day laborers in the citrus groves. With Greece's accession to the EU, tobacco subsidies were increased to 350 drachmas per kilo. At the same time, the socialist government under Papandreou lifted production limits. The result was that tobacco producers could produce as much as they liked and were guaranteed a good price. In addition there was very lax supervision of the subsidy program, so that farmers, especially those with positions or connections in the cooperative, were able to embezzle large amounts of money. For example, farmers would sometimes deliver 500 kilos and be certified by cooperative officials for two tons. Under this policy the mountain villages benefited enormously, gained wealth, and stopped working for the valley farmers.

In addition to direct subsidies and price supports there are also development programs that provide support to agriculture in the area. For example, the recent expansion of the national highway system that was aided by EU development funds has made it much easier for local truck farmers to commute to the Athens farmers' markets. Other programs focus on developing infrastructure in targeted communities. In the community of Dimena in the northeast of Argolida, a program was underway in 2003, funded by the EU, to upgrade the irrigation and road systems. These programs benefit local farmers by making it easier and cheaper to produce. In Midea township one such project, started in the early 1990s, was the construction of a roadway to connect the major archeological sites of Mycenes, Tirintha, and Midea, with the goal of increasing tourism in the area by facilitating travel between the sites. However, the project was abandoned in midstream for reasons that are unclear, and the roadway now ends at an orange grove on the outskirts of Agia Triada. At the time the government announced that funding for the roadway had been depleted, but there was also some opposition from valley landowners whose land was in the roadway path. Some residents of the higher-elevation villages assert that local politics played a role and that the project was stopped because it would have increased their economic independence. The villagers of Gerbesi are still hoping for completion of the roadway, as they consider this to be crucial for the development of a local tourist industry.

Finally, there are also programs aimed at developing local industries and modernizing agricultural production. The New Farmers program gives aid and privileges to young farmers who establish themselves on a professional basis. Young farmers must start off with a minimum amount of land or livestock and farm on a full-time basis. They are then eligible for grants in order to purchase equipment and build facilities, and are also exempt from certain restrictions on production. A herder, for example, must start with at least 70 head of livestock. Through the program he can get grants to build stables and milking facilities and is also exempt from the restrictions on herd increase. Other grant programs are available that pay a substantial amount of the start-up costs for small businesses that open in mid- or high-elevation villages.

The implementation of the CAP has had a number of effects on social relations within and between villages. First and perhaps foremost it has helped to disrupt traditional patterns of patronage. State aid has become an important source of income for villagers, who have effectively used it to bypass the old patronage system linked to political parties. On the one hand, since a substantial part of the farmer's income comes from EU-regulated funds, he or she is no longer required to establish relations with local political operatives and other power brokers. This has contributed to the decline in the relevance of political parties and the rise of a technocratic political administration. Party affiliation was once a crucial aspect of community membership and defined one's social identity. Today it is difficult even to find the local offices of the political parties.

On the other hand, the graft that accompanied the introduction of EU subsidy programs in the 1980s effectively discredited many local and national institutions like farmers' cooperatives and political parties. All the farmers I spoke with agreed that the early days of EU subsidies were characterized by graft and corruption. Lax rules and supervision on the part of the state made embezzlement easy. One farmer described the situation thus: "When we went into the EU, there was a lot of money that went to the farmers. At that time there was opposition, people were unsure how things would work. The government basically said, 'Here, take this money and shut up.' There was no way to organize it, no way to distribute the money fairly, so they just said, 'Here, take the money, divide it up however you want.' And so of course everyone just took as much as they could through various schemes and tricks. The ones with connections to the cooperatives were in a position to steal the most." Virtually every farmer I spoke with remembers the 1980s as a time when people with the right "connections" (*mesa*) were able to embezzle huge amounts of money from EU funds. A common explanation was that when it came to the Greeks the Europeans were naïve and were taken advantage of. "We have only ourselves to blame," said one man: "Our leaders ate and ate [the money] with no thought of the future." The result, according to local farmers, was that many cooperatives collapsed from internal graft and resulting bankruptcies, whereas the EU finally wised up and tightened control over the disbursement of subsidies. A few farmers see a more conspiratorial explanation, a form of entrapment by EU largess that effectively decapitated local leaders. Whether intentional or not, local cooperative leaders were discredited, and many cooperatives collapsed.

In addition, state aid has altered the relationship between villages by eliminating some of the economic inequalities between them. The tobacco money especially benefited the poorer mountain villagers in Argolida who had previously depended on day labor in the valley to supplement their incomes. Dependence on EU subsidies lessened the traditional dominance of the valley by eliminating the poverty of the higher villages. Much of the money was spent on consumer goods, like household appliances and automobiles, and on constructing new houses. A resident of Gerbesi described the change:

> In the 80s the socialists came to power and a lot of money fell on the upper villages. Money, I tell you! The tobacco market opened up and people were producing as much as they wanted. In the high village they had a contest to see who could build the most opulent house. Those people, they used to be total hicks. They would come down in old clothes, uneducated, none of them could read or write and they lived in shacks. Poverty, I tell you. Then the money hit, and bam! You go there now and it's all new houses in the village. Don't get me wrong, we have good relations with them. P.'s mother is from there and so is M.'s father. We have close relations with them and they were all leftists too. But they were very backward, worse than here. Today you go there and the whole village is new, but you go into these big beautiful houses and they are all peasants sitting around. A peasant in a big beautiful house!

As the speaker indicates, new wealth from EU subsidies did not completely erase the lower status of mountain villagers. However, the economic independence and access to consumer goods greatly reduced the kind of class subordination that existed in the postwar period.

The infusion of wealth into the rural communities of Greece came at a price, for along with subsidies came regulation. Since the 1980s, crops that receive direct subsidies have also had indirect production quotas. In the case of sheep and goats, subsidies are limited to the herd size declared when the quota went into effect. Herders may have more animals, but will be subsidized only up to their quota. Tobacco farmers are limited in the same way, and also cannot pass on their quotas to others. Olive producers too are being required to register their production, the first step toward regulating oil production.[10] In these cases EU policy makers, interpreting market needs, indirectly regulate what is produced and how much. Rather than intervening directly in markets, for example by setting prices or buying excess production, EU subsidies go directly to the producer, both enabling the transition to free markets for agricultural products and preventing the social dislocations that would normally result. The EU can also influence how crops are produced, for example through the organic produce certification process and various environmental regulations. Thus the options and decisions available to farmers and national states are indirectly shaped by EU policies. For the farmers, there is also a sense that global consumers are increasingly influencing the market at the expense of producers. One orange farmer in Manesi remarked to me that "these days the German consumer is setting the prices." Another lamented that consumers preferred large oranges, even if they were of inferior quality, saying that he was thinking of changing his trees because of the size of the oranges.

Despite the increased surveillance and regulation of producers entailed by subsidy programs, farmers participate in them because of the protection they offer from the market. Market forces are experienced by farmers in Midea township in an anarchic manner. The downward pressure on prices exerted by global markets is a constant and faceless threat to local farmers. There is little in terms of an organized response. Early attempts by state and state-affiliated organizations to mediate market forces have mostly ended in failure. For example, the predominance of Merlin oranges has made the area vulnerable to market fluctuations and kept prices low, since the whole crop must be harvested and sold within a relatively short period of time. In the mid 1980s there was a concerted effort by the EU and the Greek Ministry of Agriculture to diversify the orange crops in order to spread out the orange harvest and minimize threats of overproduction. However, at the same time the EU and USSR signed new trade agreements that opened up the Soviet bloc to citrus imports. Trade credits stimulated exports and propped up the price of oranges, but also had the effect of discouraging diversification among farmers, who were making good money and saw no reason to lose income by replacing their trees. When exports to Russia declined in the mid 1990s, farmers were left with the same problems, but by then the EU was no longer interested in funding diversification programs. Local officials assert that the failure of the first program has made EU policy makers hesitant to grant new funding. As of now, although new programs are being discussed, none have materialized.

In general, the capacity of state bodies to carry out long-term planning in agriculture has declined since Greece's first decade of EU membership. A local official in charge of agricultural development in Argolida bitterly complained in an interview of the lack of planning:

> In the past the Ministry of Agriculture did have some policy-making and planning process and was involved in the politics of production, but unfortunately that has broken into fifteen pieces, as we say. Private industry has taken on some of that role, but the ministry no longer really functions in that capacity. Agricultural policy, in other words, is left to chance. In general we are in a situation where there is absolutely no planning. There was once the ability on the part of the government to make policy, even if it wasn't always successful. At least there were some attempts. Now there is nothing. It is just the free market. But even a free market has some rules. We don't even have that. Of course that is partly the Greek character. We operate on instinct and have an aversion to rules.

The same official went on to explain that the lack of planning has put Greek agriculture at a disadvantage compared to other producers like

Spain and Israel. There was an attempt in the early 1980s to organize the Greek citrus market. A semiprivate export company with state funding, AGREX, was established in order to standardize production and market Greek citrus products in Europe. The committee that directed the company included exporters, representatives of farmer's cooperatives, government officials, and the Agricultural Bank. Steps were taken to standardize exports, impose quality control, and establish a market identity for Greek products. However, AGREX was dissolved in 1987 for reasons that are still obscure. Like the farmer's cooperatives, there were financial scandals involving the company, but it has also been claimed that pressure was exerted by multinational companies that wanted more open markets.

Lack of long-term planning has made farmers even more dependent on subsidies as a way to weather the anarchic conditions of the market. In a sense the relationship of farmers with EU institutions has become a new form of patronage in which political support is bought through favors that enable agricultural families to prosper. Farmers are faced with a fundamental contradiction between their participation in a free market economy on the one hand, and their continuing dependence on state subsidies on the other. Subsidies, ostensibly intended to promote a smooth transition to an efficient and "rational" agriculture, have actually had the opposite effect of sustaining an agricultural system that, in market terms, is inefficient and disorganized. The result has been an incomplete transition to a form of "capitalistic" farming and the continuation of the peculiar nature of Greek agriculture, characterized as it is by small, dispersed landholdings and the pluriactivity of agricultural households.

Household Economies and the Mobilization of Agricultural Labor

The agricultural economy is diffused through most of the households of Midea township. Indeed, there are few families that do not participate directly in agriculture. At the same time, there are few families whose livelihoods derive exclusively from agriculture, and these tend to be among the poorer families in the area. But while agriculture is the foundation of the local economy, agricultural labor has a very low status. Local residents attribute this to the low profit levels of agricultural production, which are seen as inadequate for contemporary needs. Commodity consumption has risen steadily in the villages, as have the costs and amounts of supplies for farming. Market prices for agricultural products, on the other hand, have remained flat as a result of pressures to provide the lowest cost to urban consumers. Subsidies from the EU help to improve the low profitability of agricultural labor, but in order to maintain profits labor costs are squeezed. In addition, traditional pools of low-cost agricultural labor, particularly women, children, and land-poor peasants, are no longer available. The solution to this labor crisis has been the massive immigration of Eastern European laborers.

The household has historically been the basic unit of production in rural Greece, in terms of both subsistence and production for markets. In the household, the politics of production were governed by the elaboration of strong ideologies of kinship and gender that organized the division of labor and defined social relationships. Despite the postwar modernization of the Greek economy and the changes initiated since accession to the EU, the household continues to be an important unit of production, particularly in agriculture. This can be seen in Argolida, where there is an almost total absence of large-scale production. Farms are family owned and operated. Yet while the household has remained the basic productive unit in agriculture, its nature has changed. Household production today is oriented almost exclusively to the market, at the expense of subsistence production. Families still produce a substantial part of their own consumption and many families have small kitchen gardens or a few chickens. But in most households I observed, the bulk of the food consumed today comes from the supermarket. As a villager explained to me, the costs of production are too high: "Say I want to raise my own meat, for my family. That meat is not free. I have to buy the lamb and buy feed for the lamb, I have to buy medicines, I have to take the time to take care of it. In the end it is not much cheaper than the supermarket. My mother grows a few vegetables, but mostly out of habit. In the end she only saves a few euro." The elderly members of households continue to provide much of the food on the table, but this share is dwindling, especially among families with young children, who tend to be avid consumers of store-bought foods.

The accessibility and low cost of foodstuffs available in the supermarkets, as well as a demand for commercially produced and packaged foods, has made subsistence farming more and more impractical. A major exception to this is olive oil, which is still produced by many families for household consumption. Oil is produced for home consumption because it is a significant expense, given its high cost and the quantities consumed, and also because for many Greeks oil is a powerful cultural symbol embodying both an elementary foodstuff and a connection to the land.

In Midea township today there are three basic patterns of household economy. Each of these patterns has been affected by processes of globalization in slightly different ways. I distinguish between these three by using the terms *elderly* household, *pluriactive* household, and *agriculturalist* household in order to illuminate the different interests of each. There are of course significant variations within the categories, as well as overlaps between them. Household production strategies are partly influenced by the geographical constraints on market participation outlined in the preceding section. For example, agriculturalist households are much more common in the higher-elevation villages, where truck farming is a more attractive strategy. Likewise, in the valley the rhythm of citrus production and accessibility of service industry jobs tend to make pluriactivity a more attractive option. The different markets that farmers can participate in influence household organization, and conversely, the structure of the household influences the type of market farmers can participate in. Patterns of household economy also have implications for social relations beyond the household, particularly concerning immigrants. Some households establish ongoing relationships with a small number of regularly employed workers, while others employ anonymous workers as harvest crews.

Elderly households are those made up exclusively of retired couples with children who no longer live in the area. I estimate that in Midea township such households make up around 30 percent of the total.[11] Elderly households depend on a combination of pensions and agriculture for survival, and sometimes receive small amounts of aid from grown children. Pensions tend to be low, particularly agricultural pensions, which average around €400 per month. Agriculture is thus often an important source of supplementary income. Because their children are far away, usually working in Athens, labor is in short supply. Sometimes elderly households rent out their lands, but it is common for people to work their land into their seventies and even eighties. They can sometimes count on help from friends and relatives, but this is rare. For strenuous work such as harvesting, it is necessary for these households to hire labor, almost always immigrants. Elderly households vary most significantly in the amount of pension they receive. Those who have retired from high-paying jobs in Athens live relatively comfortably on their pensions and spend little effort on farming, sometimes renting out their land. Those who retire on agricultural pensions face more economic difficulties and generally must continue to farm.

The large number of elderly households in the village, and of elderly persons in general, often gives the impression that the villages are dying out. Declining birthrates and urban migration both act to push the average age of village residents higher. However, on closer inspection the situation is more complex. In many of the elderly households I interviewed, almost half in fact, members reported that they had spent substantial parts of their lives outside the village, returning for retirement. Many, for example, had worked in Athens for at least part of their lives. Upon retirement these couples had decided to return to the village for several reasons. Peace and quiet was the most common, but residents also cited the sociality of the village and the ability to live more cheaply. Thus, the high proportion of pensioners is not necessarily indicative of a quickly aging population, but is also partly a reflection of urban-rural movements over the life span.

Pluriactive households—those that combine agriculture with some other productive activity such as wage-labor, a profession, or a small business—make up the majority of households in Midea township. More households are pluriactive in Agia Triada than in the higher villages because of the centralization of civil administration and businesses there. In pluriactive households, agriculture tends to be the domain of the older generation. Children, even if they live at home, usually do not take over management of fields until their parents are incapacitated. For example, a civil servant in Agia Triada, who supplements his income with 40 stremmata of oranges, tangerines, and olives, complained to me that his grown son who has graduated from university and is looking for a position as a teacher "doesn't even know where all the fields are." These households also vary greatly in the degree of dependence on agriculture. For those heads of household with high-paying jobs, mainly professionals, agriculture provides only a small additional income, while for others the wage labor of wives and children in service industries supplements the main income from agriculture. In general, the less dependent a pluriactive household is on income from agriculture, the more likely it is to use immigrant labor for farming. Those who depend heavily on agriculture are loath to spend money hiring workers and will only do so at times of peak labor demand, such as the harvest.

In most pluriactive households I visited, members cited the need for consumer goods as the driving force behind pluriactivity. This is especially true for families with children, who are perceived to require great amounts of expenditure. While children in all households are encouraged to go into the professions and service industries, this is particularly true for pluriactive households, whose status rests on their foothold in such activities. Pluriactive families are more likely to spend money on after-school tutoring (*frontistiria*), fashionable clothing, motorbikes, and pocket money for their children. In addition, as adult family members become more involved in economic activities outside of agriculture, they themselves require more consumer goods. In the professions and service industries, workers are expected to maintain a degree of status through consumer goods such as clothes, appliances, cellular telephones, and automobiles that agriculturalists do not necessarily require.

Finally there are agriculturalist households, those that depend exclusively or nearly exclusively on agriculture and its subsidies for a living. These households are more common in the higher villages such as Manesi and Gerbesi, where they account for around 30 percent of households. In Agia Triada they account for only around 15 percent of households. A few families live almost exclusively from growing oranges, but these are the exceptions. Most agriculturalist households are involved in truck farming or herding, occupations that require steady, intensive labor. There are about twenty households that live from truck farming in Agia Triada. Some of these sell oranges, but most operate hothouses and sell their produce in farmers' markets in Athens. Hothouses require labor that is especially difficult and uncomfortable, and immigrants are used almost exclusively. In the upper villages there are fewer hothouses. There vegetables are grown in fields and trucked to farmers' markets. In this type of truck farming more family labor is used. For example, a family I interviewed in Gerbesi that produces vegetables for farmers' markets rarely hires immigrants. Most of the work is done by the husband and wife, sometimes aided by their 25-year-old son. I found only a few cases of daughters working in agriculture.

Herders are found almost exclusively in the higher villages where there is adequate land for grazing and planting of feed crops. Among all households, herders tend to rely the most on family labor, generally a husband-wife team sometimes helped by grown children. Immigrants are seldom used. Herds require milking twice a day during most of the year, and milking the average herd just once takes two people several hours. With such labor requirements the hiring of day labor is difficult, as the job is not a full day's work yet precludes other employment. Herding families also tend to be among the poorer households in Midea township, along with some of the pensioners. Of all the households, herders tend to have the most difficulty financing their children's status consumption. Their children are less likely to attend private after-school tutoring and lack many of the luxuries enjoyed by other children in the village, especially teenagers.

The gendered division of labor varies between the types of households. In households that depend heavily on agriculture, such as the poorer elderly households and agriculturalist households, women participate and often take on the bulk of the farm labor. In pluriactive households and the wealthier elderly and agriculturalist households, women are less likely to participate in agriculture. In most pluriactive households women (except the older generation) work outside the home in service jobs. Most are wage laborers in the local service industries, civil servants, or professionals in education, medicine, etc. At the same time there is a strong feeling, expressed by both men and women, that women's primary responsibility should be caring for children. The education and care of children receives a great deal of attention from families, and it is generally the mother that spends the most time in childcare tasks such as preparing food and helping with homework.[12] Thus women often take on a "double duty" of wage labor and the bulk of housework and childcare. Men who work in jobs outside the household, on the other hand, generally replace their household labor by hiring immigrants.

The departure of women and children from agricultural labor is generally seen as a mark of upward mobility. The withdrawal of family labor from agriculture is reinforced by strong perceptions that menial agricultural labor is inappropriate for Greeks. Labor tasks are commonly separated into "Greek work" and "Albanian work." Albanian, or immigrant, labor generally requires the least skill and is the most difficult and strenuous. Harvesting oranges, for example, is something that no Greek will do on a day-wage basis. Only the landowner and occasionally his or her family and friends will stoop to harvesting oranges. Tasks like pruning, which require more skill and care, will sometimes be done by immigrants, but Greeks complain that they want too much money (€40-50 a day as opposed to €30 a day for harvesting) and cannot be trusted to take appropriate care with the trees. The low status of "Albanian" tasks means that even unemployed Greeks will refuse such work. There are some exceptions to this pattern. Two families I met make efforts to harvest without hiring immigrants, relying instead on family and friends, but even these resorted to hiring a few immigrants during the peak weeks of the harvest. Others claim to not hire immigrants on principle. One older man in Gerbesi told me he has never hired a single Albanian. But when I asked who harvests his apricots, he replied that he sold them on the tree to merchants. The merchants then bring their own crews, immigrants of course, to harvest.

The perception of value in agricultural labor is worth a closer look. Greeks routinely look down on agricultural work as having little value. The reason given is almost always the low prices offered for agricultural products, as a herder in Gerbesi explained: "Look, agriculture is just not profitable anymore. My herd occupies a family of four; it's a full-time job for four people. If we all had regular jobs we would be making more money, even if we were making the basic salary. Plus it's a constant headache, you never get off work. We have to work 365 days a year, twenty four hours a day." Orange picking is a more extreme example. Wages for picking oranges, at €25-30 per day with no benefits, are considered low for Greeks, and the work is hard and uncomfortable. Greeks do work for €25 per day in the local fruit packing factories, but this work is considered easier, and companies pay full social security taxes. Packing factories rarely employ immigrants. The difficulty and discomfort of work in the fields thus seems to be a primary reason that local Greeks avoid working the harvests at the present wages.

Most farmers say that it is the low market price of oranges that keeps the wages down, although others, unemployed workers in particular, cite the availability of low-cost immigrants as the reason. Each argument uses a different calculus. From the data I collected, I estimate that a worker harvesting oranges produces €150-180 per day for the farmer at the peak season, and up to twice this much in a good year. Of this sum, €30-35 goes to the worker at the present rates. I estimate that on average, another €15-20 goes to maintenance costs such as pruning, fertilizing, water, etc. The rate of profit for the farmer is then somewhere around €100-130 per worker day. Per stremma profit rates for Merlin oranges average around €400-500 on expenses of €180-220, although this can vary widely depending on weather, age of trees, etc.

Greeks claim that agricultural wages are very low, well below what is needed to live, especially given the seasonal nature of the work. Based on interviews with young people and the underemployed, wages would have to be at least double in order to attract Greek laborers. For the Greek farmer, such an increase in the cost of labor would significantly reduce profits, reducing the ability of the household to keep up with consumption demands. The solution to this dilemma has been the large-scale immigration of Eastern Europeans, who are willing to work for much less due to their poverty and the lower costs of social reproduction in their homelands. Through a variety of pressures, immigrants have been "accustomed" to a much lower standard of living. The squeezing of the farmer by low market prices on the one hand and increased production costs on the other has thus been accommodated through reducing the price of labor by the use of immigrants.

The perception of the declining profitability of agriculture has encouraged families to reallocate their labor into other areas, such as skilled wage-labor, small businesses, and professions, while maintaining agriculture as a secure economic base. Most parents I spoke with actively discourage their children from going into agriculture. This redirection of family labor is strongest in pluriactive households. As one farmer in Agia Triada told me: "No, I don't want my sons to go into farming. Let them do something else. There's no future here. It is impossible to make a good living here and in a few years this will all be gone, it will disappear. If they can't get in anyplace else, OK, they always have farming to fall back on, but I wouldn't wish that even on my enemy."

In many households I interviewed even unemployed grown children were discouraged from helping out in the fields. For example, a civil servant with orange groves in Agia Triada said he gave his 24-year-old son an allowance for spending money, but did not ask him to help in the fields since he was inexperienced and had no interest in agriculture. In agriculturist households children were encouraged to work in the fields only if they were unsuccessful in school. When I asked a herder in Gerbesi about the future he foresaw for his children, he responded: "It depends on school, how well they study. My older boy does not like to read. School, zero. So I have him working the herd with me. Maybe I'll be able to put him in a civil service position, otherwise he will be a shepherd."

In addition, there is a demographic aspect to the exclusion of family labor from agriculture. The average number of children in the families I interviewed was under two, a significant change from just a generation ago.[13] Parents told me that having fewer children allowed them to use more resources, such as social connections or money for private lessons, in establishing their children in well-paying jobs.

The strategy of excluding family members from agricultural labor encourages the formation of pluriactive households, but it is only possible because of the presence of a large number of immigrants willing and able to work. Immigrants subsidize the pluriactive household by providing labor at a cost that enables such families to continue to make a profit from agriculture while pursuing other, more lucrative occupations. Given the smaller family size, the low prices of agricultural products, and the increased opportunities for jobs in the commercial, service, and government sectors, it is difficult to imagine how agriculture would be possible without immigrant labor. And yet agriculture still provides the foundation of the local economy. Thus immigrants, who are marginalized and denigrated by Greeks, are a necessary part of the local economy and instrumental to the functioning of local households.

Farmers in Midea township as well as local officials almost universally express anxiety about the future of agriculture in the area. Farmers are well aware of the difficulties they face in the global market. Competition from other countries that produce citrus, especially Spain, Turkey, and Israel, has led to falling market prices, and there is an awareness that the subsidy programs of the EU are under economic and political pressure. At the same time there are obstacles to the modernization that Greek agriculture needs to become globally competitive. Local communities have resisted pressure to "rationalize" agriculture into larger industrial units, which planners and policy makers almost universally argue will facilitate more efficient production,[15] as this would also almost surely put many small farmers out of operation. Farmers are reluctant to sell their land and at the same time are unwilling, or unable, to make the kind of capital investments needed to become "professional" farmers. As local farmers look to the future, they often predict a rise in "boutique" agriculture, with greater crop diversification and specialization. Another possibility often discussed is organic agriculture, which has increased in recent years. However, in their current state, agricultural markets are far too disorganized to make these options practical now.

The anxiety of farmers in Argolida arises from the perception that family farming no longer provides sufficient income, but at the same time there are few acceptable alternatives. Given the plot sizes and prevalent market prices, it is difficult for a farmer to make more than €20,000-30,000 per year. While in the past such a sum may have been adequate, in the last several decades household needs have grown much faster than income. Farmers need modern houses, appliances, automobiles, and cell phones. Their children require expensive clothes and private after-school tutoring. The increased consumption of consumer goods and commodified services has become an important part of status claims in rural communities, especially, as we shall see, with the growing dependence on immigrant labor. All these things have increased monetary pressures on households to maintain an "acceptable" standard of living. Meanwhile, there is a lack of well-paying jobs outside of agriculture. The service sector and civil service provide steady, but low-income, employment. Households usually try to combine the two strategies, giving rise to the ideal of the "pluriactive" household.

Changes in the mobilization and organization of labor within the household, which have occurred within a context of shifting relationships to external markets, have important implications for social relations both within and between households. Since the incorporation of Greece into the EU in the early 1980s, there have been noticeable shifts in the ways that inequalities within and between households are produced and maintained. Historically, class, gender, and kinship were important distinctions that structured relations of production in rural society. More recently, with the introduction of immigrant laborers, the deployment of household labor has been transformed. The following chapter examines how "traditional" modes of inequality have been transformed.

Notes

1. These figures are based on the 2001 census published by the National Statistical Service of Greece (http://www.statistics.gr/gr_tables/s1100_sap_5_euro38%20lau%201.htm).

2. The effects of deregulated agricultural markets are not confined to Greece. In South Africa market liberalization in the citrus industry has also had grave social effects, including an increase in seasonal labor at the expense of a permanent workforce, leading to a more impoverished and marginalized workforce (Mather and Greenberg 2003).

3. All figures on citrus production were obtained from the Office of Agricultural Development in the Argolida State Offices (*Nomarhia*) in Nauplio.

4. These memories are surely selective. Most local historians agree that higher villages were almost always poorer than the valley. Memories of economic superiority most probably reflect the competition and shifting fortunes of villages over time. Still, tobacco was an important crop for the higher villages and allowed them a certain amount of independence when prices were relatively high.

5. After rising steadily, the market price of oranges peaked in 1996 at an average of 63 drachmas per kilo (source: http://www.minagric.gr/en/agro_pol/SERIES/TREES/Orange_tree.htm).

6. Prices here are approximate because they can vary slightly not only by market factors but also by the quality of fruit, difficulty of harvesting, and the social relationship between buyer and seller.

7. This generally takes the form of labor exchanges. Among the few families that continue to harvest citrus themselves, that is, without paid workers, it is common for kin and friends to help out. It is generally understood that this assistance will be reciprocated in some form. In previous times, before the 1980s, many informants reported that such labor exchanges were more frequent and more organized, with several families or households working together to harvest groves collectively. However, I saw no instances of such a formal organization in my fieldwork.

8. All land use data for Midea township were obtained from the official agronomist of Midea township, who collects the data from each village. He provided me with a more detailed breakdown than was available from the Greek Statistical Service.

9. Tobacco leaves must be threaded, or sewn together at one end with string. The leaves are then suspended from drying racks for curing.

10. The effort to register production is a means toward greater surveillance and management of rural space by the EU administration. Scott (1998) has argued that the effort toward greater "legibility" through statistics is a basic tactic of the state as it tries to expand control and regulation.

11. According to the 2001 census, 40 percent of households in Midea township have one or two members (http://www.statistics.gr/gr_tables/S1100_SAP_1_nik2001_mon.htm). Based on my observations, the vast majority of these are elderly couples whose children live elsewhere or retirees from urban areas. My estimates are somewhat lower because my own incomplete census of the villages indicates a lower figure, which I attribute to the tendency of some elderly people to live separately but adjacent to grown children and thus functionally in a larger household.

12. There are exceptions to this pattern. In some households men contribute to cooking, light housework, and (more often) childcare. In one household that I interviewed where the mother worked as a teacher, the agriculturalist husband and the retired grandfather took on many of the childcare responsibilities, including some cooking and cleaning. In general, though, village men avoid such tasks.

13. From 1960 to 1981 the birthrate in Greece was fairly stable at around 2.3. Since 1981 the birthrate has declined significantly, to 1.3 in 1998 (Simeonidou 2002).

14. It is not clear that industrial agriculture would necessarily be a more "rational" strategy, given the resulting strains on the water supply, pressures from global production, and lack of employment alternatives. Agicultural "rationalization" usually takes into account only a limited set of goals, such as production levels and rates of profit, and excludes social and environmental effects.

— *Chapter III* —

Immigrant Labor in the Villages

In 2001, as I was beginning fieldwork, I sat at a sidewalk café on the main street of Agia Triada. It was early summer and I was drinking coffee with a few farmers I had just met. As we talked, two men walked down the main street, which was still deserted in the late afternoon sun. From the long-sleeved flannel shirts they wore and their sunburned faces it was clear that they were immigrant laborers, generically referred to as "Albanians" by the local Greeks, regardless of their country of origin. As they passed the main square the two men stopped at the kiosk and began to rummage through the ice cream bin. Immediately our conversation stopped as the farmers I was with turned their attention to the two laborers. The kiosk man emerged and stood by the two men as they rummaged through the bin and finally made their selections. One of the farmers I was with chuckled and said sarcastically "Look, the Albanians are eating ice cream!" The others only scowled and watched the men until they had exited the square.

The hostility provoked by the simple purchase of an ice cream was palpable. It was clear that a social boundary had been transgressed. Later, I found that such episodes were often used by Greeks as examples of the irrationality of immigrants and justifications for their inferior social status. Ice cream is a small but common indulgence for rural Greeks, a treat mainly intended for the pampered children of local farmers. The gaudy ice cream bins are found in almost every small store and stocked by the trucks of several national brands, now mostly owned by multinational corporations. Ice cream is one of the countless small pleasures that have come to rural Greece as part of its incorporation into the globalized economy of the EU. However, it is not for everyone. At between one and two euros each, an ice cream bar represents a substantial amount for most immigrants, given the daily wage of €25 they typically receive. When an immigrant buys ice cream it is seen as a wasteful extravagance or worse, as a deliberate attempt to subvert the relations of domination and submission that characterize the interaction between Greeks and immigrants.

Figure 5. Kiosk in Agia Triada

As my fieldwork progressed, I realized that this ice cream episode condensed many of the changes and conflicts that have developed in rural Greece over the last several decades. Ice cream of course is a trivial example, but the episode reflects a pervasive social contradiction in the villages I studied. The incorporation of rural Greek communities into the political economy of the European Union since the early 1980s has resulted in a broad trend toward rural prosperity as represented through rising levels of consumption, particularly among groups such as land-poor peasants, women, and children that were previously excluded from direct participation in consumer markets. It has also simultaneously resulted in the incorporation and marginalization of a new class of labor: illegal immigrants from Eastern Europe. These two developments are fundamentally connected in rural Greece.

Albanian and Eastern European Immigration

Since the early 1980s Greece has been experiencing a growing flow of immigrant labor, reversing its former status as an exporter of labor to more developed countries. Immigrants come from many countries in Eastern Europe, particularly Albania, as well as from more distant countries like Pakistan and India. While accurate numbers are difficult to obtain because many immigrants are illegal, estimates place the number of immigrants at around 1 million, making up around 10 percent of the population of Greece and over 15 percent of its labor force (Fakiolas 2000; Lazaridis and Poyago-Theotoky 1999). Today immigrants live in almost every part of

Greece and make up the lowest strata of workers in both urban and rural areas. Immigrants are concentrated in agricultural (Kasimis et al. 2003) and "informal" (Droukas 1998) sectors of the labor market.

Statistics gained from working permit applications give a broad picture of the characteristics of immigrants (Lianos 2001).[1] The largest number of immigrants are from Albania (65%), followed by Bulgaria (6.5%) and Romania (4.5%). Smaller numbers come from as far away as Pakistan, India, and the Philippines. Most immigrants are male (75%), although from a few countries (Bulgaria, Ukraine, Philippines, Moldova) the majority are female, reflecting their concentration in domestic and sex work. Some four out of five (82%) are between the ages of 20 and 44, but males are younger on average (48% of males are aged 20-29 compared with 36% of females). The great majority (82%) of immigrants had secondary education or lower (32% had left school at the primary level). For postsecondary education, women had higher rates (16%) compared to males (6.4%). A large share (40%) of immigrants resides in metropolitan Athens.

The recent immigration pattern to Greece has been spurred by both "push" and "pull" factors related to the expansion of the EU and the reorganization of global capitalism (King 2000). On the one hand the collapse of socialist economies in the 1980s created social instability and poverty in Eastern European countries that encouraged the mass emigration of many toward the West, including Greece. The political and economic victory of the capitalist West over the Soviet Union and its Eastern European periphery at the end of the Cold War both opened the previously militarized borders and created a huge supply of surplus laborers searching for work. At the same time the accession of Greece to the EU made it an attractive destination for migrants. Economic development spurred by EU investments and subsidies, as well the opening of Eastern European markets for Greek agricultural products, led to a rising standard of living and a growing middle class while at the same time creating a need for flexible and exploitable labor. This was particularly true in rural areas, where a declining birth rate and urban migration had precipitated a labor shortage as early as the 1950s, although it was for several decades offset by increasing mechanization (Pepelasis 1963).

In Midea township, the recent history of immigration is tied to the orange. Recent patterns of labor migration may be new, but they are not unprecedented. The valley of Argolida has long depended on migrant labor for harvesting, whether it be cotton, olives, or citrus. Migrants have traditionally provided needed labor at periods of peak demand. As orange cultivation expanded from the 1950s on, migrant labor was often used to make up for local shortages. In the past the migrants have come from other areas of Greece, although periodically waves of immigrants from more distant lands have settled. In the 1980s orange production was further stimulated by the opening of markets in the Soviet Union and Eastern Europe. The EU aided this development by negotiating trade agreements and providing subsidies. Trade agreements were portrayed as a form of humanitarian assistance, but were also clearly efforts to colonize new markets. For the farmers of Argolida, this was a huge windfall. At the same time, however, labor was in increasingly short supply. Greek migrants and local workers became scarcer and family labor was inadequate. Hippie backpackers and Roma (Gypsies) were used as a stopgap measure, but the real solution to the problem came with Eastern European migrants. The first migrants to arrive, in the early 1980s, were Poles (Romaniszyn 2000). By the end of the 1980s the majority of migrants were Albanians. Thus, by the end of the decade a curious circle had been completed, similar to the privatization and expropriation of peasant lands in the early Industrial Revolution. The products that had been used to help destroy the economies of Eastern Europe were now being produced with the human flotsam from that same destruction.

In the early 1980s most Greeks saw immigrants as both a temporary problem reflecting social upheaval and a temporary solution to the labor shortage. Many Greeks in Midea township continue to hold this view. As one farmer explained to me: "These Albanians, they don't want to stay. They are all trying to get some money and return home. That's natural; everyone wants to live in their homeland. Besides, they don't fit in here. They are too different. They won't stay." Since the early 1980s, however, immigrant labor has become institutionalized in Greece, and many sectors of the economy, agriculture in particular, are now dependent on it. In retrospect it is clear that the temporary nature of the immigrants, their migrancy, has facilitated their exploitation. In the beginning virtually all immigrants were illegal. The Greek state did not regulate labor immigration until 1997, when a system of residency permits was instituted. Up to that time all labor migrants were subject to immediate deportation if caught. After the 1997 law, it is estimated that approximately 70 percent of immigrants have filed applications for legal status (Tzortzopoulou 2002:47).

I estimate that the total number of immigrant laborers that reside in Midea township is approximately 1,000. During 2003 the township had 914 immigrants registered as residents. Since the introduction of a work permit system in the late 1990s, most immigrants have legal, even if precarious, status. However, a small percentage, I estimate around 10 percent, continue to live illegally for various reasons.[2] Either they are waiting to get employment, cannot pay the required fees, are wanted by the police, or have some problem with their documents. During the orange harvest the number of immigrants roughly doubles, although exact figures are hard to obtain because most who are there temporarily do not register as residents. Most immigrants live in the bigger villages of Agia Triada, Anifi, and Argoliko, each housing 150-200 immigrants. In recent years, more and more immigrants have come as families, with children, but the overwhelming majority, around 80 percent, continue to be single males.[3]

Immigrants make up roughly 15 percent of the local population and a much higher percentage of the local labor force. When one takes into

Figure 6. Migrant laborers waiting for work

account the fact that the majority are male workers, we can see that immigrants make up about one third to one half of the local agricultural labor force, depending on the time of year. At certain times and places, such as the orange harvest in Agia Triada or the olive harvest in the higher villages, immigrants make up the largest percentage of the labor force. Immigrants find work in the villages in various ways. In the early morning hours the squares and main roads of the larger villages fill with small groups of immigrants waiting for passing farmers to hire them for day labor. Workers who establish a good relationship with an individual farmer can sometimes be hired for the entire harvest or even on a long-term basis. In the smaller villages, workers are generally hired through word of mouth, or in the local café. Other workers sign on to harvest crews, whose manager, usually a Greek, contracts with farmers or merchants for harvesting.

In the early years the situation for immigrants in Greece was very chaotic. With few exceptions, immigrants came illegally, with no way to acquire working or residence permits. For most, this meant passage over the mountains into Greece on foot, furtive travel by foot, bus, or hitchhiking within Greece, and constant harassment from police (King et al. 1998). One young man from Albania described the situation to me:

I first came to Greece in 1990. I was fifteen years old and I decided to go. I didn't tell my parents anything, just left. I hitchhiked and walked to the border, about sixty kilometers from my village. And after I crossed the border by walking over the mountains, I met up with some others who were doing the same and they showed me the way. Wow, was I unprepared for what I found. In

Albania we had heard good things about Greece, easy money, a rich place. I was so stupid. I thought the streets would be lined with flowers! When I crossed the border I found something different. We had no food and no place to sleep. We were sleeping in abandoned buildings and eating wild greens. Finally I made it to Kastoria and was able to find work harvesting peaches. I stayed there for a while then got a bus ticket farther south, to Larissa. I worked there for a while but then the police caught me and sent me back to the border. I had only managed to work for two months, but I saved a little money, took a bus home from the border. My parents were happy to see me, they didn't know if I was alive or dead! The next year I came back, but this time I knew what to expect.

For these early immigrants from southern Albania, the trip to Greece was dangerous and the conditions there uncertain. Deportation was a constant threat. Some turned to theft in order to survive, although in the beginning they stole mostly food, clothing, and cooking utensils.

The Greeks too remember the early years of immigration as a chaotic time. A Greek farmer in Agia Triada described his memories as follows: "I will never forget those early years. People were coming down, they looked half-dead. They all traveled at night and people were afraid to leave their houses. Things started disappearing, little things like clothing from the clothesline. I would sometimes find them in the groves, sleeping under the orange trees wrapped in plastic sheeting to keep dry. Sometimes we gave them food. They wanted work; they worked for almost nothing in the beginning, just a plate of food sometimes." Because of the shortage of low-cost labor, Greek farmers began to employ the immigrants during the harvest and later for other menial jobs. In the early days wages were very low, the equivalent of USD 10-15 per day. Sometimes farmers would not pay the immigrants at all, turning them over to the police instead when the harvest was done.

As the numbers of immigrants grew during the 1990s, so did the need for some sort of state regulation. Greece was the last country of the European Mediterranean to regulate immigration, finally doing so in 1997 (Lazaridis and Poyago-Theotoky 1999). The delay was due to Greeks' ambivalent reaction to the immigrants. On the one hand fear spread that immigrants were taking away jobs from Greeks and that they were disorderly. On the other hand their labor was clearly needed. Many Greeks demanded immediate roundups and deportation. This often occurred in urban areas as police conducted sweeps of neighborhoods. Farmers, meanwhile, demanded that immigrants be left alone during the harvest seasons. There was also a concern on the part of the state over the growing black-market labor force that was untaxed. Government officials have long seen the need to import labor as compensation for an aging population. As the illegal immigrant labor force has grown, so have problems in the taxation and pension systems, which suffer under a black market labor regime (Tzilivakis 2002b). The result, instituted in 1997 and modified several times, most recently in 2001, was a system of temporary working permits for those already employed.[4]

The vast majority of immigrant workers in Greece start off illegally, and it is very difficult for them to ever attain the same rights as native Greeks. Despite the laws, the Greek state bureaucracy makes attaining legal residence and citizenship rights a formidable task. Greece currently has the lowest recognition rate of political asylum in Europe, dropping to only 1 percent in 2002 (Tzilivakis 2003), forcing all immigrants regardless of their motivation to go through the same process. One of the peculiarities of the Greek immigration law is that work and residence permits are granted only after an immigrant has worked for 120 days. During this grace period, potential troublemakers are weeded from among new immigrants by both police sweeps of trouble spots and employers' refusal to sponsor those who are not deemed subservient enough. After 120 days, and with the signature of an employer, an immigrant can apply for residence and work permits. In many ways the immigration legislation has been an effort to tax immigrants without legalizing their entry. Under current law immigrants can receive permanent residence status after ten years and are then eligible to apply for citizenship. Because the legislation went into effect in 1997, the first immigrants will be eligible for this in 2007.

The tangled bureaucracy an immigrant must navigate creates many obstacles (Tsarouha 2002). It often takes days of waiting in line at offices. Permits are often sent out late, or are refused if certain required papers are not filed. Even though a legalization process exists, many immigrants prefer to remain illegal (Tzilivakis 2002a). Reasons given are varied. Some immigrants are not planning to stay for long and the permits require too much time and money. Others lack some required document, such as an original birth certificate. Others want to avoid paying taxes on the little they earn. Often employers refuse to give immigrants the days off needed to apply for permits. In some cases, employers prefer immigrants to work off the books so as to avoid social security payments and more easily intimidate the workers.

Most immigrants I spoke with who came to Greece after 1997 followed similar paths. First they enter Greece on a tourist visa good for three months. In order to apply for a working permit, an immigrant must first find a job and give proof of employment in the form of a signed statement from an employer. A working permit is required before an immigrant can apply for a residence permit. Technically the employer is liable for social security taxes (either IKA [Institute of Social Security], for laborers, or OGA [Organization of Agricultural Insurance], for agricultural workers) that have incurred from the immigrant's employment, but in practice these fees are either not paid or are paid by the immigrant. The laws concerning social security payments for immigrant workers have been confusing and contradictory. The result is that immigrants are often forced to purchase retroactive social security coverage (in the form of stamps) when they apply for permits (Tzilivakis 2004a). The immigrant must also pay a €150 processing fee. The working permit that is issued is good for six months, after which it can be renewed by showing proof of payment of social security taxes and another processing fee. Working papers thus represent a substantial expense for the immigrant. In addition to processing fees, most immigrants must also pay social security taxes out of their wages. Social security taxes cost an immigrant over €300 per year, a substantial sum given their low wages. Despite these expenses, most immigrants today have valid working permits because they offer security from deportation, and because of the health and welfare benefits they offer.

With the security offered by working permits, many immigrants have settled in the villages and even begun to raise families. In almost all cases they live in the older houses, often those that were abandoned as their owners moved to the cities or into new houses. In most of the houses I visited, cooking facilities were primitive, with faucets and toilets outside and no hot water. Often immigrants' houses are sheds and outbuildings located in the fields and orange groves that house at least two or three persons per room. Housing for immigrants thus tends to be spread about the villages, and there are no residential concentrations or "ghettos."[5] After work and in the evenings immigrants congregate in small groups in public areas like the village square and some cafés. In the square they may talk and drink beer from bottles. In the cafés they may play cards and have a coffee, but generally avoid consuming more expensive drinks.

Due to their low wages, the consumption level of immigrants is much lower than that of Greeks in the villages. Immigrants have little property. The most common items are a cell phone and an old bicycle, both of which are useful for work. Immigrants maintain extensive networks of contacts throughout Greece and their home countries by cell phone and often travel to where job opportunities exist. Those with more money often buy a used car or van. A few immigrants have started or bought small businesses, but for the most part buying immovable property is discouraged by high prices and the lack of long-term security. Greeks in the villages discourage each other from selling to immigrants, and the real estate prices quoted by Greeks are often doubled for immigrants. Because of the temporary nature of their work permits, immigrants are also fearful of making substantial investments that are not moveable. Instead, many immigrants try to save money for investment in their home countries. Most immigrants I interviewed told me their goal was to save enough money to buy property or start a business in their country of origin, where favorable exchange rates made prices much lower.

Greeks express an almost constant anxiety about the immigrants in their midst, whom they consider to be prone to crime and violence. The following assertion, by a Greek farmer in Agia Triada, is typical: "Before the Albanians came in, we never locked our doors. We didn't know crime here in the village. Now it is different. We lock the doors all the time. I am afraid to let my wife go out alone at night. The Albanians are dangerous, a bad group [*faro* = kin group or lineage]. You can't trust them with anything." Virtually all unsolved crimes, such as theft or vandalism, are routinely blamed on immigrants, and the crimes in which immigrants have been caught and prosecuted are inevitably held up as examples by local residents. Such views are clearly exaggerated and emblematic of a moral panic concerning immigrants. According to the local police in Midea township, the vast majority of those charged with crimes are Greek nationals.

Social Relations between Immigrants and Natives

The immigrants who have made the most successful integration to Greek society are usually those able to establish a Greek identity by claiming Greek heritage. The two immigrant families in Midea township who have bought property, one a gas station and the other a small piece of land, both claim to be Greek Orthodox Albanians, and therefore of Greek descent. They also came in the early 1990s at the beginning of the immigration wave. Both were unwilling to discuss their stories with me, insisting only that they were Greek "by blood" and that everyone in the village had treated them well. The claiming of Greek descent by immigrants was a sensitive issue in the mid 1990s. Greece has always had a special policy towards the Greek Orthodox minority in southern Albania, including the sheltering of refugees during communist rule. However, with increasing numbers it became clear that distinguishing between Christian and Muslim immigrants was difficult. The collapse of the state bureaucracy in Albania and the ensuing flood of false documents that circulated, as well as the lack of record-keeping by the beleaguered Church under communism and the historical flexibility of national identities in the region, made it easy for anyone to claim an Orthodox identity. Now most claims of Greek heritage are treated skeptically, and are applied only to those who "seem" Greek. For example, on my pressing the issue of how Greeks distinguish ethnic Greek from ethnic Albanian immigrants, an acquaintance of mine in Athens threw up his hands and said: "Look, the Greeks did not come down from Albania, they stayed there. These ones that came, they are not Greeks. You can tell by how they act."

Despite the difficulties, many immigrants try to integrate into Greek society by claiming a common religious identity. Most commonly this occurs through baptism. Immigrants who come as families with small children will try to have them baptized, if they can find a sponsor. Sponsors are almost always Greeks in a position to aid the family, most often employers. Since being a baptism sponsor is considered an honor, it is difficult for Greeks to refuse. Still, they look on it with skepticism. One farmer who told me he had been a sponsor of an immigrant child laughed and said that the child probably had several sponsors in the different towns the family had lived in. Greeks rarely maintain any sort of special relationship with the child, as they might with Greek children. Another woman who had baptized a little girl had not seen her in years even though she lives only several kilometers away. She expressed scorn for the Albanian parents, who had pulled the girl out of school so that she could watch her younger siblings while her parents worked: "They are so stupid! How is she going to make it if they don't keep her in school?"

There were some cases in which baptism did seem to cement ongoing ties between families of Greeks and immigrants. In the village of Gerbesi, two children have been born to Albanian parents, and one of them has been baptized in the local church. The father of the child has lived in the village for six years, and several years ago brought his wife from Albania. Neither parent claims to be Christian. He is employed steadily by a local truck farmer, who lets the family live on the ground floor of his two-story house. The employer served as godfather to the baby, and even paid for the reception afterward. This incident of baptismal sponsorship was cited by several Albanians in the village as evidence of good social relations between Albanians and Greeks there. The other child has not been baptized, as no sponsor has yet been found, even though he is now three years old.

The experiences of immigrants tend to differ somewhat from village to village, depending on the social organization of the local labor market. In general, immigrants fare better when they are able to secure regular work with a single employer. Immigrants who are transitory, arriving in Agia Triada for the orange harvest, for example, and then moving on, had the hardest time. Most of the immigrants who work the orange harvest are transient and thus have relatively little contact with local residents. Those who are able to become friendly with local farmers will sometimes stay on in the village after the harvest, picking up day labor from the farmers they know or, sometimes, more permanent work in a local factory or business. Transient immigrants find work either in informal "pick-up" areas or by signing on with a work crew. During the harvest season the central squares of Agia Triada and other citrus producing villages fill up with immigrants looking for work, sometimes as many as a hundred. Most are men, but some women also wait, usually in a separate area with benches. During the early morning hours, farmers drive by in their trucks and choose as many workers as they will need. If the immigrant is lucky, the job may last several weeks; in other cases it may be just for a day. Of course the immigrant may also get nothing at all and have to wait until the following day. During the period of my fieldwork there was an informal standard that immigrants receive €25 per day plus lunch for an 8-hour day of harvesting. The main point of negotiation was lunch, which many farmers tried to skimp on. Immigrants often insist on a hearty lunch, including meat, which for many is the main meal of the day.

In Agia Triada, work crews contracted by factories and merchants now do the bulk of orange harvesting. Many immigrants therefore secure work by signing on with crews. The advantage for the immigrant is steady work and housing. The disadvantage is slightly lower pay, sometimes €20 per day but more often at a piece-rate of €0.02 per kilo. Work crews are managed and operated by local Greeks, almost invariably from poor

Figure 7. Lunch break during orange harvest. Local farmer (center) with mother (his right) and hired workers.

backgrounds. I interviewed two crew operators, both from families with little land whose fathers had been day laborers. Crew operators own trucks for hauling oranges and hire about ten to twenty immigrants, whom they house in warehouses or outbuildings, providing them with basic food and water. According to operators, running a harvest crew is a brutal operation because the transient workers are of unknown character: "You can't trust the Albanians, they are ungrateful. Forty percent of them are criminals and you have to separate them out. I'm not afraid of them though. I carry a gun and I'm not afraid to use it. Most of the trouble is between themselves, different groups. I don't get involved." Crews work in groups of four, and are paid for their tonnage as a group, which encourages the workers to discipline each other. In 2003 crew operators received €0.03-0.04 per kilo, almost double what they paid to workers in wages.

In Gerbesi and other higher villages that have little citrus, the majority of immigrants are year-round residents, although transients come for the olive harvest in the fall. In Gerbesi immigrants work either exclusively for one farmer on a regular basis or for several farmers irregularly as needed. Generally those immigrants with the most seniority get the most regular jobs. Immigrants who work for a single farmer tend to take on greater responsibilities. They often work alone, unsupervised, and take the farmer's truck for errands. Gerbesi, with a fairly stable population of twenty immigrants, also maintains a more organized hierarchy among the immigrants, with those who have been there the longest assuming the role of labor managers, deciding who gets what jobs and housing arrangements. Some even employ other immigrants. In the more or less stable immigrant communities of villages like Gerbesi, senior immigrants are able to establish a degree of security. One example of this is "Ilias," an Albanian who has been in Gerbesi for seven years and is a de facto leader of the immigrant community because of his seniority and contacts with local farmers. In 2003 he rented a field in addition to his work as a day laborer, something unusual for an immigrant. He planted okra and squash for the summer and hires other immigrants by the day to assist him. This was a risky move because, lacking a vendor's license, he is forced to sell his produce to other vendors. Furthermore, he risked antagonizing local farmers through his ambitious attempt to compete with them.

Ilias left Albania at the age of sixteen in 1991 and crossed the border on foot. He remembers the journey through Greece as the most difficult period in his life. The group he traveled with ate out of garbage cans and slept outdoors. One friend he was traveling with suffered severe frostbite and had to be abandoned along the way. Ilias made his way to Gerbesi, using an Albanian woman from a neighboring village who had married a Greek shepherd as his contact. When he arrived in Gerbesi he was taken in by an older man who gave him room and board in exchange for work. He was deported back to Albania three times, but since 1998 has had a working permit. As a result of his seniority, Ilias does better than most of the other Albanians. He owns an old car and rents a decrepit house in the village. However, saving money is difficult, even though he usually works seven days a week:

> I'm the type of guy, if I have some money I'm going to spend it. €25 a day is not very much. OK, they feed us too, but it is still not much. Two packs of cigarettes a day, a coffee at the café, some little extra food, €10 a day goes just like that. Then there is rent, €90 a month, and electricity and cell phone. If I have anything left I play cards. I went to Athens last week for a day for some business and I spent €60! OK, at least I got some pussy, I can't go without that! Now I hope to make a score with this crop. I want to buy an old car with the money because I can't do the work on foot all the time. I will hire a Russian or Romanian woman from the valley to help me, and if she looks decent, I can fuck her too.

Ilias's statement reflects the social hierarchy of resident immigrants, where senior or higher status individuals have a stake in the subordination of others.

In the higher-altitude villages, although not in Gerbesi itself, Greek men have in some cases married immigrant women. Men in the higher villages, especially shepherds, have difficulty finding wives. Greek women try to avoid both the isolation of the mountain villages and the hard, dirty work of herding and milking livestock. Many young men in these places remain unmarried late in life. In the small village of Bardi, about three kilometers from Gerbesi, I interviewed a shepherd who had gone to Albania specifically to find a bride. He married a woman there and returned with her brother as well. Her brother now works for him tending the herd and milking, returning to Albania during the summer months when the work is lighter. In explaining why he went to Albania to find a wife, the shepherd stressed the cultural ties between Albanians and Arvanites and also the willingness of Albanians to work hard.

Immigrants in Greece tend to maintain strong ties with their home countries. In Gerbesi, like other small villages, most immigrants come from the same area, in this case Elbasan in Albania. As one Albanian explained, "You must know someone in the village you go to. First of all, where will you sleep? I'm not going to take in someone I don't know." In the larger villages immigrants are more diverse, but still almost always arrive with some sort of contacts in order to secure housing and work. The expansion and improvement of the transportation and telecommunications networks in Greece over the last several decades have made it much easier to travel and communicate over long distances. Immigrants stay in touch with each other and with families back home through such networks. They use cellular phones to inform others of work opportunities and keep in touch with family and friends. Immigrants who live year-round in Greece also regularly travel back home, often once a year, for short periods. Others travel across borders each year for the harvest and then return home. The ease of transportation and communication has reinforced the diaspora quality of immigrant communities, allowing them to maintain social relations in diverse locales. Greeks often ridicule the use of cell phones by immigrants, characterizing it as a needless and expensive extravagance, but on the other hand they are suspicious of those immigrants who do not travel home regularly. For example, several villagers in Gerbesi told me they did not trust Ilias, a senior immigrant there, because he rarely left the village and had not been home in years. For them this was an indication that he had something to hide, most probably being wanted by the police since it was rumored that many immigrants were fugitives from Albanian jails.

Often travel back to Albania or other Eastern European countries is justified by both Greeks and immigrants in terms of sexual activity. Several immigrant men told me they were returning to Albania for sex, since there was a scarcity of available women in Greece. There are few single immigrant women. Those who are single often work as prostitutes, and their fees are out of reach for most immigrant men. Sex with Greek women is dangerous for both the man and women. An immigrant man who makes advances toward a Greek woman is usually beaten and expelled from the village. Homosexual activity is considered to be a temporary substitute, and the passive partner risks social ostracism. Thus the trip back to the home country is often framed in terms of sexual activity. The returning immigrant is said to be rich by the standards of the home country and is able to engage freely in sexual activity.

The experience of immigration for women is substantially different, mainly because of the gendered significance of sexuality in social relations between immigrants and Greeks. While immigrant males are generally expected to express a subliminated, but dangerous sexual presence, women's sexuality conditions their integration into local society. In the villages I saw no evidence of sexual interaction between immigrant males and Greeks, although this is undoubtedly more common in the cities. The only exception to this was one case where a café owner was said to have a sexual relationship with a male immigrant who worked for him as a waiter. For female immigrants however, sexual activities and exploitation are a constant theme. In Gerbesi and the other higher-altitude villages female immigrants are always married and come as part of a couple or family. While I was there in 2003 almost a quarter of the immigrants were women and all were married, two with children. All the women either came together with their husbands to Greece, or more commonly came after their husbands had become settled in the village. Male immigrants told me that a female would never come to Greece alone unless it was for prostitution, and indeed, the Greek males in the village often commented and speculated on sexual possibilities with various immigrant women. Immigrant husbands are very protective of their wives. They tend to work together in the fields. At other times the women stay in their houses, socializing only among themselves and venturing out only for grocery shopping. One immigrant man was widely considered by villagers to be "hiding" his recent bride from the gaze of Greek males. The same pattern holds for Agia Triada and the valley villages. Among the transient immigrants at harvest time there are some lone females, but in all cases I found these were older women in their 50s and 60s who had arrived from Bulgaria and Romania for the orange harvest.

Sexual exploitation is a real and ever-present danger for female immigrants (Psimmenos 2000), even if they are with families. A particularly graphic example of this occurred during my fieldwork. During the orange harvest a family of three (father, mother, and teenage daughter) arrived from a small town in Romania. I first met them in the company of a Romanian immigrant, Petro, who operated as a small-time hustler involved in prostitution and drugs. The father had been a butcher but had closed his store from lack of work. The family had an older daughter in the city of Corinth who had married a Greek man. They initially went there, but the Greek son-in-law refused to let them stay. The family had then come to Argolida and was working illegally, picking oranges for a local farmer. The farmer had given them a place to stay, but after several weeks, when the harvest ended, the farmer refused to pay the family and threatened to call the police. Petro had taken the family in, giving them food and a place to stay. I was somewhat mystified by Petro's generosity until I met the daughter, a pretty girl seventeen years old. The next time I spoke with Petro, he told me he was having sex with the girl. When I asked how the parents reacted, he said, "What can they say? I'm like a god to them, I give them everything, food, a place to stay, clothes." The last time I saw them, Petro told me he had "found" the girl a job in a local nightclub known for prostitution. The father was with him and Petro made a point of publicly humiliating him and insulting him in Greek, which the father does not speak well. This type of sexual-economic coercion is extremely common in Greece. The illegal status of immigrants and their consequent lack of political rights make them extremely vulnerable to exploitation by both Greeks and other, more powerful, immigrants.

In the villages and small towns of Argolida virtually all prostitutes are from Eastern Europe. Many work at bars and nightclubs that sometimes feature nude dancing, and where men can make appointments with the women. Others work out of hotels in the small towns that are controlled by Greek pimps. Often these pimps hold the women's passports and charge exorbitant rent for the rooms. Women held against their will have little recourse to the police, who are often customers and have friendly relations with the pimps. "Contracts" can also be purchased whereby men can procure a female immigrant for a certain number of months, essentially a form of short-term slavery. In the summer of 2003 contracts went for €1,000-2,000 per month, plus room and board. Sometimes women are brought into the country by trafficking networks to fulfill a previously agreed-on contract. In other cases women procure contracts after entering the country on tourist visas. I witnessed two incidents where young women, one Pole and one Bulgarian, were brought into villages by pimps for "viewing" by local men.

At the same time, some young female immigrants have used sexuality as an advantage in their quest to integrate into local society. An example is the case of Vanessa, a 28-year-old immigrant from Russia who is engaged to a Greek man in the town of Nauplio. Vanessa came to Greece eight years ago, driving down through Ukraine with a friend and entering with a tourist visa. After working in several other towns, Vanessa came to Agia Triada for the orange harvest. She rented and fixed up an old house from a sympathetic farmer and ended up working in agriculture for four years. After learning Greek she was able to find work as a waitress in a café in Nauplio, a desirable job for immigrants but usually available only to young, attractive females. Her wages were the same but the work was easier and steady. Soon after she started working in the café she met a young Greek man, and the two now have plans to marry. Vanessa is enthusiastic about the wedding and the prospects of staying in Greece. She told me: "Once I have a good man I am happy. When I came here from Russia I went six years without sleeping with a man. That's a long time for a Russian girl. They tried to set me up with men, even made marriage proposals, but me, nothing! I said I will wait to find a man who loves me. I finally found Yanni and now I'm not letting go".

This is a common strategy among young female immigrants from Northeastern Europe. Indeed, Vanessa asserted that "all the Russian women here are looking to get married." In these cases immigrants can use sexuality as a strategy of assimilation and a mitigation of exploitation. Her boyfriend Yanni has intervened several times on Vanessa's behalf in altercations with café owners. Her last employer fell behind on her wages and threatened to withhold them altogether when she quit. Vanessa, intimidated by his threat to blacklist her from all the cafés, could not go to the police. In such cases immigrants get very little help from the police and can sometimes find themselves deported. When Yanni found out, he called the employer and threatened to beat him up. Vanessa quickly got her money. In Vanessa's case sexuality has been not so much a means of exploitation as one of protection. But although many female immigrants try this strategy, relatively few succeed.

The Social Marginalization of Immigrants in the Villages

Despite the fact that almost half of all immigrants come from other countries, Greeks usually collectively refer to immigrants as "Albanians." Sometimes other nationalities are delineated. Women who work in bars are rarely Albanians and are often referred to as "Russian girls" (*Rosides*), even though many are Ukrainian, Bulgarian, Romanian, etc., and male workers from countries such as Romania are sometimes singled out as being either better or worse than others. Collectively, though, they are often grouped together as Albanians. For example, to "take an Albanian" (*na paro Alvano*) is a common phrase among Greeks meaning to hire an immigrant. This effacement of immigrants into a single ethnicity is the first step in the process of social marginalization.

Immigrants live in every village in Midea township, but they remain for the most part socially invisible. Because they live in older dwellings and outbuildings and have little money to spend in the stores and cafés it is difficult for a visitor to the villages to gauge how many immigrants live there. Following the legalization of their status immigrants have begun to congregate in public areas like the main squares, but not in large numbers. When talking about the village, villagers never include immigrants in the "we" of their conversation, clearly not conceptualizing them as members of the community. With the exception of a few who have managed to claim Greek identity and integrate into village society, immigrants are almost completely socially marginalized.[6]

In Greece there is a strong and persistent anti-immigrant sentiment. According to recent polls only 8.4 percent of Greeks think immigrants are a "positive" influence and 44 percent would like to see them restricted to separate neighborhoods (Galanopoulou 2003). A more recent survey of rural Greeks by Kasimis and Papadopoulos (2005) suggests a more nuanced reaction, with older people and employers showing more toleration than younger workers. Yet even here the researchers conclude that "the wide acknowledgement of the positive implications of the migrants' employment for rural economy and society is not reflected in a satisfactory development of social and cultural relations with the local population" (Kasimis and Papadopoulos 2005: 124). Greeks justify the social marginalization of immigrants in terms of the "moral panic"[7] surrounding immigration. In Greece the massive immigration of recent years has often been depicted as a national crisis arising from the collapse of communist regimes in the East and a declining birthrate at home. According to popular discourse, which focuses on the "push" rather than the "pull" factors, the mountainous northern borders and liberal social policies of Greece have proven indefensible against this flood, and the result has been a dangerous increase in poverty, crime, and disease, threatening the fabric of Greek society (Seremetakis 1996). The following description by an Agia Triada resident of the early period of immigration is typical:

> In the beginning, in the early eighties, it was a crazy situation. Albanians were coming down, thousands of them. They had nothing, they used to sleep like wild animals, outside, wrapped up in plastic tarps. Everything was new to them, they had no civilization [*politismos*] at all, nothing. We felt sorry for them, so we gave them blankets, cooking pots, a place to sleep. We gave them work so they could eat! But it was strange, they didn't appreciate our hospitality. We would give them a blanket and they would say "Don't you have a quilt?" We would give them an old pot and they would say "Don't you have a better one?" They even began to steal from us. They would murder you for ten euro! These people have no civilization, they are like animals.

The theme of ungrateful and "uncivilized" immigrants is one that appears repeatedly in Greek people's narratives of immigration.

In the moral panic surrounding immigration, many social problems have been blamed on immigrants. Crime and disease are commonly attributed to immigrants and more specifically to Albanians. Many villagers insist that doors were never locked in the villages before the immigrants arrived, but that now people sleep with loaded guns for fear of being robbed or murdered. The "crime wave" brought about by immigrants is almost certainly exaggerated (Mouzelis 2002). Statistically, immigrants are charged with between 25 and 30 percent of crimes, depending on the category (Eleutherotipia 2004). Arrests, however, can be misleading, given the tendency of police to blame immigrants for many crimes even without evidence. Analysis of convictions for all serious crimes in Greece in 1996 shows that immigrants were responsible for 15 percent (Kourtovik 2001: 190), a percentage roughly analogous to the percentage of immigrants among the Greek population. However, crimes committed by immigrants tend to get much more attention, both in the media and in people's conversations. Unsolved crimes are often attributed to Albanians. A typical example occurred during my fieldwork when five sheep were stolen in Gerbesi during Holy Week. Following the theft one local resident publicly claimed to have seen a strange BMW in the area with Albanians inside. The thief later turned out to be a shepherd from a neighboring village.

The fear of an immigrant crime wave is largely fed by the mass media (Pavlou 2001). Newspaper and television reporting tends to paint an exaggerated view of crimes committed by immigrants. When immigrants are charged in crimes, the media stress the ethnic identity of the suspect. Stories of immigrant crime are given more prominence in the media than equivalent stories involving Greek perpetrators. In the context of privatized media, sales and market share are the prime motivation for editorial policies. Immigrant crime stories play to the fears of many Greeks, who are ready to have their fears confirmed and eager to have scapegoats for the contradictions and dislocations they experience as Greek society undergoes transformation (e.g., Cohen 1980). The anti-immigrant frenzy whipped up by the media and others also seems to benefit elite interests by justifying increased policing, deflecting class antagonisms, and producing vulnerabilities on the part of immigrants (e.g., S. Hall 1978).

Immigrants are also said to be responsible for prostitution in the villages. The larger villages usually have bars where immigrants work as hostesses, and from here informal prostitution is said to occur. Agia Triada had two such bars, one a café-bar where women serve drinks and sit with customers, and the other a late-night dance hall where women sit or dance with men for overpriced drinks and tips. Stories circulated through the villages of men who had been enchanted by immigrant women and lost substantial sums of money to them, although in all probability it is the bar owners who profit the most through the exorbitant prices of drinks in such dancehalls, €10 and more. Immigrants are also thought to play a major role in the drug trade as smugglers of marijuana and heroin, although in Midea township Roma are said to be the major traffickers. Among marijuana smokers, low-quality marijuana is referred to as "Albanian" while higher-quality is said to be produced in Greece.

The scapegoating of immigrants as criminals creates fear among Greeks and makes it much less likely that Greeks and immigrants will form direct personal relations. It is also a way of elevating the self-image of Greeks, by projecting negative social phenomena outside the social body. Greeks in the villages often advised me to be careful around immigrants and not to trust them. This fear and distrust limits the range of jobs available to immigrants. A housepainter in Agia Triada who told me he has difficulty finding Greeks willing to work for the basic wage of €25 per day also told me he refuses to hire Albanians. He said: "I just don't want to hire them, I don't trust them. Look, I often work inside people's homes and they would steal things and create problems for me." The fear of immigrants discourages Greeks from hiring immigrants for jobs that require trust or responsibility.

Immigrants are also actively discouraged from settling permanently or establishing businesses in the villages. Sale prices and rents for houses are often increased when an immigrant inquires, sometimes after the seller is pressured by neighbors. When immigrants do rent houses, they generally have little contact with their neighbors. When I asked a civil servant and part-time farmer in Agia Triada about his Romanian neighbors he responded: "I don't know much about them. We don't get involved much with them. They listen to their own music and do their own things. They are always disturbing the neighborhood. Hopefully they won't stay long". Immigrant residents are generally ostracized from the normal, everyday sociality of village neighborhoods and usually maintain their own, dispersed social networks. In addition to meeting with outright hostility from villagers, immigrants are loath to invest in real estate or businesses, even if they can afford it, because of their precarious legal status.

Those immigrants who try to achieve a social status equal to Greeks' invariably encounter problems. Even Ilias, the young Albanian man who rented a field in Gerbesi for his own production, faced difficulties. One evening I witnessed a conflict between Ilias and another farmer. Ilias had hired another Albanian man to work for him in his field the following day. A Greek farmer approached the worker and tried to hire him for the same day. The worker, clearly uncomfortable, referred the farmer to Ilias. Ilias resisted the farmer's request at first with a show of bravado and cursing, but the farmer made it clear that he would not relent and engaged Ilias in a round of play-fighting to assert his determination. A short time later Ilias relented, even though the lack of a worker created problems for him.

Play-fighting or mock aggression is often used to publicly demonstrate the social superiority of Greeks. Once as I was sitting with two farmers in a village café, Ilias came and sat down at the same table. Ilias is a frequent target of play-fighting and aggression because he socializes more with the Greeks in the café and is beginning to compete with them in production. One of the farmers gave Ilias a hostile look and said, "Get the fuck out of here" (*fige gamo to apo 'tho*). Ilias took up the challenge and replied, "Ah, fuck off," but was smiling to make it clear he considered it a joke. The farmer got up, grabbed Ilias and shoved him across the room, upsetting two chairs and pinning him against a cooler. For an instant I thought a real fight was breaking out, because the farmer was shouting and cursing. Ilias continued to smile, but was clearly embarrassed and tried to weakly resist. Finally the farmer stopped, smiled, and returned to the table with Ilias, who then sat down with us. Ilias had tried to assert himself as an equal, but the farmer, partly or wholly for my benefit, used this mock aggression as a public means of asserting Ilias's inferiority, for he knew full well that Ilias could not fight back without serious consequences.

Ilias is a target of this type of aggression because he challenges the divide between Greek and Albanian with his attempts to establish himself as an independent producer. Other Albanians, who do not try to cross this divide and remain publicly submissive to their Greek employers, are not usually targets. However, the violence displayed against Ilias is readily available for use against others. While I was in Midea township, I heard accounts from local residents and immigrants of three incidents of group conflicts, none of them in the villages I worked in. In the nearby village of Prosimni, there have been at least two occasions when immigrants were beaten and expelled *en masse*. The first occurred after a burglary in which immigrants were suspected. All the immigrants were gathered into the main square by the men of the village, beaten with sticks, and chased away. In the second incident, a group of Kurds were heard criticizing and insulting Greeks and were beaten and chased out of town by a group of Greeks. In another neighboring village, Panariti, Albanians were gathered into the square and beaten after one Albanian boy was rumored to be courting a local Greek girl. When the local police arrived, the villagers reportedly told them, "It's nothing, just a little problem that we will sort out ourselves." The police then left the village.

A more recent incident that happened on the island of Crete while I was conducting fieldwork is a telling example of the kind of violence that can break out between Greeks and immigrants in the villages. On 2 February 2003, the village priest in the village of Antiskario rescued a young Albanian man from a crowd that had beaten him into unconsciousness. According to newspaper reports (Papadokostaki 2003), the young man was one of a group of Albanians who had recently arrived in the village looking for work. One of the men owed some money at the local mini-market and their credit there was cut. Another Albanian man, who apparently had lived in the village for some time, told the mini-market owner that the others were planning to rob the place, possibly in retaliation for the newer arrivals' acceptance of lower wages. Relations between Albanians and Greeks were already tense because some of the Albanians had begun asking for higher day-wages. In addition to the wage issue there was also a "romantic conflict," and on the same day unknown thieves had stolen a car in the village. As rumors of the planned robbery spread, the village exploded in violence. Greeks chased and beat any Albanians they could find, almost killing the young man who was saved by the priest. In the aftermath, all the Albanians fled, even those who had been in the village for years, leaving the village without workers and the Greeks afraid to go to their fields. This incident reveals some of the political and social fractures that operate between and within ethnic groups in the villages, and the way these fractures can erupt into violence under stress.

Because of their lack of social ties to native villagers, immigrants are also at a disadvantage in personal conflicts. Two incidents I witnessed, again involving Ilias, illustrate this point. The first involved Ilias's car. Shortly after he purchased a decrepit Toyota, several local farmers confronted him in the village square. One said to him: "Look, I've seen you driving through the village and you should slow down. I'm just telling you for your own good. If you happen to run down some kid it will be the end for you. If you get entangled like that in the village it will be the end, especially for you. You understand that, right?" Ilias protested that he was a good driver, but the others just laughed and derided his "fake" Albanian license. The Greeks had made their point, however, and it was clear that if some accident did occur, Ilias, with no relatives or friends to intercede as is normal in tragic accidents, would be assured of harsh retribution.

Overt violence against immigrants in the villages is the exception to the normal course of events and is avoided by both sides because of the damage it can do, both economically and socially. In general, Greeks rely on more subtle means of regulating the behavior of Albanians. Often, when talking about relations with Albanians, Greek farmers would say: "They don't cause any problems. After a while we can tell which ones are trouble and we send them on their way. We have our means." Immigrants who are suspected of being troublemakers by the Greeks are first of all not sponsored for working papers. In order to get papers, an immigrant must first have some sort of personal relationship with a farmer who in effect guarantees his behavior. At peak labor times of course, this may not hold, but at harvest time the transient population is less organized and easier to deal with by means of police.

Illegal immigrants make for a particularly vulnerable and docile work-force because they have none of the legal protections of native workers. Working conditions and wages are essentially the prerogative of the employer. Illegal workers have no recourse to police or the courts. Job actions by immigrants are rare, although not unheard of. In 2002 Pakistani hothouse workers in the town of Marathon, outside of Athens, struck for higher pay, causing problems for farmers there. They eventually won a small wage increase. After the strike the mayor of Marathon conceded that "without immigrants the cost of produce would probably double" (Tzilivakis 2002b). This is undoubtedly one reason the Greek state has been reluctant to legalize immigrant workers and grant them full protection under current laws.

In addition, lack of citizenship rights excludes immigrants from access to agricultural markets and the subsidies that are distributed by the EU and the Greek state. Ilias, the immigrant who attempted to become an independent producer by renting a field, ultimately failed. Because he lacked citizenship he could not sell directly in the farmers' markets and was forced to sell his produce to other truck farmers at a lower price. At the end of the season his profits were less than he would have made by day labor. When I last spoke to him, he had given up the field, saying: "I'm not doing it anymore, too many headaches. If I work for a day-wage at least at the end of the day I can go home and relax."

As we have seen, immigrant laborers are filling a growing need for labor in the villages of Greece. Traditional sources of labor have dried up due to a declining birthrate and the growing pluriactivity of agricultural households. This labor crisis is largely a product of the integration of rural Greece into the consumer markets of the EU and the expanding service economy. At the same time the local economy remains based on heavily subsidized agricultural production. Households have thus been squeezed between growing consumer needs and flat or declining productive capabilities. As a result, immigrants have been integrated under conditions of social and political marginalization, conditions that produce their extreme vulnerability.

"Neoracism" and Cultural Fundamentalism in Argolida

The dependence on immigrant labor has created a class antagonism between Greek landowners and immigrant wage laborers as they struggle over the profits from agricultural production. This struggle is largely manifested through the elaboration of neoracist and anti-immigrant ideologies of naturalized inequality that act to construct "Albanian" and "Greek" as distinct and incommensurable racial and social categories. The exploitation of immigrant labor is facilitated by legal and social constraints on immigrants, but it is also reproduced in the daily life of the villages through a pervasive and blatant form of anti-immigrant racism expressed by almost all Greeks.

The social isolation of immigrants in the villages is maintained through a self-conscious racism. Many farmers openly subscribe to racist views. One truck farmer in Manesi told me: "I admit it; I am a racist [*ratsistis*]. I hate the immigrants. I can't stand them at all." Others however, express anti-immigrant sentiments on the basis of cultural, rather than physical differences. In general, though, both ideological expressions contribute to a systematic marginalization and subordination of immigrants as a group within the villages, based on ascribed differences that are perceived as both natural and immutable. This system is distinct in many ways from the types of racism found in other regions, such as North America, or in other epochs. Indeed, there is debate on whether contemporary anti-immigrant ideologies and practices constitute a type of racism or a fundamentally different type of exclusionary rhetoric. We shall return to this argument shortly. For the moment, though, I will employ the term to denote the totality of discourses and practices that ascribe genetic differences to Greeks and Albanians.

There are many cases of extraordinary kindness shown by some Greeks towards immigrants. Some farmers, particularly those in the higher villages, have established strong personal relations with immigrant workers and their families. In some cases, individual immigrants have become "like family." I witnessed instances when immigrants joined in family meals and when Greek families cared for sick immigrants. On the whole, however, immigrants are treated by native Greeks with the brutality, rooted in a firm belief in natural inferiority, that characterizes racialized notions of inequality. More often than sympathy or care, native Greeks greeted the sufferings of immigrants with indifference or even amusement. Once, as I sat in a village square at night with a group of farmers, an immigrant worker known to be an alcoholic appeared out of the darkness and collapsed in the square, bleeding profusely from a head wound. As I got up and went to help him, the others laughed and one said: "What are you doing? Leave him alone. He'll be dead soon anyway." He was carried home by a group of Albanians.

Racism in Greece is an ideology lacking a formal coherence. It is not a new phenomenon. Since at least the emergence of the modern state,

Greeks have claimed a biological as well as cultural distinction between themselves and Turks. In addition, racism toward Roma and Jews is widespread. There are several words that Greeks use to denote groups with inherited or genetic differences, and each can in certain contexts be translated as "race." *Faro* is used to denote "race" or "lineage," indicating a group of closely related families. *Fili* is used to denote "race" or "tribe," in other words a group of related lineages. On other occasions, Greeks will use the imported word *"ratsa"* to denote "race." I heard all three words used to describe immigrants, and Albanians in particular. Part of the racialization of immigrants is based on the firm belief among Greeks that there exists a Greek "race" (*fili*] that is genetically distinguishable from other "races" such as Turks and Albanians. Greek genes are thought to have been passed down from ancient times, and many Greeks are proud of what they believe is a "gene" for "civilization" (*politismos*].

In practice, the concept of race often slips between biological and culturist assumptions. In some cases, I heard explanations for the inferiority of immigrants based on biological characteristics, such as the following:

> Albanians are different. They are a different race [*faro*]. You can always tell them by the shape of their head. They are lazy and deceitful by nature. You must always be careful with them.

In other cases, Albanians were characterized by a lack of "culture" (*koultoura*) or "civilization" (*politismos*). For example, as an explanation for why Albanians are "stupid" and "without morals," a small business owner in Manesi asserted that

"[Albanians] have no civilization; they have no religion, no state, nothing!" Others attributed the "backward" (*kathisterimeni*) state of Albanians to the isolationism of the communist regime. In both cases, however, such statements had a finality that precluded the ability of Albanians to adapt and change, at least the current generation. Albanians were seen as unredeemable barbarians, the development of their faculties stunted by a culture of poverty and isolation.

The alleged stunted cultural and intellectual development of Albanians is used by residents in both upper and lower villages to justify and legitimize the superior social position of Greeks. Albanians and other Eastern Europeans are thought to be unfit to participate in Greek society or enjoy the prerogatives of modern citizens and consumers. The low living standards of immigrants compared to Greeks was often justified with the argument that immigrants were "not accustomed" (*den ekhoun sinithizei*) to modern lifestyles and would be "spoiled" by too much wealth. In other cases farmers assured me that immigrants were able to "endure" (*andehoun*) poor conditions and hard labor because of their history of deprivation. The exploitation of immigrants is thus naturalized by a belief in different intellectual and cultural levels between Greeks and immigrants. Because "culture" is assumed to be a quasi-hereditary quality, immigrants carry the burden of underdevelopment with them into Greece, where it is used to justify a kind of cultural racism.

One manifestation of the kind of cultural racism experienced by immigrants is the anger expressed by many villagers concerning the consumption of commodities by immigrants. Immigrants are thought not to "need" many of the commodities enjoyed by Greeks. Ridicule of and even hostility to the consumption of inappropriate commodities by immigrants was common on the part of Greeks. Many Greeks thought it ridiculous that immigrants should have cell phones. They often cited commodity consumption as an example of the stupidity of immigrants. One labor crew operator explained the difference by saying: "When the Greeks left as emigrants, they worked hard and saved their money. They improved their lives. These Albanians aren't that smart. They waste their money on silly things. Cell phones, jewelry, those things. They should be saving their money to improve their lives, but they aren't that smart. What can you do for them?" Other times, conspicuous consumption by immigrants aroused outright hostility. Immigrants driving cars, especially relatively new or expensive cars, immediately provoked suspicions of criminality.

Commodity consumption, like land ownership, is a right claimed by Greeks and denied to immigrants. Along with the segmentation of the labor market, the segmentation of rights is a key expression of social inequality that is conditioned by the cultural racism at work in the villages. To claim these rights is, in effect, to claim a Greek identity. Those who are successful generally take on the identity of diaspora Greeks, that is, "Northern Epirotes"[8] (the Greek name for Southern Albania) or "Pontics" (Greeks from the Black Sea region). This process was driven home to me one afternoon as I talked with a group of young men. After one of the group left, a young man I had met for the first time, the others turned to me and asked if I had noticed anything strange. They laughed and one said: "He is an Albanian! You wouldn't know it to look at him. That is, he is a Northern Epirote. He has been here a while and is trying to get his papers, to become Greek. He looks like a Greek, right?" I understood immediately that he "looked like a Greek" because he had all the expected commodities: cell phone, nice clothes, a nice car. Despite the fact that many Greeks claim a biological difference from immigrants, in reality it is the trappings of commodity consumption that provide the essential "physical "difference.

There is a large body of literature on the rise of anti-immigrant discourse and the resurgence of far-right ethnonationalism in Europe over the last several decades. One point of debate is whether these discourses of exclusion constitute a revitalized and resurgent form of racism, described by Balibar (1991) as "neo-racism," or a distinct form of "cultural fundamentalism" (Stolke 1995) more akin to nationalism. Balibar argues that contemporary practices, discourses, and representations of immigrant subordination constitute a form of racism because they are organized by discourses of fear and segregation that mimic scientific discourse and are articulated around "stigmata of otherness" (1991: 17-18). The effect is the construction of stereotyped identities that are assumed to reflect "natural" differences. What is "neo" about it, however, is the substitution of "culture" for "race." For Balibar this is not important in itself, because, as he argues, "culture can also function as nature" (1991: 22). Neither is it simply a more "politically correct" racism that reflects the discrediting of racial ideologies in postwar Europe. Rather, the emphasis on culture arises from the context of decolonialization. For Balibar, traditional racism in Europe was an ideology of domination within the context of colonialism (see also Stoler 1992) where racialized groups were excluded from European nation-states. Neoracism is being constructed within a very different context of social relations as capitalism has moved from colonialism to globalism, and thus reflects both the changing nature of the nation-state and changing technologies of social subordination. In short, neoracism denotes notions of genetic inferiority ascribed to subordinate groups that have become politically and economically integrated, but socially segregated, within European nations.

Stolke (1995), on the other hand, considers the characterization of contemporary anti-immigrant rhetoric as a neoracism to be misleading. Stolke focuses on the pervasive "cultural fundamentalism" of European anti-immigrant discourse that legitimizes the exclusion of foreigners through a reification of culture as a bounded, historically rooted entity and reflects a resurgence of the primordial sense of identity associated with the rise of the nation-state. Working with a "rhetorical model of reversal" (Taguieff 1990: 112) of liberal cultural-relativist discourse, cultural fundamentalism argues for the incommensurability of cultures and the incompatibility of immigrants through a discourse of respect for difference. Whereas racism naturalizes relations of domination, cultural fundamentalism legitimizes xenophobia as a "natural" reaction to cultural difference. The effect is that "instead of ordering different cultures hierarchically, cultural fundamentalism segregates them spatially" (Stolke 1995: 8).

While Stolke's argument is useful, in my view it does not go far enough in interrogating the reification of culture as a bounded, homogenous entity. Nationalism has long used notions of national "culture" to not only exclude other nationalities, but also dominate subaltern groups within the nation (B. Anderson 1983). What seems different today is the way that cultural fundamentalism acts to condition the subordination of immigrant groups within the nation-state through cultural exclusion rather than inclusion. In this sense it is closer to the neoracism described by Balibar. For Balibar, "in neo-racist doctrines, the suppression of the theme of hierarchy is more apparent than real" (1991: 24) and becomes manifest in its practical application. The other problem with Stolke's argument is her characterization of cultural fundamentalism as a resurgence of primordial nationalist identity. In the context of an increasingly transnational Europe such a resurgence is clearly reactionary. However, if this is the case, it is difficult to explain the growing dependence of Europeans on immigrant labor. The simultaneous dependence on, and rejection of, immigrants appears as a paradox. The key to unlocking this paradox, which Stolke does not address and Balibar treats only indirectly, is the relationship between anti-immigrant rhetoric and the exploitation of immigrant labor.

The analysis of cultural fundamentalism and neoracism in Europe tends to overemphasize its ideological production at the expense of its political-economic context. The rise of xenophobic and racist movements in Europe is associated with the rapid social and economic transformations of the last several decades. These changes have particularly hurt the working class and lower middle class, making them fertile ground for anti-immigrant movements. Some have argued that immigrants become scapegoats for the falling wage levels and loss of job security formerly enjoyed under Fordist or social democratic regimes (Solomos and Wrench 1993), or that immigrants represent a "tactical weapon" (Kwong 1997: 15) in economic restructuring by displacing native workers and negating their social and economic gains. Others consider the nationalistic character of anti-immigrant discourse to be an attempt by these downwardly mobile groups to reassert their position in the social fabric of the nation-state in the face of growing unemployment and decreasing access to state resources (Wimmer 1997). Indeed, such arguments are common in the villages, as many complain that immigrants are "stealing" jobs by working for much less than Greek workers demand and competing for state assistance, thus damaging villagers' livelihoods.[9]

The problem with treating anti-immigrant rhetoric in Europe as a form of reaction is that doing so tends to obscure the issue of social labor. Studies of racism often veer toward a kind of psychological reductionism in which ideology becomes a historical subject in itself. A more productive analysis takes into account migrant *labor*, and not just migrants themselves, as the focus for the production and articulation of racism (Miles 1982: 5). As Robert Miles (1987) has argued, capitalist production continues to be dependent on the reproduction of "unfree" labor by means of the manipulation of cultural criteria or symbols. Racism is merely a variant of the process of producing the necessary constraints on labor that guarantee the extraction of comparatively high levels of surplus value. Others have also pointed out that immigrant labor tends to be concentrated in jobs that natives either refuse or avoid and subsidizes the creation of certain kinds of employment, such as supervisory positions, among native workers (Harris 1995: 195). In this sense, neoracism is seen as the consequence and site of struggle between classes, and class fractions.

In his ethnography of anti-immigrant sentiment in urban Sicily, Cole (1997) shows the complexity of contemporary racism. As in Greece, immigrants in Sicily are concentrated in the low-wage and informal tertiary sector, occupying jobs that are undesirable for working class Sicilians. Cole's analysis finds significant differences in the expression of racism among different classes. Urban workers tend to be somewhat ambivalent regarding immigrants, sometimes empathetic with their plight but for the most part pessimistic and resistant to their assimilation. Cole attributes this to the competition over state support and services rather than direct competition over jobs. Among middle- and upper-class Sicilians Cole documents a sophisticated liberal antiracist ideology existing even as economic and political domination is legitimized through an ideology of cultural difference. The middle and upper classes can afford magnanimity toward immigrants, who conveniently provide a pool of cheap labor without threatening bourgeois political or economic power (1997: 97-98).

Variation in the ideologies of racial difference can also be seen in Argolida. At the end of the summer of 2003 the Gerbesi Association (Sillogos Gerbesioton), an organization of Athenians who come from the village of Gerbesi, hosted a feast in the village. The goal was to raise money to plant trees along village roads, just as other social events hosted by the club had raised money for village improvements. The association is generally left-leaning politically, and as part of the program, in addition to music, they booked a lecturer to speak on the historical roots of Arvanites as an Albanian-speaking ethnic group, with the objective of mitigating the pervasive racism among the villagers. The choice of speaker aroused controversy in the village as some perceived the presentation as a patronizing attempt to foster understanding between villagers and immigrants. In general, the cultural relationship between Arvanites and immigrant Albanians is highly controversial in Arvaniti villages (Gefou-Madianou 1999). While some applauded the efforts of their urban kin, others were ideologically opposed to the proposition that local Arvanites and Albanians shared a common ethnicity. The president of the village cultural society was vehement: "There is no relationship between us and the Albanians. We are the original Greeks. We are more Greek than the Greeks! Our ancestors have been here for thousands of years, back to ancient Greece and the Mycenaeans." For the most part, the attempt to promote multicultural understanding was met with derision and even hostility on the part of villagers.

The debate over Arvaniti identity is a common preoccupation in the upper villages of Midea township. Villagers strongly identify as Arvanites and often discuss the distinctive features of Arvaniti "culture" (*koultoura*) and their differences from the "Greeks" of the valley. In comparison to the valley Greeks, Arvanites are considered to be more clever and "sly" (*poniri*) as well as more militant and resistant to authority. At the same time Arvanites consider themselves to be more truly "Greek" than the Greeks. They claim to have provided the impetus for the Revolution and to continue to hold more closely to tradition, while the valley villagers are constantly adapting to foreign rule, corrupting their culture. Valley residents are often referred to as "Turk-lickers" (*Tourkogliftes*) and fascists. Stressing their ethnic difference is a way that high villagers have organized their resistance to the political and economic domination that reaches them via the valley villages and towns.

Villagers in Gerbesi and Manesi often assert that valley residents are descended from Arvaniti stock, but that they lost their identity under the yoke of national and foreign domination. For their part, except for families that have kin ties to the upper villages, most valley residents reject these claims. In fact, most valley residents are somewhat mystified by Arvaniti claims of ethnic difference and tend to downplay the distinction. As one valley resident told me, "Arvanites, they are really Greeks. They were just more isolated and developed their own kind of Greek culture." Arvanites are considered to be somewhat backward, their pride a cover for their lower social status. Valley residents see themselves as more modern and closer to the urban culture of the nation-state.

Arvaniti identity is sometimes used as an explanation of the different relationship between immigrants and natives in higher and lower villages. Early in my fieldwork a farmer in Gerbesi explained the difference to me:

> In Gerbesi, we have more sympathy for the immigrants because we are Arvanites, we have common roots and also because we too worked for day wages not too long ago. Our ancestors came here just like them. In Gerbesi they eat at the same table with us. We don't take them food to eat alone. Even if they are dirty from working or whatever, it doesn't matter, they'll sit right at the table.

Many immigrants seem to agree. One told me:

> The Greeks here are better, they're Arvanites. They used to be Albanians. The ones in the valley are shit. They won't even talk to you.

In some ways, I confirmed this view through observation. The residents of the upper villages do have more ongoing social relations with immigrants. They do sometimes eat at the same table. In the valley, people have much less personal contact with immigrants. It was rare to find a valley resident who maintained an ongoing relationship or to observe Greeks and immigrants sitting together. However, this seems largely due to the relations of production dominant in each area. In the upper villages farmers were much more likely to employ immigrants on a regular basis. The familial style of their relationship is used to hold the immigrants under obligation and thus claim a right to their labor. In the valley most residents are insulated from contact with immigrants because of the seasonal nature of labor needs and the use of work crews, which precludes the need for ongoing reciprocal social relations. However, even in the upper villages, in numerous interviews and observations I encountered hostility toward immigrants in general, even on the part of individuals that maintained strong ties with particular individual immigrants.

I did collect evidence that in the early years of Albanian immigration, the late 1980s, immigrants were greeted with hospitality in the upper villages. This initial friendliness seems to have been based on villagers' feelings of solidarity with Albanians. Being both leftists and Arvanites, and speaking in fact a dialect of Albanian that was somewhat intelligible to the new immigrants, many villagers had long felt a common bond with Albania. One young woman from the village, a university student at the time, had volunteered to participate in an exchange program. She spent a semester in Tirana in 1989 and learned Albanian. She reported that she was disappointed that the Albanian she learned in Tirana was so different from the Arvanitika that she had learned from her parents, and was even more disappointed with Albanian society, which she found to be corrupt, bearing little resemblance to that of the village. Back in Athens, when the immigration to Greece began in earnest in the early 1990s, she received numerous requests for assistance from arriving immigrants who remembered her from her stay in Tirana. She gave some help to the first few, but after a while she "stopped answering the phone."

The development of anti-immigrant rhetoric and practices in the villages over the last several decades tends to argue against Stolke's (1995) view of cultural fundamentalism as primarily a technique of spatial exclusion and segregation. While spatial segregation is certainly an important element in the subordination of immigrants, it has occurred in a context of economic integration. That is, anti-immigrant rhetoric has arisen as immigrants have come to play a fundamentally important role in agricultural production, but at the level of a highly exploitable, flexible source of labor. The high degree of exploitation is fueled by the farmers' own precarious situation of being trapped between the downward pressure on prices in the liberalized markets for agricultural products and the growing consumption needs of their households. The conditions of immigrants' integration and the strict enforcement of hierarchical relations required to guarantee these conditions provide a fertile environment for the development of the kind of practices, discourses, and representations that characterize systemic racism. However, as Balibar (1991) has pointed out, there are significant differences between what we see in Greece and more "classical" forms of racism. If Balibar's hypothesis is correct, these differences can be explained by the changing role of the nation-state in the production of inequality, and the transition from colonial to neoliberal techniques of domination in the capitalist world-system.

In rural Greece the discourse of racism that conditions the economic integration of immigrants tends to naturalize their social inequality in ways that both resemble and differ from older forms of domination. One example of this is the degree to which it resembles the construction of gender difference. In both cases the subordinate group is considered to be inadequate for participation in the public sphere, and its exclusion is enforced through the solidarity of the dominant group. This gives rise to a paradoxical relationship of simultaneous hostility and dependence between the two. Just as men exhibit a hostile misogyny together with domestic dependence on women, Greeks socially reject the attempts of immigrants in their midst to assimilate, while at the same time they have become completely dependent on their labor for agricultural production.

The difference is, however, that women were always socially integrated with men through marriage, kinship, political parties, and myriad other ways that acted to mitigate the effects of male sexism. Immigrants enjoy few of these mitigating factors, arguably leaving them even more vulnerable to exploitation and violence than women ever were.

Thus it can be argued that social inequality in rural Greece under the influence of neoliberal globalization has become even more extreme, despite the perceptions to the contrary among local residents. As we shall see in the following chapters, this veiling of social inequality through anti-immigrant racism has been accomplished through the spread of neoliberal concepts and practices of citizenship on the one hand and the framing of local resistance to the EU project on the other. I will argue that both of these developments are aspects of the changing nature of the nation-state and national identity in the context of the global hegemony of neoliberal capitalism.

Notes

1. These figures should be taken as approximate. They are based on applications for legal employment status after the implementation of the 1997 regularization program (Lianos 2001:6). Applications numbered 352,632, representing (depending on estimates of illegal population) between 30 and 50 percent of the total immigrant population.
2. Due to the risks involved for the subjects, I did not collect data on immigration status. My estimates come from the estimates offered me by immigrants and local residents. The actual number may be well above 10 percent. In some cases I suspect that immigrants who claimed to have permits in fact did not, or had incomplete, expired, etc. papers.
3. Overall 70 percent of immigrants to Greece are male (Tzortzopoulou 2002:47-48), but female immigrants tend to be concentrated in urban and touristic areas, a reflection of the gendered patterns of migration in Southern Europe today (Anthias 2000; Anthias and Lazaridis 2000).
4. Despite legalization and the implementation of working permits, the system remains chaotic. Gathering the various papers and stamps is extremely time-consuming. Permits are routinely issued late; in some cases permits have already expired by the time they are issued. The chaos of the bureaucracy and the delays in issuing permits keep even legal immigrants in a precarious position (Tzilivakis 2004b).
5. The dispersal of immigrant housing is also a characteristic of urban areas that has become an important element in the marginalization and "invisibility" of immigrants (Lazaridis and Psimmenos 2000).
6. Such patterns are typical of contemporary illegal migrations. According to DeGenova (2002: 429), "undocumented migrations are constituted in order not to physically exclude them but instead socially include them under conditions of enforced and protracted vulnerability."
7. The term "moral panic" denotes the way that perceived social problems carry significance beyond their "real" effects and thus highlights their social construction (Goode and Ben-Yahouda 1994). Developed by Cohen (1980), moral panics are seen to represent broader social anxieties and are related to older forms of mass hysteria such as folk devils or witch hunts. S. Hall (1978) sees contemporary media-fueled moral panics as reflecting a breakdown of hegemonic control and a move toward more coercive measures on the part of the state.

8. The southern part of Albania is sometimes referred to by Greeks as "Northern Epiros." Epiros is the province of Greece bordering Albania. "Northern Epirote" is used to describe an ethnic Greek or Orthodox Christian living in Southern Albania and connotes the idea of a "Greater Greece" in the Balkans.

9. Such claims are doubtful. Baldwin-Edwards and Safilio-Rothschild (1999) argue that there is no direct link between immigrants and native unemployment in Greece. On the contrary, they argue that immigrants have bolstered employment in Greece by filling in gaps in labor supply and providing cheap labor for otherwise unprofitable economic activities.

— *Chapter IV* —

THE SOCIAL TRANSFORMATION
OF THE COUNTRYSIDE

In the previous chapters we saw that the transformation of agricultural production in rural Greece under the EU has been incomplete. Farmers continue to resist the "rationalization" of agriculture and have maintained many aspects of pre-EU production. They have been able to resist economic pressures of market liberalization largely by exploiting the labor of immigrant workers. In this chapter we will examine more closely the social changes in the villages that have been stimulated by EU integration. Here again, I will argue that immigrant labor plays a significant role in the expression of social change and the forms of social organization that have evolved.

The promise of social change was an important element in the expansion of the EU into Southern Europe. For rural Greeks, a rising standard of living and liberation from the shackles of social inequality were important incentives in their support for EU integration. One of the novel aspects of the EU as a transnational economic and political regime is its use of political consent, rather than military force, as a means of expansion. In exchange for opening of internal markets to European capital, Greeks were offered the possibility of escaping the forms of class and gender domination that characterized postwar society. Many rural Greeks perceived an opportunity to subvert the old structures of patronage and dependency that had locked them into chronic underdevelopment. Women and young people looked to European modernity to free them from the fetters of traditional gender and kin restrictions. The reality has not lived up to expectations. The initial boost to farmers' incomes from the opening of European markets has been overtaken by rising prices of consumer goods, growing pressures on CAP subsidies, and slow economic development. New opportunities available to women and young people in the service industries have been offset by high unemployment and low wages. These problems have only been deflected by the availability of low-cost immigrant labor. As with the restructuring of agriculture, the social transformation of rural Greece has been incomplete and tentative. The implicit promise of the EU was a move toward greater equality and the improvement of living conditions for all sectors of society through the expansion and liberalization of transnational markets. While there have been significant changes in the class position and consciousness of farmers as well as gender and kinship relations under the EU, it is the availability of immigrant labor rather than economic development that has done the most to stimulate these changes in the villages.

Peasant to Petty Bourgeois?

Rural Greece has traditionally formed part of the semiperiphery of world capitalist economies. In recent decades, and especially with the entry of Greece into the EU in the early 1980s, this condition has undergone a fundamental transformation. New relationships between local village economies and transnational commodity and labor markets have been established, profoundly influencing village societies. The increasingly direct involvement of Greek agriculturalists in transnational European markets has affected both what is being produced and how production is being carried out. In short, the class relations of agricultural production are undergoing change. Greek agriculture is becoming less dependent on family labor and more dependent on the wage labor of immigrants to carry out production. The growing dependence of rural Greeks on commodity markets to meet their consumption needs has created pressures to maximize profits at the same time that the value of agricultural labor is falling. This has encouraged families to diversify their labor into nonagricultural endeavors, but not to abandon agriculture entirely, leading to a contradictory position combining aspects of a peasantry and a petty bourgeoisie.

Rural Greeks are no longer dependent on their own production to meet their daily needs. The bulk of foodstuffs and other goods that they consume is procured from markets and stores in the valley and nearby towns. Certain items, such as fresh vegetables and some meats, are sometimes proudly described as "homemade" (*spitiko*) or "our own" (*dika mas*), but these items make up a shrinking part of daily consumption. While homegrown foods do help to offset household expenses, especially for elderly residents, their appearance on the dinner table often seems to reflect a stubborn nostalgia rather than thrift. For other foods, as well as clothing and most other household items, families have turned to store-bought goods. Two supermarkets, as well as several clothing shops operate in Agia Triada. A short distance away, on the main road between Nauplio and Argos, are several more large supermarkets belonging to transnational chains. This shift has increased the dependence of households on external markets and, therefore, their income needs. Families have adapted by devoting more time to cash crops and by encouraging family members to work outside the home. The family labor diverted from household production has been replaced by lower-cost labor provided by immigrants.

These changes have had a profound impact on relations of production at the village level. In the past, the surplus labor and subsistence production of the Greek peasantry was a valuable reserve for the industrial societies of the foreign capitalist centers and urban Greece. The production of this surplus was predicated on a complex web of noncapitalist, "traditional" social relationships, most prominently of gender and kinship. The advent of globalized labor markets and the increasing centrality of market economies in village life have both disrupted these traditional relationships and shifted the techniques by which the social inequalities and labor discipline necessary for rural production are reproduced. While rural Greek households are becoming more dependent on service industries and light manufacturing, they have also shifted their role in agricultural production from laborers to owners. As owners of land, rural Greeks are dependent on the exploitation of immigrant labor and access to state subsidies that have, in a sense, become a form of rent. In fact, it is problematic to speak of rural Greeks as a class of labor at all. What the EU has made possible, it seems, is the incorporation of Greek farmers, not as an urban or rural proletariat, but as something close to a petty bourgeoisie (Tsoukalas 1987).

Class has always been a problematic concept in the analysis of rural Greek society (Lampiri-Dimaki 1990). The historical development of rural Greek society has produced a number of special characteristics that distinguish it from other Mediterranean and Balkan societies. First and foremost, the series of politically expedient land reforms that accompanied the birth and expansion of the Greek state both dissolved the old Ottoman landowning class and prevented the formation of a new landed aristocracy. The result was, and this is especially true for the Argolid region, a rural society of peasant smallholders with relatively little difference between the richest and poorest. The Greek economy, both rural and urban, has been heavily weighted toward small- and medium-scale production units, a problem that continues today. In addition, the Greek state has always been relatively weak and for most of its history almost completely dependent on foreign powers. Internally, this has meant a reliance on patronage networks organized through competing political parties, a middle class dependent on civil service positions, and a weak national bourgeoisie propped up by both the state and foreign sponsors. Finally, the rich ethnic and geographic diversity of the Greek countryside has tended to compartmentalize both labor markets and social identity, further obscuring class formations and deflecting class consciousness. Historically the result has been a notable lack of the kinds of antagonistic class formations found in other Northern Mediterranean countries, as well as the lack of the type of peasant-based political party found in other Balkan countries.

Some propose that things are not much different today. Damianakos argues that Greek farmers as a whole have retained many qualities of a peasantry, and that even today "for most Greek 'farmers', agriculture is not an occupation: it is a condition to which they submit because the economy provides no credible alternative" (1997: 192). In this view, the mass of Greek smallholders has basically retained a rationality of subsistence production, but with social relations that have been distorted by the expansion of capitalist markets. Control by transnational capital has increased, but the basis of their incorporation into world markets has not provided the foundation for a transformation of either class consciousness or the structural conditions of their exploitation. The Greek farmers' pluriactivity, high debt, shifting relations of production, and continued dependence on subsistence production thus represent a disorganized reaction rather than a step up the class ladder.

Greek family farms employ a complex and heterogeneous set of productive relations between labor and capital. They are sites for both external and internal relations of production. They have also followed diverse and contradictory paths of integration with respect to global markets (Kasimis and Papadopoulos 1997). To think of them as a petty bourgeoisie glosses over the contradictory nature of their involvement, as neither labor nor capital, and the incompleteness of their transformation. It does, however, highlight the degree to which Greek rural families have decreased their direct role in production and shifted their attention to ownership and management, even if this has been accompanied by increasingly direct control by transnational institutions.

Today, Greek farmers in Argolida often characterize themselves as petty bourgeois or middle-class (*mikro-mesai*). They use this term in two senses. In one sense they refer to a perception of social equality, of belonging to the same social class. There is a strong sense that social differences between Greek farmers have declined in the postwar period. Families that were wealthy and had large landholdings slowly sold much of their land to finance their children's move to urban businesses, and land-poor peasants who did not move to the city were able to slowly gain land or small businesses. Today in Midea township I could not find a single Greek family that subsists entirely on wage labor with no property or business of its own. In another sense, "middle-class" refers to a perception of having land and property as capital to be monetized, invested, and exploited. Most of the land held by villagers is exploited for market production. Farmers are constantly strategizing for market success, and their goal is to produce a return on their investment, to live off the profits of their production rather than labor.

Orange farmers, for example, often strategize to obtain the maximum returns from their land. They choose species depending on location of the land and availability of water. They invest in fertilizers and labor to maximize production. They also choose when to harvest by weighing the risks of bad weather against the rise of market prices. Most farmers carry out little of the actual labor themselves, preferring to hire day laborers to harvest and often even to prune and fertilize. Instead they concentrate on managing their investments wisely in order to maximize returns. Other farmers operate in a similar manner. Truck farmers choose what crops to plant based on location and market prices. Even olive producers select species to maximize profits, as one olive producer in Gerbesi explained to me:

> After high school I didn't make it into university so my father set me up with 45 stremmata. I decided to plant olive trees because they need very little work and I have confidence that there will always be a demand for oil. I picked a species that produces very high-quality oil that gets a good price. This type of tree needs watering, though, so I had to invest in a well and pump. Now the trees are seven years old and produce well, but I take good care of them too, I don't just leave them to chance. Still, it's not much work, regular watering, a little fertilizing in the spring. The only hard work is harvesting in the fall, but I just get a few Albanians to do it. I clear about 13-15,000 euros a year, plus the subsidy from the EU. That's enough for me to live on because my wife has a job.

For the villagers, land is capital to be invested in wisely. The returns come not from the labor, which is generally purchased and considered a business expense, but from the management of the investment. This is somewhat less true for truck farmers and herders, though. In both of these cases the labor of the farmer plays a more direct role in the generation of profits.

Agricultural strategies have undoubtedly been influenced by availability of both low-cost labor and state subsidies. In many cases, farmers told me that they were reluctant to risk changing their production strategies as long as they were guaranteed a steady income without having to work too much. This is particularly true for citrus farmers. Making changes such as switching species or converting to organic produce entails extra work, a temporary loss of income, and market risks. Given the general pessimism concerning the future of agricultural markets, most farmers are content to continue as they are. The availability of immigrants and the floor prices set by state subsidies mean that farmers can continue to receive income with little work, essentially as a form of rent, while devoting their time to other endeavors.

The *rentier* character of many Greek farmers today helps to explain the resistance to the "professionalization" of farming. For the most part this resistance comes from the farmers themselves. One of the explicit goals of the agricultural policies of the EU and Greek state has been the reduction and specialization of the agricultural labor force and a transition to "professional" large-scale farming. In Greece as a whole, it is estimated that around half the agricultural land and around one tenth of the farms qualify as "professional agriculture of large scale" (Papadopoulos 2001: 13). In the Peloponnesos, however, where small farms predominate, this proportion is much lower. In Midea township professional large-scale agriculture

Figure 8. Farmers' market in Nauplio

is the exception, found only in few of the larger orange producers, truck farmers, and hothouse operators. One indication of this is the relatively low number of full-time farmers enrolled in the New Farmers program.

The New Farmers program is an EU program designed to encourage the transition to professional farming. Under the program, farmers under age forty who start out with a minimum amount of land or livestock are eligible for various subsidies and exemptions from production limits. In exchange they must agree to work full-time at farming. In Midea township there are only a few young men who have enrolled in the program. When I asked young men who are involved in farming why they did not take advantage of the program they described several obstacles. It is often difficult for young men to accumulate the necessary land, which is usually gained through inheritance. Because landholdings are small and inheritance is traditionally split equally among children, it is difficult for one child to inherit enough land to qualify at a young age. Parents will sometimes distribute land unequally, but only after their other children are settled in careers and it is clear that one child has greater need. For example if one child becomes settled in the city with a good job and the other stays in the village, the one in the village will probably inherit the bulk of the land. These issues are often not cleared up until later in life. In addition, there is a tendency for parents to hold on to land titles as long as they can, even if the land is worked by their grown children. This strategy enables parents to retain a measure of authority over grown children and is a constant point of conflict (Athanasopoulou 2002: 103-112). More importantly, young men, and their parents, are loath to commit to a career in agriculture, preferring a flexibility in employment strategies that is precluded under the New Farmer program. Since pluriactivity in employment is the ideal, young people are reluctant to devote themselves full-time to agriculture. In the village of Gerbesi I found only one young farmer, who had set up a honey production operation, enrolled in the program. In Agia Triada I found only two, one who has an organic hothouse and another who grows oranges.

The lack of interest in the New Farmers program is symptomatic of the general ambivalence toward agriculture displayed by villagers, the overwhelming majority of whom say that they do not want their children to become farmers. Agriculture is seen as a career of last resort, to be followed only when other career possibilities are exhausted. Villagers cite the declining prices of agricultural products and rising expenses that make it difficult to make a living with the small average acreage of the area. There is also anxiety about the future; indeed, the overwhelming majority are pessimistic regarding farming as a sustainable livelihood. At the same time, however, agriculture is seen as an important supplemental income, and land is sold only with reluctance. In fact, most farmers told me that, given the opportunity, they would buy more land rather than sell. While some of this ambivalence is based on speculation regarding the future land market for vacation homes, it also seems to be a result of the value placed on part-time farming and the lack of other avenues for capital investment.

Rather than the "professionalization" of agriculture, the last several decades have brought an increased tendency toward pluriactivity, rooted in the flexible patterns of employment and frequency of urban-rural movements that have characterized Greek society since at least the early twentieth century. Statistically, around 30 percent of farm heads, 15 percent of farmer's spouses, and 23 percent of other family members combine agriculture with other jobs in Greece (Papadopoulos 2001: 14). In Midea township, the percentages seem much higher. Based on interview data, I estimate that in the upper village of Gerbesi only around 20 percent of households live exclusively on agricultural income. For the valley town of Agia Triada the figure is even lower, below 10 percent. The majority of households combine income from agriculture with other forms of income, and are thus pluriactive. Pluriactivity can take different forms, however. In some cases a head of household combines farming with other pursuits. A café owner whom I interviewed in Agia Triada, for example, who runs the café with his brother, gets about a third of his income from oranges he grows on 30 stremmata. Many farmers, especially in Agia Triada, combine farming with a small business, civil service position, or skilled labor. Other households have pluriactive members, which seems to be more common in Gerbesi. For example, in one family the 65-year-old grandfather continues to farm a small piece of land and collects a small pension, while his son and daughter-in-law, who live with him, work in salaried positions in the nearby city of Argos, he as a truck driver and she as a physical therapist. Eventually, the son plans to take over the farming responsibilities as well. In Midea township most pluriactivity centers around the service and tourist industries. In other areas of Greece, the pluriactivity of the rural population is connected to the development of light manufacturing and the garment industry (Kalantaridis and Labrianidis 1999; Hadjimichalis and Vaiou 1987).

Pluriactivity has a positive value for households for several reasons (Zakopoulou 1999). It is perceived as a safe strategy because it spreads out the risk of economic downturns. Farming is still perceived as something to fall back on in times of hardship, whereas small businesses are held to benefit when times are good. In addition, it is widely thought that more than one source of income is necessary to maintain an adequate standard of living. The generally low income of farming, the low profit margins of small businesses, and the low pay of civil servants put pressure on households to combine sources of income. Because of its somewhat flexible labor requirements, farming is thought to be an ideal complement to the regular schedules of wage and salaried employment.

It is somewhat misleading, however, to think of pluriactivity only as the holding of more than one job simultaneously. In reality, pluriactivity signals the ability of households to exploit the labor of different individuals simultaneously. The pluriactivity of households generally reflects a strategy of diversification. Given the unstable economy and limited prospects for high-income employment in the area, families try to spread members out over a number of professions. Parents encourage children to pursue careers outside of agriculture but at the same time encourage them to stay in the household. Many people told me in interviews that "we keep the family strong here and we like to keep our children close." Indeed it is rare for an unmarried child to live outside the natal household in Midea township. Stem family households are the norm. It is very common for households to contain three generations, although in many cases grandparents live in adjacent dwellings while cooperating closely in terms of labor, childcare and meals.[1] In the households, it is generally the elderly who carry out farming tasks. Young people may help out sometimes, but are usually either going to school, working, or looking for work. Parents often complain that their children are lazy and that they expect to be taken care of by their parents indefinitely. However, in the family histories I obtained a clear pattern emerged of children taking over agricultural work and responsibilities when parents became incapacitated.

Individuals who are pluriactive, who hold more than one job, can only do so if at least one job is flexible and part-time. In reality very few individuals in Midea township can work as farmers and hold a job at the same time. Farming demands periods of intensive labor that make a regular time schedule difficult. Those who are technically pluriactive in fact do relatively little of the work themselves. For example, one man I interviewed grows oranges on 30 stremmata in Agia Triada and at the same time has a position with the town administration as a street cleaner, a lucrative civil service position. He does little of the farm labor himself, though. When intensive labor is required in his groves, such as at harvest or for pruning, he contracts with laborers. If he had to do the farm labor himself he would not be able to hold his second position, which requires that he work a five-day, 35-hour week. Thus the pluriactivity of the Greek farmer in Midea township is possible only because of the available cheap labor of immigrants. It would not be possible otherwise, and indeed I found no example of a farmer who was pluriactive *and* did farm labor himself.

Pluriactivity in Midea township tends to reinforce perceptions of class homogeneity and minimize class antagonism. Since both individuals and families tend to simultaneously pursue different economic strategies, i.e., agriculture, small businesses, and wage labor, class consciousness remains ephemeral and diffused. Attempts to support the emergence of a professional class of farmers have met with only minimal success. While such a class may emerge under pressure from EU policies, the expression of its interests are so far inchoate and muted. Pluriactivity, a strategy of evading classification, in fact represents a certain resistance on the part of farmers to their consolidation as a class. A recent attempt to define a professional class of farmer through the Registry of Farmers and Farm Enterprises (MAAE) completed in 1997, has so far been ineffective, in part because of the blurring effect of pluriactivity in farming households (Papadopoulos 2001: 20-22).

Partly as a result of this resistance on the part of farmers, as well as other pressures like GATT policies, the EU has more recently shifted to a sectoral rather than agricultural approach to rural development. The latest phase of CAP policies emphasizes economic diversification and the preservation of heritage through tourism and "heirloom" production. It has been argued that the discursive framework of CAP policies and the paradigm shifts in the underlying definitions and assumptions concerning "rural" societies play a significant role in reconfiguring local practices (Gray 2000). In Greece, the sectoral approach seeks rural development through policies that accept agriculture as a largely part-time activity. This approach inherently recognizes the power of family and community relationships in the transformation of rural areas and attempts to use them as bases for the "rationalizing" of agriculture. In contrast to previous CAP policies, pluriactivity is embraced as the norm, and attempts to promote the development of a professional class of farmers are de-emphasized. The sectoral approach also has implications for understanding the reproduction of agricultural labor in the countryside. Rather than focusing on the *labor* of the farmer through his so-called professionalization, the focus now is on the management of the farm enterprise, the recruitment of labor being left to the family and community to sort out.

The incomplete and contradictory process of "petty bourgeoisification" of the Greek peasantry has produced a number of problems and contradictions. The process has been limited by the inadequate structural conditions. Land is limited, and existing landholdings are inadequate for the basic capital needed by household economies, given current market conditions and prices. Furthermore, other economic sectors are still unable to provide enough economic opportunities for local residents, leading to a relatively high rate of rural under- and unemployment. This problem has largely been held in check by the existence of a program of state subsidies that allows families to maintain a high standard of living while propping up many unproductive rural businesses. The dependence on subsidies and bank loans, together with the control exercised by global markets, has meant that perceptions of increased autonomy and freedom, and of a corresponding rise in class status, are somewhat illusory. At the same time, the attempt to raise the peasantry into the ranks of the petty bourgeoisie *as a class*, which has been necessary to preserve the political legitimacy of the shift toward neoliberal market policies, has created a labor shortage. Rural Greeks, expecting a certain standard of living, no longer want to work as agricultural laborers. This has created the paradoxical situation in which a high level of unemployment co-exists with a shortage of agricultural wage-labor. Farmers can no longer afford to pay the wages demanded by Greek laborers and can no longer rely on other means for mobilizing the necessary labor, such as kin and gender obligations. The solution to the labor crisis has been found through the introduction of migrant laborers from the destroyed economies of Eastern Europe, a process that has disguised the class contradictions in rural Greece and obscured the ongoing problems of development.

Shifting Gender Roles

The transformation of relations of agricultural production and household economies in rural Greece has also had a tremendous impact on gender and kinship relations. Greece, like the Mediterranean region in general, has long been a focus of gender and kinship studies. Prominent gendered discourses of honor and shame and visible symbols of female subordination have been documented and analyzed by researchers from a variety of theoretical perspectives. Gender inequality has been explained by analysis of symbolic dichotomies that transcend different levels of social organization, maintaining difference by the weight of ideology (Herzfeld 1986). It has also been analyzed in functionalist terms as the expression of social power, where kinship and gender difference organize and maintain public and domestic realms of production and exchange (Dimen 1986; Friedl 1986; Vernier 1984). Others have sought to locate Mediterranean ideologies of gender difference in their wider political-economic context, as a method of social control and economic organization under weak states of the capitalist semiperiphery (Schneider 1971). Despite differences in analysis, however, most studies note important connections between ideologies of kinship and gender inequality and relations of production, especially in rural areas. This is consistent with a peasant model of production in which the household exists on the periphery of capitalist production and is maintained through the reproduction of non- or precapitalist techniques of stratification (Medick 1981). In this model, the family serves both as a reservoir of surplus labor and a means of supporting that labor cheaply. Household labor, organized through kinship and gender, can be seen as a means of reproducing and maintaining productive labor at low cost. The labor of women and children, in particular, can be seen as an early form of flexible labor, filling seasonal, temporary, and part-time positions as needed and controlled through an ideology of patriarchal domination.

However, most of this work is based on ethnographic research from the 1960s and 1970s. More recently, under the influence of globalized markets and institutions, there is evidence that these patterns of inequality have been transformed, particularly as women have entered the formal workforce of the service industries and wage labor. This has generally been seen as a process of modernization, often depicted as part of a trend toward greater freedom and equality in rural areas. The commodification of female labor and declining fertility in Greece have both served to disrupt traditional labor markets (Kottis 1990). In rural areas this has contributed to a shortage of seasonal labor. The long-term effect has been the growing dependence on foreign migrant labor. The way in which migrants have been used to replace family labor has received relatively little attention. We have made some headway toward understanding the implications of the gendered patterns of the new migration and its relationship to the commodification of female labor in host countries (Anthias 2000). However, we have only just begun to understand how access to immigrant labor in rural areas has led to shifts in the discursive production of social inequality.

While gender differences remain strong and inequality persists in many areas, such as the formal workforce, it seems clear that traditional gender constructions have been disrupted. In Greece, the social and economic position of women has undergone rapid transformation in the last several decades. These changes have been both ideological and material. As women have made progress towards legal equality under neoliberal regimes and increased their presence in formal, public arenas, their association with the private sphere of household production has weakened. In addition, as we have seen, female labor in pluriactive households has tended to focus on wage labor in response to the increased dependence on commodity consumption rather than household subsistence production. The participation of women (aged 15-64) in the labor force increased from 42.6 percent in 1990 to 49.7 percent in 2000, although unemployment figures for women have risen as well, from 12 percent to 16.9 percent, over twice that of men (Ketsetzopoulou 2002: 127-128).

Rising rates of women's participation in the labor force are characterized by several important developments. There has been a general expansion of the service sector, where female employment is most concentrated.

Educational attainment levels have also been rising much faster for women than for men. Despite high levels of unemployment, there is a definite trend among women away from agricultural labor. With the expansion of nonagricultural sectors and the increasing need for two incomes, female agricultural work as a percentage of all female employment fell from 21.5 percent in 1960 to 1.4 percent in 1995 (Crouch 1999: 433-439). At the same time informal "family work" (chiefly agricultural) as a percentage of employment for females dropped from over 20 percent to under 10 percent during the same period (Crouch 1999: 89). These figures suggest fundamental changes in the mobilization of female labor, in particular a shift from kin-organized household labor to wage labor.

National statistics provide a framework for understanding some of the macroeconomic shifts in labor markets. If we look at figures for Midea township, the picture becomes somewhat more complicated. In the 2001 census,[2] 72 percent of males and 46 percent of females aged 15-75 are listed as economically active. Of economically active males, 51 percent are employed in the primary sector (agriculture), 14 percent in the secondary sector (manufacturing and production), and 24 percent in the tertiary sector (services); 6 percent are unemployed. For economically active women, 55 percent are employed in the primary sector, 6 percent in the secondary, 27 percent in the tertiary, and 8 percent are unemployed. From these figures we can discern that female employment still lags considerably behind male employment. Among economically active females, however, there is higher unemployment and less concentration in the secondary sector, which in Midea would be mainly packing and juice factories and various utilities, such as the telephone, electric, and water companies, all of which are considered to be good and stable sources of income. These figures, however, may not capture several important elements of the labor market. They exclude "off-the-books" labor, which is prevalent. They also do not capture pluriactive individuals, in particular men who combine a formal job with part-time agriculture.

The changes that have occurred in gendered labor patterns in Greece are mostly consistent with patterns of development in other European countries. The mid-century model of social organization in Europe was characterized by a gendered occupational structure in which men were associated with formal industrial and distribution sectors, while women were associated with informal household sectors. That model has been undergoing a transformation since the early 1960s as more women have moved into the expanding service sector. The increased participation of women in the formal economy has been accompanied by the development of a "bicephalous gendered occupational structure" (Crouch 1999: 112) in which the concentration of women in the lower-paid and more flexible service sector has balanced out the declining rates of male employment in the industrial and manufacturing sectors. This development has formalized many household tasks as staples of the service economy and has created incentives for the shift of domestic tasks from a private informal arena of the household to a public informal arena increasingly staffed by immigrants.

Greece is somewhat of an exception to this pattern due to the continuing prominence of the agricultural sector and the weakness of manufacturing. As a result Greece has a relatively high rate of self-employment characterized by a high degree of household production and multiple occupations. But even here the same type of transformation can be discerned. Agricultural production in Greece has long been characterized by small-scale household production. In this context, men's labor has been associated with formal, "public" networks of exchange, while women have been tied to informal, "private" arenas of production (Friedl 1986). In the last decade, women have entered the service sector, even in the villages. The result has been a reconfiguration of the family in relation to other social institutions, along with a reorganization of household economies. Traditional patterns in relations of production and the mobilization of labor have undergone a transformation. Taking this into account, we can better understand the articulation of migrant labor in a new order of inequality. In Greece and other areas of the Southern European semiperiphery, the hegemonic position of ideologies of gender and kinship traditionally employed to organize relations of production are under pressure to change. However, this has occurred within a context of continued, and even growing, social inequality, which is increasingly legitimated and reproduced through constructions of ethnic identity and citizenship.

Collier (1997) has described the transformation of gender relations and family organization in an Andalusian village since the 1960s. Much of her analysis can also be applied to Greek rural society. Comparing two models of family organization, one of the 1960s and the other of the 1980s, Collier analyzes changing modes of social reproduction under the increasing intrusion of the capitalist market. The 1960s model was characterized by an emphasis on duty and organized around patriarchal authority and a well-defined code of kin and gender relations. Kin and gender relations organized relations of production through the ownership and inheritance of property and were thus crucial to the local production of inequality. Villagers could be divided into status groups based on property holdings, with a small aristocracy of landowners dominating smallholders and landless peasants. The household division of labor was largely organized by gender and age. By the late 1960s, however, this model had begun to disintegrate as competition from capital-intensive mechanized farms drove down prices for agricultural products. Urban migration followed, particularly among lower-class villagers who could no longer survive on day labor.

By the 1980s Collier detects a shift in the discourses of economic and moral inequality. As villagers became increasingly entangled in capitalist industrial relations and alienated from the means of production, discourses of ownership and inheritance give way to discourses of earning and achievement. Increased value was placed on personal character, hard work, ambition, and education. This shift did not necessarily result in greater freedom or equality for women. In fact, Collier argues against a reading of modernization as increased freedom. In many ways, modernization represented a loss of power for women and their increased dependence on their husbands, particularly with the relative decline in the importance of dowry. Rather, Collier argues that this process of modernization more importantly resulted in a new subjectivity, where identity is made or achieved instead of inherited. At the same time she notes a shift to ethnicity (i.e., Andalusian) as opposed to local village distinctions of genealogy, age, and gender as primary markers (1997: 195). Here Collier's ethnographic evidence is rather thin, but I suspect that this new experience of ethnicity is crucial to understanding new forms of social inequality, and is related to what Stolke (1995) terms "cultural fundamentalism." Collier does not mention the immigration of North African laborers into Andalusia in the 1980s and 1990s, but it seems that local inequality there is now organized by ideologies of ethnic and racial difference. In recent years extensive hothouse agriculture has developed, worked by low-wage North African immigrants who are also subject to violent racism from native Andalusians (Hoggart and Mendoza 1999; *New York Times* 2000a, 2000b).

The development of rural Greece has been somewhat different. Greece for the most part lacked a powerful class of rural large landowners, and the extensive mechanization of rural agriculture was limited to certain crops, such as cotton. However, rural Greece has also undergone a similar transformation of gender and kin relations in recent years. The most noticeable development in rural Greece has been the departure of women and, especially, children from agricultural labor. While Greek men have continued to work in the fields, even if often as managers of immigrant labor, women have turned to either service industries or the growing demands of childcare. Women and children have also emerged as important consumers of various commodities. A vivid example of this is seen in the transformation of the traditional coffee shop, or *kafeneio*, into the *kafeteria*. Cowan (1991) has documented the proliferation of kafeterias as a disruption of traditional gendered forms of sociality. Kafeterias, or coffee and pastry shops frequented by both males and females, explicitly transgress the traditionally male public arena of the coffee shop (*kafeneio*) as a center of village life. Cowan argues that kafeterias represent the "hegemonic penetration … by urban Greek and European institutions, symbols, and forms of sociality that are effectively displacing their indigenous counterparts" (1991: 202). Today kafeterias in rural Greece are full of males and females, but few immigrants frequent them, as they are more expensive than the kafeneio.[3] Although some bars and cafés catering to migrants are beginning to open, they remain segregated and out of view. This is not to say that gender inequality has disappeared. Indeed, what is more surprising is the ways in which discourses of gender difference have persisted in the face of changes in relations of production and consumption.

The ideology of gender inequality in rural Greece has always had a complex and often contradictory relationship with actual practice of gendered behavior, as has been noted by numerous anthropologists. Despite its importance in organizing relations of production, gender difference has never been reducible to economic relations. Gender has been used not only to define a division of labor within the household economy but also as a discourse for negotiating the complex relations between levels of identity, from the individual and family to the nation-state (Dubisch 1986; Herzfeld 1986). Despite the changes in the organization of household production, gender continues to be a strong and visible basis for inequality in rural Greece that even conditions the integration of immigrant labor into the household. In some ways, we can discern similarities in the techniques by which immigrants are, and women were, excluded from the public domains of social power.

The Politics of Gender and Family in Argolida

Despite women's increased access to political and economic rights under the EU, social spaces in the villages of Argolida still tend to be segregated by gender. This is especially true in the higher-altitude villages.[4] In the towns of Argos and Nauplio women move freely, and there are few places or professions that are off-limits to them. Couples often go out together, and men can be seen engaged in mundane tasks of childcare and domestic errands. The villages, by contrast, are considered more conservative and "traditional" (*paradosiaka*). Whereas in the valley villages there is somewhat more public mixing of unrelated men and women and the gendered division of labor is not as strictly enforced, on the whole daily activities and the use of space continue to be segregated by gender. This fact had implications for my own research. As I was a single male working in the villages, my ability to interview women or participate in their activities was severely limited. Thus most of my information comes from interviewing and observing men or family groups.

In the villages the traditional bastions of male authority have been strongly defended, especially in the upper villages. In Manesi and Gerbesi, and to a lesser extent in Agia Triada, kafeneios and *tavernas* tend to be almost exclusively male, although they will sometimes be staffed by women, usually female relatives of the owners. Indeed, men have successfully defended their monopoly on much of the public space of the villages, including the village square, roads, and surrounding countryside. Men freely travel from village to village at all hours of the day and night. Groups of boys (age 9-10 and up) freely roam the village until well after dark. Not all men participate in the public male spaces of the village, but most do. By my estimate approximately 60 percent of village males regularly visit the coffee shops and taverns, many on a daily basis. Men who frequent the public spaces of the village tend to define the political discourse of the village as well, and constitute what Loizos (1975) calls "political action groups." Women, on the other hand, rarely venture outside of their homes, other family properties such as fields, or the homes of their relatives. When they do venture into public spaces it is almost always for specific errands, such as purchasing bread, going to church services, or going to and from work. Within the home, however, women exercise a great deal of authority. This gendered division between "public" and "private," often documented by anthropologists in the past, continues to define village life in Argolida today.

In the upper villages the division between male and female spaces is strictly enforced by the villagers, especially the men. Young girls are often seen playing in the public square when the weather is nice, and are often sent to the coffee shop or the store on errands. However, as they get older the older men will begin to chase them away. Several times, as I sat in the square in Gerbesi watching groups of children play in the early summer evening, men would approach and let out a sharp "*Oust!* Home!" that sent the young girls scampering. Boys, on the other hand, were free to roam the village until very late. When I asked a local man why he did that, he replied, "Girls have to learn. Their place is at home, not in the square." After puberty, village girls are rarely seen loitering in public areas of the village, except in the company of relatives. Men maintain a strong ideology of female inferiority, despite somewhat contradictory practices. They insist that women are inadequate for many diverse tasks, such as driving cars or public leadership, even though in practice women frequently carry out such tasks. I frequently heard statements such as: "Women are lower than men. That is a fact and you should remember." On the other hand, women are thought to be capable of exercising power over males through the creation of dependency, giving rise to the view that "a man without a woman is nothing." Often this takes the form of expressions of sexual dependency. On several occasions men repeated a common saying among males in the villages that "one pussy hair [*mounotrikha*] can pull an entire ship. If you see a ship up on the mountain, it was pulled there by a pussy hair." On another occasion an elderly man confided to me that "we have a saying here: 'Let the women depart first and leave us peaceful,' but if that really happens we suffer." Thus men exhibit both hostility to and dependence on women, behavior typical of the Mediterranean "machismo" complex.[5]

The exclusion of women from public spaces is usually justified in terms of sexuality. Men are widely considered by villagers to be naturally promiscuous, and their promiscuity is even a badge of honor, entitling them to respect from other men and even many women. Women's promiscuity, on the other hand, is considered shameful, and most will avoid giving the impression that they are available for extramarital sexual activity. When I asked one young Agia Triada couple in their thirties about the difference, the wife replied: "Look, if my husband had an affair I would be angry, but I also understand that it is just their instinct [*instincto*]. That's just the way they are, it doesn't mean that much to them. With women it is different; it is more of a betrayal. Women can't separate sex from everything else." In practice, this means that many men spend much of their time pursuing, or at least talking about, potential affairs with other women (usually married) while at the same time jealously guarding their own wives from the predations, real or imagined, of other men.

The gendered division of space and definition of sexuality provides an underpinning for the gendered division of labor within families, but it is also a frequent point of conflict. There is great variation in how families divide labor and the amount of conflict that this division provokes. However, through interviewing and observing many families in both the valley and mountain villages I could discern tendencies that correlated with household economic strategies. Agriculturalist households, not surprisingly, tend to maintain a stricter division of labor. Women's labor in the fields is a necessary component, and their tasks tend to be sharply delineated. Among tobacco farmers, men handle most of the plowing, fertilizing, irrigation, and other "heavy" or "dirty" tasks. Both men and women harvest the leaves, but women are mainly responsible for the tying and hanging of leaves to dry. Among herders, men do most of the herding and women do most of the milking. Among truck farmers, women help with harvesting and usually handle the sales at the farmers' market, while men handle the plowing, fertilizing, irrigation, lifting, and packing. In most cases women's tasks keep them close to home or to their properties, seldom working alone, while men are often on their own for much of the day, running errands and carrying out solitary tasks. This freedom of movement often insures that many a man will end up at a coffee shop or tavern to drink and gossip with his friends on a daily basis. As they pass through the village on various errands, men often run into friends and end up sitting for hours drinking and smoking. The men's ability to escape from the house is generally tolerated by women since it leaves them "peace and quiet" (*isihia*) to carry out their own tasks and visit with other female relatives and neighbors. Thus men often leave in the morning, return for the midday meal and nap, and depart again in the early evening, turning over the house and garden to the authority of the women. While women often complain about their husbands' "laziness" (*tembelia*) and excessive drinking, they generally seem grateful not to have them around constantly.

The division of labor tends to be more fraught with conflict among pluriactive households, especially those in which the wife is employed. It is more and more common for women, especially younger ones, to live in the villages but work in nearby towns. Village women hold a variety of positions, from wage laborers in shops and small factories to salaried workers in civil service, teaching, or other professions. In most cases they provide a significant, sometimes the most significant, part of the household income. At the same time they continue to carry the burden of housework and childcare, even if generally there are older female relatives around to assist them. Most women in this situation suffer from a high level of stress. In the villages men sometimes step in to assume part of the responsibility for childcare and housework, but most often they do not, at least partly from fear of losing status in the eyes of other men. For example, when I attended the Easter feast at a house in Gerbesi one of the men there, who was visiting from Nauplio, became the butt of ribald jokes when he got up to help his wife wash the dishes at her request. In his defense he said: "That's the way we do it in the city. We both work, we both share the chores."

In households where women work outside the home, men will generally take on agricultural responsibilities, even if they also work another job. They are able to make up for the wife's absence by hiring immigrant laborers to carry out necessary tasks. Women, however, do not have this option with housework and childcare. Immigrants are not trusted by families to work inside the house or to take care of children or frail elderly relatives, so women must take on double duties. Women are judged by the quality of their housework and the condition of their children much more than men are. In fact, several times villagers attributed unruly behavior of children to the fact that their mothers worked outside the home. This causes great anxiety in women, who feel that they are constantly behind in their housework and neglecting their children. In addition, many of the women who work outside the home are not native to the village but have "married in" and so lack the support of relatives and childhood friends. At the same time, they feel that their economic contribution gives them a certain entitlement to the freedoms that, in the villages, are male prerogatives, such as going out to cafés and tavernas. As one woman said: "Look, the other women in the village, they can't raise their heads or their husbands will cut them off. I'm not like that. I work. Why should he go out all the time and leave me at home. I want to go out too, I want to go to a café, the cinema, to visit friends in town. He doesn't understand that." Despite her bravado, however, this woman rarely socializes with friends on her own. Instead her "free time" is generally devoted to catching up on housework or watching television. "Going out" was a constant source of friction in pluriactive households. Most of the men avoid taking their wives out, claiming they don't want to spend money and prefer to socialize with their male friends. Men are clearly uneasy with the prospect of their wives having public social lives not connected to themselves or family. This is a constant theme of women's complaints in the villages.

Men try to hold on to their differential access to the public sphere by restricting the movements of their wives and monopolizing their labor, but at the same time are increasingly dependent on their involvement in the formal, public economy. This is also reflected in changing marriage strategies and dowry practices. For some agriculturalists, particularly herders and those in the higher villages, it is increasingly difficult to find wives. Most young women, and their families, see marriage as an opportunity for upward mobility. In the neighboring village of Bardi, for example, a 35-year-old herder has been trying unsuccessfully to find a wife for several years. He is fairly well-off, with a large herd, but few women are interested in the monotonous and "dirty" duties of a herder's wife. He has few opportunities to meet women socially, and attempts at arranging a marriage have been unsuccessful. One of his friends told me: "I found a shepherd girl over towards Epidavro. She wasn't much to look at but she could handle a herd of goats like a man. So I found out who her father was and went to talk to him. I told him this and that, that I had a nice boy. But he said 'What? She's a shepherd now! What shall I do, give her to another shepherd?' That was the end of it." In many villages herders are turning to Albanian women as brides, but this has yet to happen in Gerbesi or Manesi.

Other agriculturalists, such as truck farmers, have an easier although still difficult time. Girls' situation is a little easier since they are not expected to carry on the family business and properties and parents are often willing to invest substantial dowries in a "good" match. Given the low number of children, there is more pressure on boys to stay in the village, unless they have other brothers. Thus while girls are often pushed to marry out of the village, boys are more often expected to remain in the village, something that a bride's parents may resist if it is considered a step down. Often, rather than a formal courtship with parental approval, village boys must resort to "stealing" brides.

In the past, most marriages were within the villages, but villages often took brides from poorer villages and gave their own daughters to richer ones. For example, boys in Gerbesi and Manesi often took brides from the poorer villages of Bardi and Limnes further up the mountain, while girls were often married to boys in valley villages or towns. The same was true of Agia Triada, whose men took brides from Gerbesi and Manesi but more rarely gave them. The parents' first choice was to marry off their daughters outside the village if possible. Young couples could circumvent this pressure by bridetheft, whereby the couple publicly displayed a sexual relationship, thus forcing the hands of the parents. Young men sometimes employed this strategy to obtain wives they could not have gotten formally. For example, a farmer in Manesi from a relatively poor family described to me how he got married:

> I got married young. I was twenty years old and we had some problems in the house. My mother died and my father, you know, he was drinking. My younger brother was getting wild. It fell on me to take care of things, to cook, everything. So I said to myself, 'this is not making it.' I decided to marry. I knew my wife from around the village. She was younger and used to go up the hill with a few sheep for her father. So I started following her, talking to her nicely, and soon we were having sex. She was crazy about me. Then I went to her father and said this and that. He went crazy, said he would kill us both. He wanted to marry her in the valley. She only had a sister and so she had a nice dowry. But what could he do? Everyone knew about it by then.

The disadvantage to stealing a bride is that the dowry is at the discretion of the parents, since it is not negotiated beforehand. In this case, because the only other sibling was a sister who had already married in the valley, the dowry was more or less assured. But in other cases a stolen bride may receive very little as parents may take the opportunity to bolster the dowries of her sisters or the inheritance of the sons. For this reason, some parents facilitate the theft of daughters by turning a blind eye to budding romances.

Today bridetheft of a sort continues. Some marriages today still entail large dowries. In a recent example, when a young woman from Midea township was married to a doctor in Nauplio I was told the dowry was valued at close to a quarter million euro. My informant quickly added, "but he is a doctor." However, as more and more daughters select their own husbands, either through socializing in the cafés and discotheques of nearby towns or while studying in the cities, dowries have become after-the-fact gifts rather than incentives. As one local farmer explained to me: "My daughter is studying at university. When she finishes she will be able to get a good paying job. She doesn't need a dowry to find a good husband. She will probably stay in the city. For her dowry I will probably give her some olive trees. That's why we have the olive trees, to give them as dowry. The rest, the fields and the house, will go to my son. We like to keep sons close and he will need all the property in order to find a good wife himself." As this statement implies, many villagers have come to see the expenses of education as a kind of dowry. As women have entered the formal economy, dowries have become less important for marriage and have been replaced to a certain extent by the financing of young women's education. Instead of dowry, women's skilled labor is considered more valuable, something that helps to explain why in recent years more females than males in the higher villages are going on to higher education.[6] Except for parental support during their education, women essentially earn their own dowries. The alternative for females is to find a husband through romantic sexual relationships. At the same time, this has allowed parents to endow sons with enough property to survive and prosper in the village.

Changing dowry practices also reflect changing practices in how children, in particular daughters, are raised in the villages of Argolida. Since the marriage prospects of daughters are perceived to be improved with education, parents generally encourage schooling and readily pay high fees for after-school tutoring. After secondary school, those who pass the exams attend postsecondary institutions. If they make it to university they will go off to live in cities far from the day-to-day surveillance of their parents. Such freedom for girls still in their teenage years was rare as recently as a generation ago. Even if they do not go away to school, girls in the last years of secondary school are afforded a remarkable amount of freedom from parental control. Village girls dress attractively, affecting the latest urban styles, and, particularly in the summer, regularly go out to discotheques and cafés with their friends, often staying out until the early morning hours and traveling home by taxi. Most parents continue to insist on modesty and decorum for the girls while they are in the village, but often they turn a blind eye to their romantic adventures in the nearby towns. This period of freedom is considered to be a time of experimentation preceding the duties of marriage, but is also a way that girls can find potential husbands. As one woman in Agia Triada explained to me: "When I was a student, before I was married, I lived alone in Athens. It was a great time; I could do whatever I wanted. I could go out with boyfriends without any problems. Then I met my husband and settled down. It is important to have that experience, otherwise you think you are missing something and you have regrets." Compared to the experiences recounted by older women, such freedom is in stark contrast to the conditions usually faced by previous generations of women in the villages.

Sons have always enjoyed the kinds of freedoms that daughters are beginning to experience in the villages, but they too have benefited from new child-rearing practices. From my interviews with parents I detected a sharp decline in corporal punishment of children by parents. While most parents, particularly men, told me they were regularly struck or whipped by one or both parents when they were young, few would approve of such punishment today. Two parents told me of incidents when they had recently whipped their children with belts, but they always told the story with expressions of guilt and regret, saying they had "lost control." Also, in both cases the punishment was of older children who had failed to properly look after younger ones. Parents often threaten to beat children, sometimes carrying out an elaborate theater of taking off a belt in an attempt at scaring them into behaving, but they rarely carry out the threat. In explaining the change in practice, parents will often attribute it to a concern with the "psychological" wellbeing of the child and the harmful effects of parental "repression" (*katastoli*). Psychological problems are usually attributed to parents' behavior. One mother told me in an interview: "I saw a show on television and there were psychologists talking about children. They said that if your child is anxious [*nevriko*], look to yourself. In other words it is the parents who make children anxious by being anxious themselves. This really seems true to me." Boys, however, are still encouraged to be aggressive and, by American standards, quite willful. In the villages, it is common to find boys of four or five years of age who curse fluently and threaten their parents when they are denied sweets or other things. Such behavior is usually greeted with laughter and approving comments such as, "He's such a tough fighter [*tsampoukas*]!"

Most Greek parents readily assert that children today are much more "spoiled" (*kakomathemena*) than in previous generations. Parents, in particular mothers, go to great lengths to accommodate the specific demands of their children, often preparing special dishes for them or buying them treats and toys. One young mother, as she bustled through her kitchen preparing special snacks demanded by her two sons, told me: "Look what I do for them! They are my masters [*kirioi*], that's what I call them."

Figure 9. Tobacco farmer and daughter

However, parents also often complain that as they reach their adolescence children become "lazy" and refuse to work or help out around the house.

In the last several decades children have become significant burdens on households. For parents the cost of freedom for their children is mainly economic. Education is expensive, given the necessity of private tutoring to overcome the perceived deficiencies of the public school system. In addition to schooling, children demand an increasing number of commodities in order to acquire and maintain social status. Cell phones, brand-name clothing, spending money, and for boys, motorbikes and cars are all considered necessities by young people, who rarely work before finishing school. Most of these things have to be provided by parents, even if it stretches their budgets. Parents refuse requests for money with great difficulty and feelings of guilt. Once I was with a shepherd when his son, a student in Athens, called on the cell phone to ask for 300 euro for some expenses including a trip to an island with some friends for the weekend. Even though I knew the shepherd was short on cash, he agreed. I later accompanied the shepherd as he borrowed some money from his mother-in-law and got the rest from the bank before sending it via the bus company to Athens. "Let him have fun while he is still young" was his only comment. The expense of raising children was the main reason villagers gave for the precipitous decline in birth rates over the last several decades.[7]

Besides costing money, children have also generally ceased to contribute to household production. In most families children rarely help out in the fields. Again, this is in stark contrast to the childhood conditions described by older and middle-aged villagers, who vividly remember being awoken before dawn to accompany their parents to the fields to work. Today such treatment of children would be considered abusive. Collier (1997) describes a similar change in Andalusia, where children, who once were raised to carry out familial duties and obligations, are now encouraged to desire their work as a form of self-actualization, a sort of Foucauldian internalization of social discipline. Besides altering the mechanics of social discipline, however, this shift in child-rearing practices and discourses, along with the departure of female labor, has contributed to a serious labor crisis in the traditional patterns of household production, a crisis that has so far been solved only by the importation of immigrant labor as a replacement.

Notes

1. The most common arrangement in Midea township is for new couples to construct their own dwelling either above or next to the husband's parents' house. While technically separate, the two households generally function as one, pooling labor, resources, and to a certain extent, income.
2. Figures from the 2001 census published by the National Statistical Service of Greece (http://www.statistics.gr/gr_tables/s1100_sap_5_euro38%20lau%201.htm).
3. In Midea township kafeterias are found only in Agia Triada, where there are three. Agia Triada has two kafeneios. In Manesi and Gerbesi there are only kafeneios: one in Gerbesi and two in Manesi.
4. In general, the gendered segregation of public spaces increases the further one goes up the mountain.
5. "Machismo" in rural Southern European societies has most often been analyzed as a psychological expression of male dominance (Brandes 1980) and/or a reflection of male ambivalence and psychological fragility in the context of female-centered households (Gilmore and Gilmore 1979).
6. In Gerbesi, for example, three young women and one young man were studying at university during my fieldwork.
7. Among families in Midea township today the average number of children is around two. This is a marked decrease from the previous generations.

— *Chapter V* —

THE STATE, CITIZENSHIP, AND IDENTITY IN ARGOLIDA

During my fieldwork, I was often struck by the stark contradiction between the perception held by many people that social inequality had decreased and the reality of a growing dependence on impoverished and marginalized immigrant labor. Many people, even those bitterly opposed to what they saw as the destructive force of "globalization" (*pankosmopoi-isi*), often conceded that Greek society today was much more equitable than the past. In particular, perceptions concerning the status of women and children have changed dramatically. Women are perceived to have greater political and economic power. Children are perceived to have more freedom, now being less oppressed by parents. Children of what was the rural peasantry have greater opportunities for education and upward mobility. For the population as a whole, conditions have also changed. The rural population is less isolated and less dependent on urban elites. Patronage networks have weakened. Many of these developments are attributed to Greece's membership in the EU, which has opened up trade[1] and promoted a shift toward more liberal techniques of governance on the part of the traditionally patriarchal, authoritarian, and clientelistic Greek state. At the same time that this rural "liberation" has occurred, however, there has emerged a new, and arguably more oppressed, class of labor made up of non-Greek immigrants. That both these things, the perception of greater equality and the creation of a new exploited class of labor, have developed simultaneously is, of course, dependent on the concept of a Greek "nation" that includes some and excludes others. Thus, despite the apparent weakening of the Greek state that has followed its incorporation into the EU, the production of a Greek nation continues to be instrumental in defining and regulating social relations.

Just as the emergence of the modern Greek nation was conditioned by the development of a state apparatus within the fractures created by the declining Ottoman Empire and expanding European mercantile capitalism, contemporary processes of Greek nationalism are shaped by the context of the Greek state and the EU parastate. In many ways, the persistence of Greek nationalism in the face of the transformation of the state under the regime of the EU is surprising. After all, for most of the twentieth century the political principle of nationalism was based on the assumption that "the political and the national unit should be congruent" (Gellner 1983: 1). Many believed that as the EU developed, some form of pan-European national identity reflecting the new reality of the state would slowly replace ethnic nationalism. The fact that this has not happened is often attributed to the defensive reaction of those classes and class fractions most threatened by the transnationalization of state power. I will argue in this chapter that, far from being a defensive reaction to new forms of state power, nationalism in rural Greece is being conditioned by the particular characteristics of the EU state system and is in fact an integral part of the political economy in the context of EU-style globalization and neoliberalism.

Greeks in Midea township are constantly preoccupied with defining themselves vis-à-vis others in terms of gender, kinship, community, political affiliation, ethnicity, nationality, and class. It is largely the definition of these differences that, taken together, constitute what we call "Greek culture." Today these social differences are being produced under a particular form of globalized political economy that is often termed "global" or "late" capitalism. Swyngedouw (1989), among others, has argued that social relations under global capitalism continue to be inscribed at the local level, a process he describes as "glocalization." By now it is clear that globalization acts to condition the local production of difference in ways that benefit global markets. In this process, it is often assumed that the nation-state has weakened or been "hollowed out." I argue that the organizational level of the nation-state continues to be vital to the production of inequalities under contemporary globalization, and that the nation-state is being transformed rather than weakened. In this chapter I document some of the ways in which global forces have influenced the production of difference in Midea township through a reorganization of the relationship between nation and state.

Labor Migration and the Nation-State

The transformation of the role of the state can perhaps best be seen through a comparison of immigration policies and practices of today with earlier models. The current patterns of labor immigration from Eastern Europe are not without precedent in Greece. In the 1920s and 1930s the massive forced immigration of ethnic Greeks from Asia Minor and the Balkans swelled Greece's population by approximately 10 percent (Giannuli 1995; Ladas 1932; Pentzopoulos 1962), a figure comparable to the share of immigrants today. Of course, the historical conditions for this immigration were somewhat different. The earlier wave of immigrants was stimulated by a series of nationalist wars and provided a solution to the national question amidst the debris of the Ottoman Empire. Today's immigrants are stimulated by the destruction of their native economies and the labor needs of Greece and other EU countries. Regardless of the differences in cause, however, the two waves of immigration pose certain structural similarities in terms of their relationship to the Greek nation-state. Like the immigrants of today, those of the 1920s became a resource for the state and provided the impetus for important political and economic changes. Socially marginalized and the subject to overt racism by native Greeks, immigrants provided both a vulnerable labor force for early urban industrialization and the driving force for a comprehensive land reform program that fundamentally altered rural relations of production. However, the relationship of the state to immigrants was drastically different. Whereas the early state facilitated their incorporation through *legalizing* their existence, the contemporary state has *illegalized* them, despite the necessary and important role they fill in the national political economy.

It may be said that the early Greek state had no choice but to legalize immigrants in the 1920s and 1930s, given the conditions under which they arrived and the impossibility of return to their native lands. But such a posture on the part of the state was characteristic of most immigration patterns during the mid twentieth century. The transnationalization of labor markets is not a new phenomenon, and indeed has been a characteristic of capitalist economies since their early development, even if it is only a recent focus of anthropological studies. In terms of sheer numbers, today's immigration is still dwarfed by the numbers of migrants during the period 1850-1914, when the capitalist core, especially the United States, industrialized (Hatton and Williamson 1998; Potts 1990). During that period, however, the capitalist states actively facilitated immigration and the movement of labor through a legalistic policy of granting citizenship rights and encouraging, through various means such as public education systems, the assimilation of immigrant workers. Despite currents of nativist racism, nationalism also acted to promote the cultural assimilation of new populations and to alleviate some of the social pressures of class conflict that labor immigration engendered.

In the post-World War II period European states continued to facilitate labor migration, but at the same time they erected partial bulwarks to cultural assimilation. Immigrants provided between 10 and 25 percent of the industrial labor in the capitalist core of Western Europe, but were managed through various "guestworker" programs that legalized their labor and guaranteed partial citizenship rights (Berger 1975; Piore 1979). Immigrants, although protected by the state, saw themselves as temporary citizens, even if in fact many ended up staying and second generations went through at least partial processes of assimilation (Portes 1998).

By the end of the twentieth century, however, the relationship of the state to immigration had undergone a radical change. While numbers have not significantly increased, the labor markets immigrants participate in have changed, with the bulk of immigrants now consigned to what has been described as "informal" or "irregular" economic sectors rather than the "formal" industrial sector (Castells 1989; Kloosterman et al. 1998; Wilpert 1998). Most importantly, immigration is now characterized by its *illegality* (DeGenova 2002). The prevalence of illegal labor in European countries, including Greece, reflects a fundamental transformation of the state and its role in reproducing relations of production. As we have seen, the state is instrumental in the marginalization of immigrants, a significant difference from previous policies that supported, at least ostensibly, their assimilation. Today the state is in the apparently paradoxical situation of *illegalizing* the very labor on which it depends in order to subsidize economic development and social liberalization. This position reflects the state's fundamental shift to neoliberal practices of governance as well as a transformation of the relationship between state and nation under advanced or "globalized" capitalism.

Politics and Anti-politics of the Contemporary State

The European Union is constituted by a diverse set of institutions, practices, and ideologies. It is experienced by the people of Argolida in three distinct ways, which we can roughly separate into political, economic, and social dimensions. On the one hand it is experienced as a sort of supranational state with a set of laws and policies that sometimes supplement and sometimes supersede local and national ones. On the other hand it is experienced as a form of mini-globalization where economic markets and capital flows are separated from national-state controls and consolidated into economies of scale, at least within the confines of an expanding Europe. Finally, it is also experienced as a cultural or social project representing the convergence and strengthening of a "European" model of society, a process that some have termed "Europeanization" (Borneman and Fowler 1997). Each of these political, economic, and social domains is an arena of negotiation, conflict, and accommodation for local residents as they confront social changes.

One important effect of EU membership has been the weakening of the Greek state in certain respects (Ioakimidis 2000). Direct state control over the economy has decreased through the transition to "free" markets and the privatization of formerly nationalized industries. In terms of laws and policies, the Greek parliament remains the primary source of governmental power, and local residents are much more interested in national elections than in those of the European parliament. However, in certain areas EU laws and regulations are seen to supersede or "tie the hands" of Greek parliamentary decisions. This is especially true in areas such as the exercise of citizenship rights, travel, government spending, business practices, and environmental regulations, to name a few. In other areas EU policies are seen as supplemental to Greek state policies. For agriculturalists this is especially true of the various programs of price supports and economic aid that are more and more administered and funded by EU institutions. The EU has also promoted the decentralization of state power in Greece and has provided substantial funding for NGOs and other citizens' associations. Overall, EU membership is seen as having strengthened "civil society" in Greece through a "redefinition of the boundaries between the state and society in favor of the latter" (Ioakimidis 2000: 90).

In economic terms the EU is seen by local residents in Argolida as the driving force behind the creeping deregulation of markets. The Greek state, in many ways a classic example of an authoritarian state managing a semiperipheral economy (Mouzelis 1978), has historically taken a strong role in the capitalization and support of industrial development as well as the regulation and administration of domestic markets. This role has been rapidly dismantled by the EU's insistence on "free" markets integrated into a European core economy. In urban areas many industries have been shut down or absorbed into transnational corporations as government support has evaporated. Small businesses have also been under pressure as large corporations such as supermarket and electronics chains have moved in to displace small owner-operated shops. In Argolida real market prices have declined as crops such as citrus have been subjected to international competition and price supports have declined. The perception among agriculturalists is that, as several farmers told me, "prices are now set by the German consumer." On the other hand, the deregulation of markets has also brought in a flood of lower-priced consumer goods, such as clothing, electronics, and automobiles, which were formally subject to high tariffs by the Greek state.

Rising levels of consumption have contributed to the perception among rural Greeks that their society is becoming increasingly "Europeanized." This development is viewed with a mixture of satisfaction and apprehension. People perceive that the widespread poverty and "idiocy" of rural life has disappeared, yet at the same time they are troubled by the erosion of what they perceive as traditional values of family and community solidarity. The participation of rural Greeks in European and global consumer markets, as well as the introduction of the euro currency and European passports, has tended to promote a kind of European consciousness among Greeks, who now see less difference between themselves and other Europeans. Often this is displayed in the common assertion that "in a few years Greeks won't exist anymore, only Europeans." This consciousness is generally promoted through practices of consumption. One young woman told me that after riding on the new, French-designed Athens Metro she "felt like a European for the first time." Even in the villages, Greeks feel that through television and other media they have become more "European."

When I conducted fieldwork in 2003, Greece had been ruled by the socialist party PASOK for almost twenty years, with the exception of

1989-1993, when the conservative New Democracy (ND) party was in power. PASOK, guided to power by the charismatic Andreas Papandreou, oversaw the entry of Greece into the EU as well as the increasing liberalization of what had been a traditionally conservative and at times strongly repressive state apparatus. In many ways, PASOK was well suited to the modernizing project of the EU despite the clientelistic character of Papandreou's administration. Rural development was given a high priority, as were women's rights, the expansion of educational opportunities, and social welfare programs. Throughout this period in Argolida PASOK gained support both in the valley, which had traditionally been conservative, and the mountains, where many villages were traditionally communist. Local residents attribute this shift to the pro-agriculturalist stance of the PASOK government and its success in attaining EU funds in the form of subsidies and programs (Fouskas 1997), as well as to the increase in civil service positions that in Greece have traditionally served as a form of political patronage.

Ironically, the success of PASOK and the EU has led to a depoliticization of local government. In Greek villages, where political differences were once an important aspect of social relations, local party offices are now difficult to find or even nonexistent. In Agia Triada the offices of both major parties have closed. In Gerbesi, where the Communist Party of Greece (KKE) had strong backing, the local party organization has been effectively dissolved. While people still vote along party lines, for the most part, and continue to identify with one or another party, their activity is no longer local but instead national. They vote for parties in national elections and garner information on political programs and policies through the national media. Given the lack of formal party organization at the local level, people also seem to switch their votes more readily. In local elections most people tend to vote for individuals rather than along party lines. There is only one village in Midea township where town council representatives are formally affiliated with a political party.

For the last ten years an independent bloc under the leadership of the mayor, Panagiota Nassou, has run the Midea township government. Ms. Nassou is a prominent doctor in the village of Agia Triada and has a medical office on the ground floor of the town hall. She has practiced there for over twenty years and is married to a business owner from the city of Corinth, about 50 km away. Her father was one of the largest landholders in the township. Her brother and two unmarried sisters now manage the family lands. Nassou was originally a member of PASOK, but left the party and was elected as head of an independent slate.

The township government of Midea is run by the mayor and town council. The town council consists of 25 representatives. The presidents of each of the nine villages in Midea township serve on the council together with between one and three representatives of each village, depending on size. Of the 25 council members, 18 belong to the Nassou bloc, with the remaining 7 representatives making up the opposition. Nassou's bloc is made up of representatives with a wide range of political affiliation. The vice-mayor, for example, is a conservative. Neither is the opposition, headed by a representative with PASOK leanings although no longer a party member, united by political philosophy. Instead, the opposition operates mostly as a contrarian force, opposing the Nassou bloc on the basis of its competence in carrying out various programs and public works. The Nassou bloc meets in closed-door session before every council meeting, where representatives from each village battle over funding and programs, each trying to secure a bigger share for their village. At the public meetings the bloc presents a united front, having already decided on various proposals.

Political parties play a larger role at the regional level, where representatives are elected to parliament. Argolida elects three representatives to parliament in a proportional system. In 2004, two of the representatives were from the conservative party, New Democracy, and the other from PASOK. One of the conservative representatives, Elsa Papadimitriou, is particularly active in Midea township, participating in many community events. Papadimitriou is from a family of conservative politicians. While party allegiance still tends to hold in the national elections, vote switching seems to be increasingly common. Several former communist voters I spoke with, and even some PASOK supporters, told me they intended to vote for Papadimitriou both as a protest against current corruption and because she is effective in getting funds and programs allocated to Argolida.

Most people in Midea township hold a fairly cynical view of politics and politicians. The decline in political activism and party membership in the area is generally attributed to the view that there is little real difference between the parties, and that in any case politician's hands are tied by both EU policies and the interests of big capital. In the words of a resident of Manesi, who supported first the KKE and then PASOK:

> Look, after the dictatorship fell in the 1970s everybody ran to join a party. There was a feeling that with democracy many things could change. Everyone wanted to give their opinion. When PASOK took power, it was like a revolution, people were dancing in the streets. In those days the PASOKists were like regular people, they dressed without ties and expensive clothes. Now, if you look at them, they all wear Armani, expensive clothes. Where did they get so much money? For twenty years it has been eat, eat, eat. Do you know how much money they have eaten? They turned out to be thieves like the others. So now, no one gets excited about elections. Here one group will eat well, then another group will come and eat well. But it is better not to have the same group too long, it is better to keep them a little hungry.

Political ideology plays a diminishing role in elections, particularly at the local level. Politicians are seen as technocrats whose job is to manage the country within the framework of the EU while keeping corruption within tolerable limits. A certain amount of corruption is seen by most as inevitable and even desirable as long as it is not concentrated in a few hands. One former communist told me "it would be better if everything belonged to the state, then we could all steal from the same source, we could have a democracy of thieves."

Until the late 1980s, political parties were highly visible in the villages and towns of Greece. Party offices were usually prominently located along main streets and marked by large signs and flags. With the declining importance of patronage networks and greater restrictions on the parameters of state policies under the EU, these offices have, for the most part, disappeared. Since 1989, the main political dynamic has been not so much the different policies and programs of political parties, but the struggle between "populists" and "modernizers" within each party (Fouskas 1997). Both major parties are undergoing a struggle between the "old guard" of populist leaders who continue to exploit clientelistic networks of political support and a "new guard" of modernizing technocrats. Since the passing of the regime of Andreas Papandreou, a consummate populist, in 1995, the modernists have had the upper hand. With the PASOK government under the leadership of Simitis from 1995 to 2004, there was a concerted move to reorganize and modernize the state and economy along European lines while preserving some elements of the welfare state. Since the ascendancy of a technocratic, European-oriented political class elections have become less about policy and more about personality. People I spoke with in Argolida generally cast their ballot in favor of the person they thought would perform better. Frequently they based their vote on a calculation of which politician was more "hungry" (*peinai*). A typical statement was: "There is not much difference anymore. But these in there now, they have gotten too lazy. They have eaten too much. This time I will vote New Democracy because they are hungry, they have been out of power for ten years. It is not good to have the same group in power all the time."

The constraints imposed by the EU model of economic development have led to conditions similar to the "anti-politics" described by Ferguson (1990) for Lesotho. In the case of Lesotho, Ferguson argued that international development projects facilitate particular kinds of intervention that narrow the parameters of possible social changes and reinforce the bureaucratization of state power. While Greece is a weak comparison to Lesotho, parallels can be seen in how the imposition of a bureaucratic discourse of economic and social development, a "European" model, has served to limit political options and even suppress political debate and struggles. "Development" is seen as a technical rather than a political problem. Political management is increasingly seen as an administrative skill rather than a creative act, hence the rise of a technocratic political class of university-trained managers.

The European Union and Neoliberal Governance

The development of the European Union as a political and economic system is the latest chapter in a long history of state development in Europe, which is in turn tied to the emergence and spread of capitalism as the dominant mode of production. As the European bourgeoisie rose to social dominance, first through the mercantilist expansion of the seventeenth and eighteenth centuries and then through the industrial revolution of the nineteenth century, the old feudal social order crumbled and disappeared. The new economic order required new forms of state regulation and administration that differed from the powerful and centralized monarchies that had risen with the decline of feudalism. The modern state, which, though it first emerged in the Americas, was the product of a long struggle in the Northern European mercantilist kingdoms, was characterized by a philosophy of liberalism that provided a fertile environment for the development of capitalist relations of production.

Liberalism, as an ideology of government, essentially acted as a mode of regulating society that facilitated the expansion and consolidation of capitalism by setting limits to formal powers of government. Liberalism was not so much a plan of government as a set of guiding principles that arose from the problematization of the relation between a free market and political sovereignty (Burchell 1996). The emergence of the liberal state was accompanied by a new source of political legitimacy, the nation, which made the liberal state possible as a functioning entity. The early liberal capitalist nation-state system of Europe was hobbled by a pattern of periodic crises, however, which resulted in several important corrections. After the destruction wrought by successive world wars in the early twentieth century, capitalist economies entered a period of Keynesian intervention whereby states sought to stabilize the fluctuations of capitalist production and regulate the intensity of class conflict. This period, often described as "Fordist" (Arrighi 1994; Gramsci 1971; Harvey 1990), culminated in the postwar establishment of "welfare states" in many parts of Europe. During this period European states became more dependent on the expertise of positivist social science to engineer social integration and exercise rule (Rose 1996: 39-40). The Fordist resolution to the contradictions of liberal capitalist political economies proved to be temporary. By the late twentieth century a new round of economic crises and social conflicts provoked a political-economic shift to "advanced liberal" (Rose 1996) or neoliberal states and a globalized capitalist mode of production. In Europe, this move was embodied in the expansion and deepening regionalism of the EU.

The neoliberal turn in global capitalism has been reflected in a paradigm shift within the capitalist core countries away from a Fordist-Keynesian state model to one that has been variously described as a "competition state" (Cerny 1995) or a "Schumpeterian post-national workfare regime" (Jessop 2002). As a revitalization of classical liberalism, neoliberalism "proposes that human well-being can best be advanced ... within an institutional framework characterized by strong property rights, free markets and free trade" (Harvey 2005: 2). Older forms of state regulation and intervention are rolled back and limited to creating and protecting social conditions for the free functioning of markets. As a general trend, neoliberalism is reflected in pressures to privatize state enterprises and services, the use of market proxies in what is left of the public sector, and the shift towards viewing public welfare spending as a cost of production rather than a source of domestic demand (Jessop 2002: 454). This does not necessarily result in a weakening of the state, but rather a readjustment as states seek to adapt to global trends and forces. The state acts to manage political consent and social stability "without generating policies that interfere with the free play of internationalized market forces" (Crouch and Streek 1997: 12). Often this takes the form of a resurgent nationalism that absorbs citizens' discontent, but also obscures the declining control of national governments over economic policies.

Neoliberalism, as an overarching philosophy or "rationality" (Foucault 1991) of governance, has been implemented in different ways. The EU, because its development has been shaped by a context of market deregulation and globalized production and trade, represents a particular manifestation of neoliberal governance. The European experience of neoliberalism differs significantly from that in other parts of the world, such as Eastern Europe, largely because of the social democratic history of the core European states and their ability to continue to provide a measure of social protection for the more extreme forms of market predation. As Vivian Schmidt observes, "Europeanization has acted both as a conduit for global forces and a shield against them, opening member states up to international markets and competition at the same time that they protect them through monetary integration and the single market" (1999: 172). In this way, the EU has developed as a unique combination of both neoliberal economic principles and traditional European social policies.

Even though the EU maintains a relatively strong social policy, the primary dynamic of European integration since the 1980s has been the adaptation to global neoliberal trends (Laffan 1998). A single European market was envisioned in the 1957 Treaty of Rome. Its implementation in the 1990s after the Single Market Act of 1986 and later with the European Monetary Union (EMU) was clearly aimed at furthering regional cooperation as a means of maintaining global competitiveness and restructuring the economies of member states in a politically acceptable manner (Schirm 2002). Economic restructuring in member states has been stimulated by the rising costs of neo-Keynesian policies and enhanced incentives of market liberalization in the present global environment. Because the EU operates at the supranational level, it has also been able to effectively "tie the hands" of member states to make restructuring seem all but inevitable. The fact that this has, in many cases, been accomplished under the stewardship of social democratic political parties attests to the social opposition the move to neoliberalism has provoked and the special ability of leftist parties to survive the political consequences (Hamann and Wilson 2001). Social democratic parties and leaders are able to deflect responsibility to the European or global level, as well as more easily ease or manipulate the economic costs of restructuring.

There is still debate over whether the neoliberalization of the European economies can really be achieved. Many European states continue to blend liberal and social democratic policies, and significant differences remain in national markets. While European firms have been consolidated, they have often done so on a consortium basis and have not been restructured as truly transnational enterprises (Calleo 2001). Others argue, however, that the potential for producing a "social market" version of capitalism under the EMU is weak at best (Whyman 2001). So far market stability and growth have been given priority over social protections. The stringent conditions of fiscal policy effectively prevent a return to neo-Keynesian policies, and the emphasis on low inflation seems certain to support continued high unemployment rates.

The ideology of neoliberalism has proven to be as important as its practice. Besides the implementation of specific policies and market conditions, neoliberalism also works in a more ephemeral way as a discursive framework, a kind of rationality, whose effects have gone beyond forms of *government* to modes of *governance*. As part of this new model, new techniques in the production of social discipline have evolved. In one sense, neoliberalism represents an extension and intensification of basic liberal techniques of governance. According to Colin Gordon:

> The fulfillment of the liberal idea in government consists—over and above the economic market in commodities and services, whose existence founds the classic liberal attribution of an autonomous rationality to the processes of civil society—in a recasting of the interface between state and society in the form of something like a second-order market of governmental goods and services. It becomes the ambition of neoliberalism to implicate the individual citizen, as player and partner, into this market game. (1991: 36)

Neoliberalism also involves some novel shifts in the liberal paradigm. Nikolas Rose analyzes the move to "advanced" liberalism through three characteristic shifts. First, there is a new specification of the subject of governmental rule embodied by the citizen-as-consumer so that subjects "fulfill their national obligations not through their relations of dependency and obligation ... but through seeking to fulfill themselves" (1996: 57). Second, there is a shift from social theory to accounting and economic expertise as techniques of critical scrutiny. Finally, there is a pluralization and detaching of various regulatory technologies. The government is "de-statized" and the state is "de-governmentalized." Devoid of political struggle, the state is increasingly seen as a technical apparatus appended to market operations.

One of the most important underpinnings of European neoliberal governmentality is the principle of subsidiarity. Douglas Holmes (2000) describes subsidiarity as a "surrogate discourse of power," a guiding philosophy that shapes the organizational structure and technocratic practice of the EU. Subsidiarity is a principle of selective centralization that seeks to centralize only those state functions amenable to an economy of scale while at the same time constructing an interdependence of social groups and levels of regulation. Extending the classic liberal skepticism of state authority, subsidiarity constitutes a principle for circumscribing domains of governmental action and devolving authority to the lowest possible levels while making as much room as possible for the construction and functioning of civil society.

The idea of civil society as a diverse set of institutions operating between, and checking the power of, the market and the state on the one hand and individuals and families on the other, is a key concept of liberal society. While it has been linked to the peculiarities of the emergence of Western European modernity with its dispersed authority (Gellner 1995; J. Hall 1995), in recent years the idea of civil society has regained currency as models of "democratic" Western society have been exported to other areas of the globe (Keane 1998). As a concept it has been employed by a diverse set of social philosophers, from the architects of the EU and the economists of the World Bank to those further left such as Gramsci (1971).

Given the historically contingent nature of civil society (Hann 1995; Mouzelis 1995), we should be skeptical of claims that the liberal mode of governance embodied in the EU has been, or can be, seamlessly exported into what have historically been semiperipheral societies. Instead, we need a frame of analysis that can take into account the particularities of different paths and experiences of integration while enabling some generalization of their convergence. In this respect it is useful to think about Foucault's notion of governmentality (1991) as a way of understanding the social transformations underway in European globalization and the role of nonstate institutions.

In order to avoid ethnocentric assumptions of the relation between the state and other national-level social institutions, the notion of governmentality is useful. Building on his analyses of the microphysics of power embodied in such institutions as the prison or discourses such as sexuality and psychiatry, Foucault proposed to analyze the macrophysics of power relations within a nation-state in a way that transcends particular institutional divisions. Thus Foucault defines governmentality as the totality of institutions, procedures, and techniques that allow the exercise of a form of power or rule over a population (1991: 102). In thinking about governmentality the contours of the state as a formal institution are relatively unimportant for understanding how societies are ruled and power is exercised. Governmentality foregrounds two ways of understanding the power of the nation-state. First is an analysis of "governmental rationality" (Gordon 1991) or the "conduct of conduct," the ways of thinking or acting that shape and regulate individual behavior toward certain principles or goals. In this sense liberalism and neoliberalism constitute particular forms of rationality that guide the interpretation of social reality and shape individual behaviors. Secondly, it focuses on the technologies of rule, the array of techniques, procedures, institutions, and strategies through which authority is communicated and reproduced in the individual. The power of the state is an effect of the technologies of rule rather than a cause, and should be seen together with civil society as part of a totality rather than analytically distinct (Rose 1996: 42-44).

While the concept of governmentality is inherently vague as an analytical tool, it does help us to avoid reifying both the state and civil society as distinct, coherent, purposeful actors. As an array of technologies loosely integrated under a pervasive rationality (a term we would sometimes define as "culture" in anthropology), the exercise of social authority lacks a strict unity or functionality. This perspective is useful in understanding the dialectical relationship between resistance and state authority in a way that goes beyond the simple oppositional relations entailed in some Marxist theory. It will also be useful as we try to understand the role played by resistance in Argolida as rural agriculturalists confront the neoliberal capitalism of the European Union.

Practices of Neoliberal Governmentality in Argolida

Neoliberal governmentality is enacted through a complex system of beliefs and practices concerning citizenship in the polity of the nation-state. The concept of citizenship in Argolida is increasingly egocentric, focusing on rights and privileges of consumption rather than production. As we have seen, such changes are particularly apparent in changing attitudes toward children and, to a lesser degree, women. In both cases we can detect a shift in the technique of imposing social discipline, as Collier (1997) has suggested, from "duty to desire." Social self-actualization is increasingly seen as a product of autonomous individual subjectivity rather than the imposition of identity by society. In this sense citizenship is more than a legal distinction. It is also a practice by which individuals claim rights and privileges within a society.

Evidence for a shift in the practice of citizenship can be seen in the changing significance of public education. Public schooling has always been an important factor in the creation and reproduction of national identities. Indeed, public schools were critical tools for the forging of national consciousness together with the "print capitalism" of early state-affiliated mass media (B. Anderson 1983; Weber 1976). In speaking with older residents of Argolida about their early experiences in public school, I was struck by the predominance of memories concerning civic mythology and state rituals. By their accounts, public schools placed great emphasis on teaching narratives that illustrated the origins and nature of the Greek nation-state, such as stories of the Revolution and its heroes, religion, and duties to the "Fatherland" (*patrida*). Until the mid 1970s teachers were responsible for encouraging church attendance among students. School discipline was maintained through corporal punishments administered by teachers, a fact still remembered today with some fondness. Yet now there is a perception that such efforts on the part of schools have been dropped in favor of a focus on skills and individual development. A farmer in Agia Triada gave me a typical criticism of schools today: "They don't teach patriotism anymore in school. There are too many foreign kids. My son, when he sees the flag, he doesn't feel patriotic. Most of the kids today, they don't know about the heroes of the Revolution, about the suffering of the people under the Turks. They are too easy on the kids, if they don't want to learn they don't punish them. We are getting soft! We are losing our culture!" There is a pervasive sense among the residents of Argolida that schools have begun to abandon their role in the reproduction of national identity. This is often blamed on the requirement that schools take in and educate increasing numbers of immigrant children.

The perception that the nationalist character of schools has weakened is largely shared by teachers as well. Two local primary school teachers I interviewed both told me that in the last decade there has been a move away from memorization and factual recall in the curriculum. Currently there is a push towards what is termed "biometric education" (*viometriki paideia*), a curriculum that emphasizes thinking and research skills. Such a curriculum is consistent with developments in other countries, such as the United States, toward a more student-centered educational model. The student-centered model entails a shift from emphasis on students' duties as citizens to their skills. Students are increasingly viewed as "consumers" of education in the same way that citizens have come to be viewed as "consumers" of governmental services.

For their part, the teachers complain of the lack of a knowledge base among students, who are often unable to recite basic facts, especially concerning Greek history. The teachers I spoke with assert there has been a conscious effort to de-emphasize the teaching of national identity. One said "the system does not need to pay attention to national consciousness anymore. It was useful for much of our history, but not so much now. Now the kids need to learn how to compete in the European economy." Many patriotic rituals remain embedded in the schools, such as the annual parades on national Independence Day, but clearly the emphasis in education has changed from particularistic knowledge of the Greek nation and culture to more liberal, universalistic notions of individual development and self-discipline, as well as skills considered necessary for students' incorporation into transnational capitalist markets.

The diminishing role of education in the production of national identity has not, however, resulted in a noticeable decline in nationalism among Greeks in Argolida. The sense of a Greek community and the definition of a Greek nation continue to be a preoccupation of mass media, especially television. Virtually every Greek household I visited in Argolida contained at least one television, and most people watch television on a daily basis. Television is also used as an "electronic babysitter," and many children watch five or more hours of television every day. There are many channels to choose from, including two local stations, six national stations, and one international channel (CNN) that are available with a modest antenna. Many more are available through satellite servers.

The importance of television in the villages has grown steadily over the last several decades. Until the late 1970s, television viewing was limited to two national stations, which broadcast for only part of the day. As was the pattern for Europe, both were government owned (one was run by the armed forces). In the early 1980s, as Greece entered the EU, television was deregulated and many private stations appeared, some financed by European capital. In the early years the privatization of television, the power of the American media market, and the rise of the EU led many to predict both a transnationalization of television through the rise of a "European" television market and a fragmentation of national into local or regional markets as technology became more accessible (Morley and Robins 1995). For the most part, however, such predictions remain unfulfilled. While production is increasingly outsourced, conforming to the economic principles of flexible accumulation, and distribution is increasingly monopolized by global media giants, privatized media production and consumption still tend to conform to national boundaries (Stevenson 1997). As Schlesinger observes, "the short history of attempts to fashion Europe-wide public-service satellite television channels has been above all a tale of casualties" (2002: 43). It has been argued that this is due to cultural and linguistic differences, but even in Latin America, where linguistic diversity is less evident, television has not been a very successful midwife to global or transnational identities (Waisbord 1998).

In retrospect, the persistence of national identities in Europe is not surprising. The expectation that the development of a European "state" will lead to the development of a "European" national identity represents a simplistic and uncritical assumption that the early capitalist period's relationship between "print capitalism" (B. Anderson 1983) and the nation-state will hold for late capitalism as well. In fact, with some exceptions (most notably among media directed to youth and business elites), mass media continue to be organized around national markets. Even though television has been largely severed from direct state control, the audience, as media consumers, is still constructed in national terms. This can be seen clearly in the television viewing of Argolida residents. Except for foreign (usually American) movies, dubbed children's programming, and international sporting events, the vast majority of programs are Greek productions. Most commonly these include serial comedies or dramas and news and interview programs. In both cases these types of programs are self-consciously "Greek" in character and provide viewers with an experience of national belonging.

Serial comedies and dramas tend to focus on what are perceived as common dilemmas and characteristics of Greek cultural life. People tend to closely follow whatever program is most popular during a particular season, often discussing plot developments or the antics of characters with great relish. From my observations I found that women were much more likely to engage in discussions about such programs, with the explanation that the subject matter focused on family and love affairs. In discussing programs that they had seen on television, people were very conscious of their participation in a national audience of viewers. Viewers also frequently pointed out to me the "Greekness" of the narratives with assertions such as "That's the way Greeks are!" (*etsi einai oi Ellines*). Thus, television viewing can be seen as a form of ritual (Ettema 1997) in which the representation of narratives of shared beliefs, and challenges to those beliefs, helps to construct a common sense of identity.

News programs and interview-format talk shows, which tend to be more heavily viewed by males, also contribute to the sense of a Greek community in Argolida. Except for news on the local stations, which tends to be directed at specific groups like farmers, news programs operate in a national format. They focus on events in different parts of Greece as well as issues of national government while also presenting a self-consciously "Greek" interpretation and analysis of world events. Current news stories are avidly followed and hotly debated among village residents. It frequently happened that different people would recount to me the same story, gleaned from television reporting, to back up their interpretation of the state of Greek society. For example, news stories of crimes committed by immigrants were frequently invoked to justify anti-immigrant sentiments. In another example, after widespread news coverage of an incident in which Greek troops participating in peacekeeping operations in Kosovo were attacked by protesters and an Orthodox church was burned, hostility against Albanian immigrants in Argolida noticeably increased. One young man told me: "When I saw that on the news my blood boiled. These Albanians are animals! It made me want to go out and thrash one."

Television has also had an important effect on the functioning of local governmental and civic institutions. In June of 2003 I attended a meeting of the Herder's Association (Sillogos Ktinotrofon) of Midea, called to deal with recent incidents of sheep theft. A culprit had been identified and the meeting was held to publicly condemn him and recommend punishment to the court. As is usual, a cameraman and a reporter, a woman in her thirties, showed up from one of the local television stations to cover the event for the local news program. The president of the association, who happened to also be the brother-in-law of the culprit, led the meeting. There was little debate over the recommended punishment, as it had been previously agreed to through informal negotiations among those most affected. The presence of the news media clearly excited the herders with the prospect of being shown on the evening's broadcast. After about fifteen minutes the reporter, exasperated by the slow pace of the nervous president, took charge of the meeting from the sidelines. As the cameraman recorded the proceedings she urged the president to follow a narrative format with orders such as "Make an introduction now," and then "Now you have to make a proposal and the guys should vote." which the president duly followed. She clearly wanted to package the meeting in a way conducive to television news reporting. After the recommendation was made for compensation and an official warning of community banishment in the case of further thefts, the reporter and cameraman interviewed individual herders for their reactions and quickly departed. On the evening broadcast the video from the meeting had been edited into a coherent narrative led by the voiceover of the reporter, who concisely described the conflict and resolution. Later, I heard several people compliment the president on his performance. Despite the fact that the court case was still to happen, and possibly a year or two away, the conflict seemed to have reached closure and ceased to be a topic of conversation.

In the case of the herders' meeting, the narrative requirements of television served to structure an official public process of conflict resolution. Local government has been affected in a similar way, with the demand for "transparency" through the standardization and broadcasting of public meetings leading to a particular, media-friendly format and processual structure. The interest of the television producers lies in attracting an audience in order to market advertising time to sponsors. Therefore, there is pressure to "package" news and events in a standardized, easily accessible narrative format. Through this process a particular form of governmentality is promulgated that provides both a rationality for social interactions and a technology for the exercise of social power. Furthermore, this process has the effect of channeling political behavior and conflict into well-defined, highly structured forms that reinforce the neoliberal nature of the contemporary state system. In the case of the herders' meeting, what had been a contentious issue was resolved peacefully. At the meeting there was little real debate or anger. The participants were pleased to be on television, and what comments they made were *pro forma* and self-consciously performed for the benefit of the camera. The potential social conflict arising from the sheep theft was effectively deflected.

The relationship between mass media and audience is crucial to understanding the constructions of citizenship under the neoliberal governmentality of global capitalism. Despite a pervasive functionalist paradigm that assumes media shapes and maintains cultural patterns primarily through transmitting information, most studies show that people learn relatively little from television. Instead, television tends to reiterate and re-enact what is already known. Even though viewers often claim television as a source of information, ultimately it creates an "illusion of being informed" (Buckingham 1997: 352). More importantly, television acts in important ways to construct the "we" of nationalist discourse, the audience becoming the imagined community of the nation. Besides this positive notion of community, television also serves as a defensive mechanism of community closure, acting to create the excluded "Other" through its totalizing discourse. Thus television does not so much link people into global networks as provide a new technique for the construction and defense of national boundaries.

Television has become an important instrument of neoliberal governmentality in Argolida in the sense that it embodies a representation of a particular rationality, a "conduct of conduct." Since the privatization of television, the rationale for its existence and the motor of its development and expansion have not been its role in educating and informing the population, as was arguably the case with state-controlled media. Instead television's main purpose is to sell advertising. Under the commercialization of television, stations and programming are evaluated by the numbers of viewers they can attract. Viewers constitute a market of consumers, rather than a population of citizens. It is precisely this rationality that has come to define the neoliberal subject as a "consumer" of government services, part of the proliferation of capitalist-economic rationality in previously "non-economic" domains of social life (Burchell 1996). Television viewers expect to be marketed to, and their participation in the networked community of mass media is constituted and internalized as a product of their own desires as consumers, despite the fact that the expression of these desires is more and more regulated. Thus television has come to embody the logic by which individuals participate in the neoliberal nation-state, as consumers of national identity and state services.

Television serves as an important technology in the exercise of governmental power. John Thompson (1995) has argued that the impact of mass media in the modern age has been most pronounced in the transformation of the public sphere and the relationship between power and visibility. Starting from a notion of "mediated publicness" (1995: 126), a concept similar to Anderson's "imagined communities," Thompson argues that "modern" social identity is no longer defined by physical co-presence in a common locale. This development has changed the relation of power and visibility. In a counterpoint to Foucault's theory of the exercise of power through increased surveillance, categorization, and visibility of its objects, Thompson argues that the visibility of power itself through the mass media is an important element in its effectiveness. While the state then is concerned with the "legibility" of its domain and subjects (Scott 1998), the nation and national identity are produced through the spectacle of power in which the state and nation become legible to their subjects. The visibility of social power through spectacle has been a common technology throughout the modern era (Debord 1995), but under the regime of neoliberal capitalism television has increasingly become the primary performance venue for such spectacles. In recent decades, there has been a growing disarticulation between the technologies of state surveillance and regulation on the one hand, and the spectacular production of national identity on the other. This development points to a reorganization of the nation-state project.

Citizens and "Others"

The disarticulation of nation and state under the European Union has had important ramifications for issues of identity and rights. To the degree that the institutions and policies of the EU have altered the form and function of national states in Europe, there has also been a concomitant shift in the concept of citizenship among Europeans. Soysal (1994, 2002), among others, has suggested that a new form of "postnational citizenship" has emerged that differs significantly from previous forms. In her view "modern" citizenship, associated with the rise and consolidation of nation-states in Europe, was characterized by territorially bounded populations with specific sets of rights and responsibilities. Beginning in the late twentieth century, however, modern citizenship was transformed through the influence of the EU, the intensification of a global discourse of human rights, and the growth and institutionalization of transnational labor migrations. Under the postnational regime of the EU there has been a decoupling of rights and national identities.[2] While the materialization of rights is still vested in the nation-state, the EU and other transnational or global forces guarantee their legitimacy.

In addition to the shift in sources of legitimacy, a multiplicity of status, especially vis-à-vis rights, has developed. Soysal argues that whereas modern citizenship presupposes the relatively uniform access to rights based on a territorial definition of national identity, the presence today of large, permanent communities of immigrants in European countries has led to an uneven distribution of rights. In other words, the incorporation of immigrant labor into European economies, beginning with the "guestworker" programs of the post-World War II period, created certain contradictions for liberal definitions of citizenship. Although immigrants have established de facto membership in European polities by virtue of economic necessity as well as the attribute of human rights, they have continued to be excluded from the full rights of citizenship. This situation has led to a two-tiered system of rights in which some rights are increasingly abstract and legitimated at the transnational level, while others continue to be tied to national identity and so are particularized and territorial. Ultimately Soysal argues that immigrants have achieved rights to membership in European societies without achieving citizenship.

The main problem with Soysal's analysis is that it takes for granted an abstract concept of rights without regard for gender, class, and racial distinctions that have always made such rights problematic. Following Wallerstein's dictum that "citizenship always excluded as much as it included" (2003: 674), we can be skeptical of Soysal's assumptions about modern citizenship. For example, in most European countries women were not granted full citizenship rights until the postwar period, when immigrants began to replace them as "second-class citizens." In addition, strong class-based social inequalities have always made the exercise of citizenship rights problematic for many, despite their existence on paper.

Based on the ethnographic evidence from Argolida we can also take exception to Soysal's (1994: 45) rather rosy view that immigrants have gained "most rights," even though full citizenship has eluded them. Even though technically immigrants may exercise basic human rights to free speech, movement, and religion, among others, in practice such rights are extremely limited or non-existent. The exclusion from citizenship still remains a powerful tool for disciplining and making vulnerable a crucial source of labor.

That being said, the main point that Soysal makes, that the economic integration of immigrants into European societies has led to a new conception and new practices of citizenship, does seem to be true. The exclusion of immigrants from the rights of citizenship simultaneously conditions their vulnerability and at the same time renders them invisible in the discourse of Greek society. Thus, for example, residents of Argolida can assert, quite honestly, that their communities have become more affluent and less stratified over the last several decades despite the poverty and marginalization of the immigrants on whom they depend. The discourse of citizenship that often served to disguise and mitigate class differences in nation-states through *inclusionary* tactics is more and more used to disguise class difference through *exclusion*. The result has been a move towards a sort of neofeudal, or as James Anderson (1996) suggests, "neo-medieval" social structure. As sovereignty has fractured into different levels, the class of immigrant labor has become fettered with a distinctive set of social and political rights, obligations, and restrictions. This is especially apparent in rural areas like Argolida, where Greek landowners and immigrant laborers operate under completely different sets of rights and obligations and are bound together largely through personal relationships of patronage and obligation.

The neofeudal character of citizenship in Argolida is displayed not only in the structurally differentiated relationships to the land between Greeks and immigrants, but also in the different rights to consumption. As noted before, consumption among immigrants is kept at low levels, not only by low wages and legal restrictions that make it difficult for them to get credit, for example, or purchase land, but also by social sanctions. Conspicuous consumption of commodities such as cell phones, cars, or brand-name clothes among immigrants immediately arouses suspicion, ridicule, and even physical aggression on the part of Greeks. For Greeks, however, such modern commodities have become necessities. Silverman (1996) has described a similar process in France. Silverman argues that citizenship, which has always conflated principles of individual and community rights, has more and more come to conflate individual and consumer rights. The rights of citizenship have come to be measured by consumption. In a similar vein, Canclini argues that "modes of consumption have altered the possibilities and forms of citizenship" (2001: 15). In Argolida, consumption is often described as a birthright. The vast majority of Greeks in Argolida accept as "natural" the different levels of consumption between Greeks and immigrants. This view often slips into a form of racism. Thus Greeks are thought to be lazy by nature, fond of gadgets, and too vain to appear poor. Immigrants are hardworking but untrustworthy, and can endure conditions that Greeks, by virtue of their longer economic and social development, can no longer tolerate.

Policing the boundary between citizens and immigrants is an ongoing and incomplete process, as evidenced by the widespread anxiety and hostility that transgressions provoke. While I was conducting fieldwork in the spring of 2003 a story circulated in the mass media concerning a conflict between parents and school officials in the town of Amaliada (Nodarou 2003). In what has become a regular occurrence in Greece, parents in the town were upset by the prospect of an immigrant student carrying the national flag during the school parade marking Greek Independence Day, 25 March. By custom, schoolchildren throughout Greece march in parades on Independence Day wearing traditional local costumes. The honor of carrying the Greek flag at the head of the procession is traditionally given to the students with the highest marks. In recent years, as immigrant children have enrolled in public schools in increasing numbers, that honor has sometimes fallen to students of non-Greek background, creating a conflict between legal statutes guaranteeing equality and the ideals and expectations of ethnic nationalism. Indeed, before this incident was reported in the press I had heard similar tales from several different informants. Such stories have become part of the public discourse surrounding the contradictions and ambivalence of immigration in Greece. For example, a government employee in Agia Triada told me the following during an interview: "Our culture is disappearing here, it is dying. Look at the schools. Half of the kids there are foreigners. They don't want to learn about Greek history. For them it has no meaning. They don't even teach it anymore. Children today graduate and don't even know when the Revolution happened. It's a shame. During the parades they even have foreign kids carrying the Greek flag! They are not Greek, what business do they have carrying the Greek flag?" His comments reflect a general anxiety shared by many of the Greeks I spoke with concerning immigration, the nation-state, and Greek culture.

Both the Greek government and school officials have consistently enforced the equal right of immigrant children to carry the Greek flag during parades, and the issue has often been portrayed as a conflict between the neoliberal ideals of European modernity on the one hand and traditional popular feelings of ethnic nationalism on the other. For example, several informants used the issue as proof that Greeks were not ready for the type of multicultural liberal society envisioned by the EU. However, I believe that the situation is more complex than that. One of the reasons that the story is so attractive to Greeks is that it describes a major shift in how "Greek" and "foreigner" are produced as cultural identities, and how the meanings presented by these identities act to construct social relations of inequality.

Figure 10. Students marching in the annual Independence Day parade

On the surface this is a conflict between two notions of citizenship: a neoliberal notion of *sui juris* (by law) and a traditional notion of *sui generis* (by blood or birth). Indeed, Greeks themselves tend to naturalize the problem in terms of blood. By this logic Greeks are Greeks by virtue of their genes. In the villages I found this to be an almost unquestioned premise. Being "half Greek," that is having a Greek mother, I was subject to constant comments on and judgment of the level of my "Greekness." As I became accepted into the community, people decided that my Greek genes outweighed my American genes. By the same logic, most immigrants are incapable of truly integrating into Greek society because they lack a "Greek" nature. Those that have done so almost invariably are said to be ethnic Greeks descended from the Eastern European Greek diaspora, a fact that is of course impossible to prove one way or another, given the vagaries of history. Such a view is incompatible with the contemporary discourse of neoliberalism in the EU, which holds that there should be a basic equality of citizens before the law, regardless of their ethnic or natal origins.

The notion of a *sui generis* basis for Greek identity, however, obscures both the history of citizenship in Greece and the complex politics of Greek ethnicity in general. Citizenship has always been a disputed category. During the twentieth century, for example, the concept of citizenship has expanded to include both women and children. Both women and children are assumed today to have certain rights of citizenship that they did not always possess. At the same time the concept of Greek citizenship has narrowed to exclude certain groups that have in earlier historical periods been included, such as Christian Albanians. Thus we should consider the naturalizing of Greek identity, and citizenship, as a process reflecting historical and social conditions rather than a principle of citizenship itself. In other words, the *sui generis* notion of citizenship only superficially reflects a biological principle of inclusion/exclusion. Seen in a historical perspective, the biological principle of *sui generis* is itself no less a social creation than *sui juris*.

Given the institutional ambivalence of the state regarding immigrants, we can also question the neoliberal assumption that the role of the state is to guarantee certain *sui juris* citizenship rights in face of popular "backwardness" and resistance. To be sure, in certain cases such as the school flag incident described above the state has acted to protect the equal rights of immigrants in the face of what is generally described as nativist racism. On the whole, though, state policies act to insure the exclusion of immigrants from citizenship rights through the continued enforcement of their illegal status and the erection of immense barriers to their attaining citizenship. This becomes especially clear when we compare contemporary immigration policies with those of the early twentieth century. Contemporary immigration policies in fact reveal one of the main paradoxes of the neoliberal state, which has combined an expansion of citizenship rights and perceptions of social equality among citizens with a more rigid exclusion of immigrants. This of course represents a substantial savings for Greek society—which avoids many of the costs of social reproduction of the labor force, such as education, support of children, support of the elderly and sick, etc.—and is one of the characteristics of the flexible labor force created by contemporary global capitalism (Sider 1992; see also Castles and Kosack 1973: 409).

The lack of state investment in the social reproduction of labor is accomplished by the construction of the pool of immigrant labor as a diaspora.[3] It is common to hear among Greeks that immigrants "don't want to stay in Greece" and that their goal is to save money and return home. In talking with immigrants I found this sentiment to be less pervasive. Many immigrants did indeed plan on returning home, but not because they missed their homeland or felt they "belonged" there, which was the explanation usually offered by Greeks. Rather, immigrants felt that their position in Greece would always be precarious and dependent on the shifting needs of the state. Most immigrants felt that investing in local communities through the establishment of families or the buying and improving of property was not a very wise strategy, given the lack of long-term security and citizenship. Most felt it safer to invest, if they were able to save money, in businesses or properties in their home countries. I found this to be an important motivation for the maintenance of social ties with home communities as well as kin and friends who had immigrated to other parts of Greece. The social and political situation of immigrants in Greece encouraged them to organize as a diaspora with strong ties to home communities.

The organization of immigrants into diasporas also has a technical basis. Ties to home communities are facilitated by regular travel to and from Greece. Most of the immigrants I spoke with made a point of going home once a year, and few go for many years without returning home. The state has encouraged this cyclical travel both indirectly, through the modernization and expansion of transportation systems and links between Greece and other Eastern European countries, and directly, through the regulation of immigration and the system of work and residence permits that allow periods of travel to non-EU countries. Regular contact with home and other immigrants is also maintained through the expanded networks and lowered cost of telecommunications.

The organization of immigrants as a diaspora reduces pressures for assimilation that accompanied previous patterns of migration. Immigrants are mobile and dispersed, preventing them from establishing corporate communities and forms of local solidarities. At the same time, it is easy for them to maintain social relations with their home countries, which deflects immigrants' aspirations for upward mobility away from the host country. The diaspora organization of immigrants not only provides a measure of protection and security to immigrants, but also acts as a safety valve, deflecting potential resistance and demands for social and political inclusion.

The presence of immigrant diasporas within Greece has created a novel problem in the production of Greek national identity. Whereas historically the task of the Greek state and civil institutions has been to unite the different ethnic groups living within the borders of Greece into a single nation, now great effort is spent on constructing differences between national groups within the same state. This is partly accomplished through the regulation of immigration and citizenship by the state, which creates different sets of statuses, rights, and privileges for individuals living in the same communities and participating in the same economies of production and consumption. It is also accomplished through social relations at the local and personal level that position subjects differently according to perceived differences in nationality.

Notes

1. Before the liberalization of trade under the EU, the Greek state imposed high tariffs on imported consumer goods, such as electronics and automobiles, pricing them out of reach for many rural households.
2. In Greece, for example, it has become much more difficult for immigrants claiming "Greek ethnicity" to automatically acquire Greek citizenship.
3. "Diaspora" denotes the transnational movement of groups constructed as a deterritorialized "nation" or "ethnicity." It has gained currency in the social sciences as a way of avoiding essentialist notions of race and culture, especially around issues of transnational black identity (Gilroy 1993; S. Hall 1990). Clifford (1994) has extended the concept to describe the contemporary subversion of the nation-state in the era of globalization. In this sense diaspora acts to challenge the cultural hegemony of dominant social groups and provide subaltern groups a degree of autonomy and protection. Others, however, have criticized the diaspora model for obscuring internal dynamics of class and gender in transnational communities (Anthias 1998).

Chapter VI

THE POLITICS OF RESISTANCE

In Argolida, "resistance" to the intrusion of global political and economic forces is a complex and contradictory process. Many residents consciously think of behaviors intended to subvert or deflect what they perceive to be external threats in terms of "resistance" (*antistasi*). In fact, though, these behaviors, as we shall see, often have the contradictory effect of furthering the entanglement of individuals and communities with global political-economic forces. Given the absence of an organized force of resistance or feasible alternative to the EU, we could perhaps more accurately categorize acts of resistance as simply reaction. Indeed, local residents do sometimes describe their tactics as "reaction" (*antidrasi*). However, their term "reaction" carries with it a conservative connotation of acting to preserve an existing social order and resisting change. While in Argolida such a description is not completely inaccurate, at least as expressed by residents, it fails to capture the extent to which residents try not so much to resist change as to manipulate and subvert social changes to their own benefit at the expense of outside interests. Following local usage, I will use the term "resistance" to denote acts and activities intended to defend local group and individual interests against elite outside interests and to alter or negotiate the terms under which individuals and local communities are being integrated into the transnational and global networks of the EU and beyond. In this sense, resistance is partly a reactionary process, but it is also *proactive* in the sense that it conditions the practical formation and adaptation of social relations.

Paradoxically, the most vocal resistance to EU policies and objectives is found among Greek farmers, who have arguably benefited the most from EU subsidy programs. Greeks employ both passive and active methods of resistance to a process they perceive as damaging and exploitive. Indeed, one can scarcely have a conversation about contemporary issues of politics, economy, or culture without people proclaiming their opposition to what they perceive as "globalization." Regardless of political affiliation, many people I spoke with in Argolida voiced strong opposition and bitter disappointment over what they perceive as a breakdown in social order and a decline in political and economic autonomy arising from the global forces of media, transnational markets, and immigration.

In the face of such a consensus, it seems strange that, compared with other periods of modern Greek history, there is little in the way of a serious challenge to the social order. That is, while people complain bitterly and display a cynical pessimism about the future, they for the most part continue to participate in the markets of consumption and production about which they complain. At the same time, there has been a notable decline in organized resistance through political parties, cooperatives, and the like. None of the major political parties advocates withdrawal from the EU, or even seriously advocates a restructuring of EU programs and policies. Therefore, popular resistance is expressed most strongly through the institutions and arenas of civil society, from the mass media to the coffee shop.

Argolida, like Greece in general, has a rich history of strong and sometimes violent opposition on the part of rural communities to the exploitation that has characterized their incorporation into various world economies. From the revolution against the Ottoman Empire that resulted in the founding of the modern state through the civil strife of the twentieth century that often resulted in military dictatorship, rural areas in Greece have been sites of resistance and conflict. From a historical perspective, the resistance displayed in contemporary Argolida seems distinctively muted compared to earlier eras. That is, residents may complain but have by and large peacefully accepted their place in the new world order. This "culture of complaint" as opposed to a "culture of opposition" can perhaps be explained in various ways. Some interpret the "culture of complaint" as endemic to Greek society. This interpretation is favored by many residents of Midea township, who criticize the "laziness" and lack of initiative of their neighbors. In the academic literature on Mediterranean society, such cynicism and complaining has sometimes been analyzed as a defensive cultural practice in response to the exploitative nature of relations between peasants and urban elites, or a form of passive resistance (Banfield 1958). For Greek rural society Herzfeld (1986) has argued that cynical complaints reflect a "disemia" in Greek culture between "Hellenic" and "Romaic" identities that are linked to a gendered, oppositional practice of cultural discourse.

There are other explanations that focus on geopolitical conditions. The most obvious is the nature of the contemporary world system itself. In Greece, opposition to world political-economic orders has generally been shaped by fractures within the order itself. Opposition groups were almost always allied with competing world powers. The Greek Revolution was shaped and nurtured by the rise of European capitalism and its confrontation with the Ottoman Empire, and more recently the Greek civil war of the 1940s was shaped and nurtured by the opposition between the US and Soviet world systems. In short, opposition movements in Greece have historically been aided and nurtured by outside patrons, both practically through funding and military support, and ideologically through the possibility of alternative or utopian social orders. At the end of the twentieth century, the world was confronted by the novel possibility of a globally integrated economic system and a hegemonic world power, the US, with almost no institutional opposition at the global level. Today, for perhaps the first time in their history, Greeks have no global fractures to exploit.

People in Midea township do not just complain, however. They also act in a many ways to defend themselves from exploitation at the hands of outside forces. As we shall see in this chapter, this self-defense takes the two main forms. First, local residents engage in a host of illegal and quasi-legal actions, including theft, graft, and evasion, that serve to ameliorate economic exploitation. In these ways, rural Greeks take advantage of various opportunities to enrich themselves at the expense of the state, EU, and markets. Second, is the reconstitution or reassertion of an autonomous subjectivity in terms of identity and consumption that local residents employ to subvert what they see as their political exploitation at the hands of national and transnational elites. This subjectivity is often expressed as a form of resurgent nationalism. Both of these forms of resistance, however, are premised on residents' ability to both exploit immigrants and suppress any potential resistance on their part.

The Preclusion of Resistance among Immigrants

From all appearances, immigrant laborers, as the most exploited and vulnerable class of labor in Midea township, should be the most resistant to the social relations of globalization—and yet the opposite is true. In the interviews I conducted with immigrant laborers I collected few statements of animosity or bitterness toward Greeks regarding the conditions faced by migrant workers. While I did collect examples of immigrants complaining about specific Greek employers and the state bureaucracy they were forced to deal with, I recorded few examples of hostility directed toward Greeks as a group. This may be partly attributed to my inability to speak Albanian, as well as my identification within the villages as a Greek-American. I did find indirect evidence of a subaltern current of some degree of resistance among the immigrants. However, for the most part the people I interviewed felt relatively lucky to have work and grateful to the Greeks who employed them. Immigrants living in the valley villages had hard-luck stories more often then those in the mountain villages, but even here they generally attributed their misfortunes to a minority of "bad" Greeks or ultimately to the failure of their natal states to adequately support them. How are we to explain the relative passivity of the most exploited sector of the working class, and their apparent acquiescence to their own exploitation?

On the one hand, for many immigrants life in Greece is a step up from conditions in their homelands. Given the widespread social and economic destruction wrought by neoliberal policies in Eastern Europe, for many a steady job and modest income are vast improvements over the hunger and hopelessness they faced at home. In this sense many immigrants, especially recent arrivals, feel genuinely fortunate and are reluctant to agitate for better conditions lest they jeopardize their new opportunities. In addition, the favorable exchange rates for the euro in Eastern Europe mean that the little they are able to save goes a long way back home. However, for most immigrants it quickly becomes apparent that their social position of vulnerability puts them at a severe disadvantage, and that Greeks have little interest in either improving working conditions or raising their standard of living. For the immigrant, preserving their gains while resisting the more onerous forms of exploitation and seeking opportunities for advancement is a delicate and perilous process.[1]

The obstacles facing immigrants in rural areas as they try to organize and resist are enormous. As we have seen, state policies have contributed to making immigrants the most exploited and vulnerable class of labor in Midea township. At the same time, resistance among immigrants themselves is precluded by the lack of secure residency and the temporary and transient nature of their role in the Greek economy. The paternalistic method of granting permits and working papers insures that immigrants can be individually monitored, at least in rural areas, and makes them constantly dependent on the goodwill of individual Greek citizens. Thus a decentralized form of surveillance and control has evolved in rural Greece that is capable of efficiently enforcing social discipline and subservience among immigrants. Immigrants who actively resist or try to organize for greater political power face blacklisting from work, the inability to renew papers and permits, and finally deportation. The immigration system has been very effective in weeding out potential trouble-makers and promoting a form of self-discipline among groups of immigrants that makes organizing very difficult. In rural areas, the physical dispersal of immigrants further limits their ability to organize. Immigrants in the villages do not live in one area or neighborhood, but are rather scattered among the properties of individual employers who employ them or rent them outbuildings.

The result of subsuming legal status under personalized relations of obligation and privilege has been the creation of a kind of "neo-medieval" (J. Anderson 1996) political hierarchy. The relations of agricultural production have become naturalized through a discourse of birthrights. The personal dependence of immigrants on Greek landowners creates overlapping political allegiances and a complex politics of caste in which sovereignty is diffused through familial, ethnic, and national discourses. For immigrants in this situation, the possibilities of resistance become fractured between the personalized reciprocity they establish with individual landowners, their class identity as immigrant laborers, and their segmentation into ethnic or national groups.

Figure 11. Immigrant laborers taking a break during the orange harvest

As we saw in the last chapter, the techno-bureaucratic conditioning of diaspora communities among immigrants acts as a safety valve, defusing resistance among immigrants. Most immigrants support families in their home countries with savings from their earnings and plan on returning after amassing enough capital. Even those with families in Greece often plan on returning eventually to their home countries. In one case an Albanian family I interviewed described how they regularly send money to relatives in order to build up capital to buy property and open a small business in their hometown of Elbasan. They explained their actions by pointing to a favorable exchange rate as well as the difficulties they faced in securing permanent residency in Greece.

In talking with immigrants, especially those who live year-round in the villages rather than seasonal migrants, I was also struck by the general mistrust that they felt toward other immigrants. In the mountain village of Gerbesi, one Albanian immigrant told me that he would never help another Albanian get a job or find housing if he did not know him, or know of him. "You don't know what trouble you could find," he said. This mistrust is one element in the general lack of social presence in the villages. Not only are immigrants segmented into national groups (Albanian, Romanian, etc.), but fellow nationals are further segmented by region or even village of origin. In the villages there are few public displays of immigrant cultural or ethnic identity, such as religious symbols or stores catering to immigrant tastes. Albanian immigrants, many of whom are considered to be Muslim, have made little effort to assert a distinct religious identity in the villages. Nor could I find any immigrants who aspired to establish themselves as a cultural community or any immigrant entrepreneurs servicing the minority communities. Immigrants were socially invisible to those from outside the community. Migrant workers wanted to make money and move on. Those who resided for longer wanted to blend in as much as possible, and their comments about the local Greek community were almost always characterized by a tone of gratefulness and subservience.

This is not to say that immigrants in the villages are totally passive. Some turn to petty theft, drug dealing, or prostitution as a way to improve their social position and achieve independence from Greek bosses, although this is relatively rare in Midea township, where residents can keep an eye on local immigrants and quickly eliminate those who challenge the Greek monopoly on such activities. There are also informal agreements among immigrants regarding wage rates and sanctions against those who work for lower wages, and in some areas of Greece spontaneous strikes have occurred.[2] Despite their dispersed residences, certain public areas of the villages, such as sections of the public square or cafés, have become gathering spots for immigrant groups (usually separated by nationality) as fear of deportation has subsided with the new system of work permits. In these places immigrant communities have begun, perhaps, to coalesce beyond the watchful eyes of local Greeks.

In the absence of any form of labor- or community-based immigrant organizations, power has been concentrated in the criminal or "mafia" elites that have developed under the illegal and semilegal conditions of immigration. Most of these groups seem to be based in urban areas and have somewhat limited authority in the villages. Growing out of the smuggling networks of the early period of illegal immigration, immigrant mafias often control drug and sex trafficking, "facilitate" the acquisition of permits, and in some cases operate extortion and protection rackets. During my fieldwork, however, the only evidence I encountered of such mafia-type groups was in the nearby towns of Argos and Nauplio. In the villages, immigrants often organize informal groups that regulate wages and job assignments. In the larger villages established groups of immigrants sometimes come into conflict with newer arrivals, who will sometimes work for lower wages and try to take positions away from established immigrants. During my fieldwork I collected information on a serious conflict in a nearby village between two such groups that broke out into a bloody battle in the village and was only quelled by the arrival of riot police from Argos. The causes were somewhat obscure, but most attributed the battle to charges that a group of newer arrivals had been working for lower wages and taking work from senior immigrants who had been in the village for a long time.

Immigrants' rights groups and antiracist organizations in Greece are found almost exclusively in the urban centers, and are made up predominately of young Greeks with liberal or leftist perspectives. No such organizations exist or operate in Midea township. In nearby Nauplio, there was a group of young people associated with the Greek Social Forum who were considering organizing an immigrant aid center similar to ones organized in some other parts of Greece. One young woman, an archeologist working in Midea township, told me the group was interested in "doing something about the racism and poor living conditions that immigrants faced" in the area. In Athens there is more activity, such as an annual three-day "Antiracist Festival" held in July, where over a hundred groups set up information booths and panel discussions and organize cultural activities. For the most part, the planners and participants are, again, young and Greek. In 2002 only five of the booths were organized by immigrant groups, and none of these were from rural areas.

The Failure of the Left

The lack of political organizing among immigrants and the social distance between them and Greek labor organizations stands in sharp contrast to the earlier history of the left in Greece. In the 1920s and 1930s, during the founding and growth of the Communist Party of Greece (KKE) and allied labor unions, immigrants played a major role (Hirschon 1989). The Greek Orthodox refugees who arrived in Greece after the defeat of the Greek army in Asia Minor and the establishment of the Turkish national state provided the cheap and vulnerable labor force that was instrumental in kick-starting Greek national industrial development, much as today's immigrants from Eastern Europe are providing the labor for the transformation of the Greek economy under conditions of global capitalism. At that time immigrants provided fertile ground for KKE recruiters and stimulated the growth of labor unions and other working-class organizations. Refugees from Asia Minor were in fact heavily represented in leadership positions in the KKE during the 1940s and 50s (Averoff-Tossizza 1978). During the occupation and civil war of the 1940s, the KKE made a conscious effort to recruit ethnic minorities, especially among slavophone groups in the north and Arvanites in the south. In the recent wave of immigration at the end of the twentieth century, however, the left in Greece has been noticeably absent or ineffective in fighting for immigrant rights and incorporating immigrants into existing working-class organizations, especially in rural areas.

The failure of the peasant rebellion that was reluctantly directed by the KKE at the end of the German occupation, along with the incorporation of Greece into the American "sphere of influence," had severe consequences for the left in Greece. After the defeat of the Democratic Army in Northern Greece, the KKE leadership fled to Eastern European countries. The severe domestic repression of the 1950s and 1960s, coupled with splits in the party between the "outside" exile leadership following Soviet policies and "inside" factions advocating a "euro-communist" strategy, weakened the party. In Argolida during the occupation and postwar struggle for power the KKE had become associated with the mountain Arvaniti communities' traditional resistance against the urban Greek state. Afterward, the Greek state actively suppressed both communists, by jail and exile, and Arvaniti identity, by renaming their villages and suppressing their language. Communist sympathies remained strong in some of the villages and reemerged with the legalization of the party and return to parliamentary democracy in the early 1970s. However, many former partisans turned to various forms of traditional brigandage, either renouncing or changing political ideologies.

Communist sympathies have remained strong in some of the mountain villages, despite the fact the Argolida in general is a conservative stronghold. In the village of Gerbesi the KKE still garners 25-30 percent of the vote in national elections, while in the valley villages it receives less than 5 percent. Gerbesi's strong communist base has earned it the moniker "Little Moscow" from area residents. Other nearby villages like Limnes also have a strong communist base, although in the postwar period many communist families ended up migrating to urban areas in the face of local repression. Despite the continuing electoral showings, however, the party infrastructure has withered in the last several decades. The generation now in their forties in Gerbesi was the last to have an active cell of the communist youth organization (KNE). Men from this generation remember the 1970s and early 1980s as a time of regular meetings and group discipline that discouraged the use of drugs and resisted "American culture." Today the party structure consists of occasional meetings with party cadre from nearby towns attended by a handful of remaining active party members. Among the younger generation, that is, those in their twenties, I found very few individuals who identified themselves as communist or who had much interest in the leftist heritage of the village. Those who did were invariably among the few young people who had left the village and were studying in universities.

KKE policy on immigration and immigrants remains progressive, but its organizational weakness means that it has little effect on local social relations or local governmental bodies. With the exception of the communist-controlled construction trade union, there have been few attempts to organize immigrant workers. Immigrants are concentrated in sectors that were traditionally not unionized, like agriculture, and there have been few efforts to organize new unions given the defensive posture of the KKE. Local party members in Gerbesi told me that the party advocated the free movement of migrants across borders and their complete legalization. Indeed, KKE members in Gerbesi seemed to be the most sympathetic and supportive of immigrants among the villagers, and some had established friendships with them. In fact, the only times I witnessed Greeks and Albanians socializing publicly by going out to eat together at a *taverna* or pizzeria, the Greeks were villagers I knew to be KKE members or sympathizers. On the other hand, several ex-KKE members, who however still voted KKE, were very publicly anti-immigrant. One who was otherwise very left-wing in his political orientation told me: "We are all racists now. Bad, I know, but that is the truth."

The organizational structure of the KKE has weakened due to several factors. The most important is the demise of the Soviet Union and the Eastern European communist bloc that previously provided the Greek communists with both a social model and a source of moral and organizational support. The KKE was one of the last major European communist parties to end its support for Soviet-style communism. After the breakup of the Soviet Union it lost its sense of direction and purpose. In addition, the rise to power of the socialist party PASOK in the 1980s had the effect of pulling members and votes from the more moderate wing of the KKE as well as some of its leadership at the local level. In Gerbesi, for example, there were many accusations against people who switched parties, or appeared to have switched parties, in order to get jobs or secure leadership positions in local government.

Another factor was that by the 1970s the KKE's hold on the imagination of the youth was waning. Many teenagers began to listen to rock music, especially on the "pirate," or illegal, radio stations that had proliferated locally. Pirate stations acted to build networks among youth across Argolida, uniting them in a youth "subculture" that stretched across traditional village and kin boundaries. As one early radio pirate from Gerbesi told me: "I was high on the mountain so my station had the best range. I was playing all this new rock music, American music. I began getting calls from kids in the valley, from villages I had never been to and we started gathering together. We had a love for the music that united us." The growing involvement in rock music and fashions, and later drugs, also stimulated the desire among youth for money to spend on consumer goods. The same radio pirate told me: "Every time someone was going to Athens I would find some money to send along for buying records. All my money, and whatever I could borrow, went to those records. What can I tell you, I had the biggest collection in the area." Another rock music fan and sometime radio disc jockey told me: "All of a sudden everything had to be rock style. The kids in the valley had money and tried to dress cool. We had to work. I remember working for weeks in the packing factory just to buy a pair of Levi's. Those were the thing then. All my money went to clothes and records." Many of the early followers of rock music in the villages came from communist backgrounds. The official party line at the time condemned rock music as a form of bourgeois decadence and thus alienated many from the communist youth groups. Rock music represented a form of generational rebellion, and the long hair and clothing styles often met with hostility from older villagers. However, it was a form of rebellion that ultimately drew young people into transnational consumer markets.[3]

There is a sense among many ex-leftists that the potential for social change no longer exists and that the current political system holds little possibility for effective opposition. In addition people feel more and more trapped by their entanglements with commodity consumption, working harder and harder to buy more and more. When I asked a middle-aged ex-communist in Gerbesi what had happened to the left, he replied:

What really broke the left here? The television. It's all television now. Every house has one, sometimes several and they are on constantly. I watch it before I go to bed. I watch the news or some movie. If Al Pacino is on I will definitely watch. The people here used to be more revolutionary. There were about ten kids from here at the Politechnic [uprising against the junta]. Now everyone is involved with their personal problems. In the press every party gets up and says their opinion, But you know now the two big parties, they have everything set up. There is little difference between them now. It is just a question of who gets to eat [i.e., steal]. Those who are in power now, they have eaten and eaten. The others? What can they do? They wait their turn. Many leftists went to PASOK. Around here it was mostly poor kids that went to PASOK. We missed it. We were stupid, we didn't go to PASOK and we got screwed. Because when they went to PASOK they got good jobs. Like M., the jerk, he went to PASOK and now he has it made; easy job, nice little income.

When the dictatorship happened, the army came to the village and collected forty people. They kept some for a few weeks, some for several years. Our village had the record for arrests for the whole Pelopponesos! In those days out of 400 votes, 360-370 went to the left. They called us "Little Moscow." Now what has happened? We lost it. We degenerated [ekfilistikame]! We lost our reflexes! Our character changed, everyone tried to get a good job, we were co-opted. All that is gone. We lost, we got scared and we gave up. But we are still very nationalist. That has remained. And we all have property. We have our houses and our fields. We get money from the fields.

As this passage demonstrates, a strong feeling of pessimism regarding political change is pervasive in the villages. Instead, resistance takes the form of a resilient nationalism as well as a defense of property, both of which are seen as defending the local community against the intrusion of the forces of globalized capitalism.

As the KKE has diminished in importance as a local organization of resistance, some residents in Midea township have returned to a form of smuggling, this time marijuana trafficking and consumption.[4] In virtually all the villages of Argolida there are groups of marijuana smokers and dealers who constitute an underground economy in the area. They form networks that cross village and kin boundaries and often stretch across the Peloponnesos. While impossible to accurately count given their illegal status, I estimate that in the villages I studied around 10 percent of the adult population is involved in some way with marijuana consumption or production. According to informants, relatively little marijuana is grown in Midea township, due to the lack of isolated and secluded areas. Most of the marijuana consumed there is produced in the more isolated and rugged areas of the central and southern Peloponnesos. In interviewing middle-aged marijuana users in Midea township I found that most had been active in left-wing politics. As this generation, those in their forties mainly, moved out of activist politics, they moved into a social and economic network of marijuana consumption.

Marijuana is not new to the villages. Local residents claim it has been grown and smoked for at least the last eighty years. According to an elderly resident of Gerbesi, it was mainly the communists who learned to smoke marijuana: "They learned it from the [Asia Minor] refugees in the 1930s. Back then, during the Metaxas dictatorship, a lot of communists were thrown in jail, and many from this village too. In jail they got to know a lot of refugees who were there for drugs and they used to smoke a lot of hashish in the prisons then. So when the communists got out, they had acquired the habit." By all accounts, however, marijuana remained rare in the villages during the period from 1950 to 1980. This was at least partly because of the characterization of marijuana as a form of "bourgeois decadence" by left-wing groups. Then in the mid 1980s, as left-wing politics began to fizzle out in Greece, marijuana consumption surged. A middle-aged marijuana smoker recounted: "My generation, when we were young, we didn't get involved with drugs. We were hardcore communists in those days, in the 1970s. The dictatorship was over and we were all in KNE [Communist Youth of Greece]. We considered drugs to be bad. Then the 1980s came with Papandreou and it was 'take it, take it, smoke the pot!' It was then that I started to smoke, in the army. The first few times I felt guilty, but at the same time I liked it. How good it was! Now with the younger generation, the kids in their twenties, it is everywhere!" Most informants linked the spread of marijuana consumption to the liberalism of the 1980s, the decline of party discipline among the young, and the rise of consumer markets in general.

There are several other reasons for the surge in marijuana consumption and production in the villages. To start with, marijuana is simply one of many types of psychotropic substances used by villagers. Tobacco consumption is extremely high; there are few adult men who do not smoke. Alcohol consumption is also very high among men, and alcohol is consumed at all hours of the day and night. In addition, many villagers consume various forms of prescription drugs such as sedatives and painkillers for their "nerves." As such, marijuana easily fits into the social life of the village. Like alcohol and tobacco, marijuana is mainly for male consumption. Women more rarely smoke and tend to drink only with meals. The only drugs that local women take at rates that seem to equal or exceed men are various prescription drugs for "nerves" [*nevra*] and depression. In fact, many males I talked with expressed hostility towards females who smoked marijuana. Men believe that marijuana acts as an aphrodisiac on women, and any woman who agrees to smoke with a man is considered "ready for anything." There have been several allegations of rape in recent years involving women, either tourists or residents of nearby towns, who had agreed to smoke marijuana with men from the villages.

There is also a strong sense of solidarity among marijuana smokers and traffickers that transcends village and kin allegiances, much like the old underground KKE. Marijuana smokers and producers think of themselves as an underground of resistance by the fact of their illegality. Police units, including special plainclothes drug enforcement units, actively hunt them. The most fearsome of these are the EKAM (Special Interdiction Police Units), special paramilitary police that dress all in black, also called "Cherokees" (*Tserokoi*) because of the distinctive black Jeeps they drive. The EKAM often set up roadblocks where they stop cars randomly and do extensive searching for drugs. Those who are arrested face the possibility of stiff jail sentences. EKAM officers theoretically cannot serve in their home regions so that they have minimal connections to the local communities, although I knew of at least two exceptions to this in Argolida. That, in addition to their bravado and machismo, engenders an outlaw mentality among marijuana smokers and leads to elaborate evasion techniques that strengthen their solidarity and their sense of being an underground resistance movement. In the villages the cat-and-mouse game between police and marijuana smokers has largely replaced the militant communist underground of the postwar era.

Resisting "Rationalized" Agriculture

The development of marijuana production is one way that Greek farmers have evaded EU plans for the "rationalization" of Greek agriculture. While it is patently rational from an economic perspective, politically it has cast those rural Greeks who participate in it into the role of outlaws and brigands. In many areas of rural Greece, especially isolated mountainous regions hit hard by economic restructuring, marijuana production has proved lucrative. In some areas it has become the most important cash crop. It is also a very risky option, however, with heavy penalties for those who are caught. As a result, relatively few farmers produce substantial quantities. The rest, particularly those in more populated and accessible areas, must rely on more mundane strategies for evading EU attempts at agricultural reorganization.

From the perspective of the EU, Greek agriculture is hopelessly inefficient. Almost 17 percent of the Greek workforce still makes a living primarily from agriculture, landholdings are small and dispersed, and most of the crops suffer from overproduction on the world markets. The goal of the EU, then, has been to reorder agriculture along the lines of capitalist rationalization by enlarging landholdings, reducing and mechanizing the workforce, and stimulating investment in diversified crops. This has been the pattern in both advanced capitalist economies, such as the US, and socialist economies, such as the former USSR. In both the cases the consolidation of landholdings and shift to industrial agriculture was accomplished violently through land expropriation resulting in massive social upheaval, in the US by means of bank foreclosures and in the USSR by military means. For the EU with its neoliberal trope of governance such solutions are unacceptable. Instead the EU must rely on incentives and subsidies as methods for enticing agriculturalists to carry out a program of rationalization.

EU programs in Argolida are centered on two methods of pushing agriculturists toward efficiency. On the one hand various subsidy programs have been used to soften, but at the same time facilitate, the discipline of global commodity markets. For some crops, such as citrus, minimum prices are more or less guaranteed, moderating the effects of a downward price spiral and price fluctuations. In this case, price supports act to prevent the political opposition that would arise among farmers with a collapse in prices while at the same time they facilitate the slow but steady erosion of profits. In other cases inefficient and overproduced crops such as tobacco and milk have been limited, and production is being slowly bought out by EU incentive programs. In exchange for guaranteed high prices, farmers and herders essentially agree to limit and slowly reduce production. These programs mostly function in the mountain villages and have encouraged farmers to switch to truck farming for urban farmers' markets. In the valley, where citrus is protected by only minimum price supports, market pressure on agriculturalists has been greater, encouraging them to try to leave agriculture altogether. On the other hand, incentives such as the New Farmers program have encouraged the "professionalization" of farming through the capitalization of large-scale, mechanized enterprises. There have also been various efforts, both state and private, to encourage specialized production of organic or "boutique" crops that command premium prices. Other programs subsidize the diversification of the rural economy through the development of tourism industries and small nonagricultural businesses. In addition, the growing consumer markets and availability of credit have put pressure on farmers to abandon low-return agriculture in favor of the service industries.

In Argolida these attempts at rationalization have met with only limited success, faced with the strong resistance of local residents. Following their own sense of "rationality," most residents have been extremely reluctant to part with their land, even when the returns are low and land prices are high. One citrus farmer I spoke with extensively was typical. Aware that he faced large debts, a dwindling income, and a growing family, I asked him why he did not sell two unproductive plots he had that were close to a main road. He replied: "Sell them and do what? OK, I would get a lot of money and what? Buy a new car? Fix the house? Pay off my debts? In a few years I will back in the same situation. They can go to hell! No, I will save that land for my daughters. They may need it for their education or whatever. Let them do what they want with the damned land!" Farmers' reluctance to sell stems from the lack of optimism surrounding the development of the nonagricultural economy, what they perceive as a dearth of safe investment opportunities, and the dangers of consumer spending.

Local residents also view the New Farmers program and various economic development subsidies with skepticism. One local herder explained his reluctance to enroll in the program despite his eligibility:

"Yes, it has some good things. I could build a new stable. They pay 70 percent, and with overbilling it would be free. Also I could increase my herd
and get a bigger subsidy. But my parents are getting older. Who will help
me with the work in a few years? Women don't want to marry herders
anymore. I will have to hire immigrants and there go my profits. And they
kill you with paperwork. Plus I won't be able to do anything else on the
side. No, I will wait. When my parents are gone I'll probably switch to
truck farming."

Young farmers are hesitant to give up the freedom of movement that
pluriactivity allows by locking themselves into a restrictive program that
denies them the ability to work at second jobs, despite its benefits.
Residents are reluctant to invest time and money in projects that are risky.
One valley resident who operates an old olive oil press turned down the
opportunity to apply for funds to modernize his equipment, primarily
because the upgrade involved training and more work, precluding other
economic activities. Another resident who had modernized his press a
few years earlier was unable to raise production to profitable levels owing
to competition from small presses. In the end he lost his press to the
banks. Heavily capitalized and industrialized enterprises that do operate
in the area are often the target of local resentment and opposition. One
such business, a modern pig farm and slaughterhouse outside the mountain village of Bardi, has been the focus of neighbors' complaints about
toxic runoff. In another case, two fish farms that opened on the coast near
Midea township were the object of protests because of both pollution that
threatened nearby resort areas and the fact that immigrants rather than
locals were employed on the project.

Agriculturalists, then, are able to frustrate and resist EU goals by holding on to land and its flexible uses. In this regard there are some differences between mountain and valley strategies. In the mountains,
agriculturalists are more likely to avoid EU programs in order to preserve
flexibility and freedom of movement in pursuing fluctuating market
opportunities. In the valley, farmers are more likely to avoid full-time
occupation with agriculture in order to preserve the pluriactivity of the
household. In both cases, however, the main weakness in resistance
strategies arises from the increasing dependence on store-bought consumer goods and services. Residents are fully conscious of the pressures
exerted by growing household needs. Families need automobiles and cell
phones. Children need spending money and after-school private tutoring.
In addition, most food and virtually all clothing is now bought commercially, a drastic change from just a generation ago. This explosion of needs
necessitates further entanglement with market economies and a complete
dependence on EU protection and subsidies to survive that entanglement.
One of the greatest fears of agriculturalists is the loss of land due to
default on consumer debt. Despite their ambivalence, therefore, agriculturalists find themselves in a position of having little choice other than to
follow the policies and programs of the EU.

Greek agriculturalists are able to subvert the interests and goals of the free market in two main ways. The first is by taking advantage of immigrants, who have even less protection than they and have already been displaced by market dislocations. By using immigrants, Greek farmers are able to absorb the decline in profits of agricultural production both by relocating the costs of labor reproduction to other countries and by employing both state and civil violence to enforce the extraction of surplus labor. The second way is by using various frauds to "scam" the system, thereby diverting funds and negating many of the EU policy goals.

The early days of EU membership are still remembered fondly by agriculturalists in Argolida. Money was there for the taking. In a climate of large subsidies and lax controls, frauds and scams proliferated. Tobacco was subsidized, but not yet controlled or supervised, so farmers could produce 500 kilos and, with the help of friendly cooperative officers, get registered for two tons. Trucks full of oranges would get weighed and recorded, and then the same truck would circle around and get back in line. Large amounts of money were made overnight, especially by the officers of cooperatives who were placed in charge of keeping records and recording weights. On one occasion a leader of a local farmers' cooperative proudly told me: "I have forty years of illegalities. Forty years! And I don't have a single regret!"

Since those early years controls over subsidy disbursements have increased, but defrauding EU subsidy programs remains an active sport. While working with a group of citrus farmers I heard one loudly complain about delays in the per-head sheep subsidy. When I remarked, "I didn't know you had sheep," he replied, "I don't, but I'm down on paper for 100 head," and the whole group began to laugh. Shepherds are particularly adept at outwitting officials charged with monitoring subsidy claims. One shepherd described a common tactic: "When the inspector shows up we call G. [local cooperative head] and then we insist that the inspector be treated to village hospitality. We take him into the café and buy him whiskey and start telling him stories, you know, conversation. In the meantime we send out people to get the herds ready. They just inspect a few, randomly. We take him to the first and say 'this is so-and-so's herd,' then we go to the next. In the meantime the first herd is driven across the hill and he may see it again later under a different name. He can't tell the sheep apart! Especially with all that whiskey." This ruse helps to explain why shepherds in Argolida do not brand or tag their herds. Recently, however, the EU has disclosed plans to require the tagging of livestock, ostensibly to track diseased animals, which will likely make this practice more difficult. In another instance I attended an afternoon conference on rural development programs with some local residents run by a local Ministry of Agriculture official. The residents incidentally knew the official also as a former Communist Party local leader. The program offered 50 percent capitalization for small business start-ups in specified higher villages like Gerbesi and Manesi. The residents were mostly unimpressed.

Several expressed interest, but as I learned in discussions afterwards, they were mostly exploring the potential for scamming the system. In the words of one resident: "It's not bad. I could transfer the old house to my son, say we are starting a 'traditional' hotel, get half the money to fix it up and then he would have a nice house. Fuck them, what will they know?" By the time I had left the field, no one at the meeting had actually filed the required paperwork, however.

As EU programs sought in the early years to work through existing channels of cooperatives and the state Ministry of Agriculture, opportunities for graft and corruption grew, making many wealthy. The downside of this graft for the communities, however, was a loss of credibility for indigenous farmer organizations. One cooperative leader told me that the biggest mistake of the cooperative movement was taking up a role in subsidy disbursements. The temptation to engage in graft has ruined many cooperatives, dividing boards and creating suspicions among members. Some former leaders have been charged with crimes in subsequent years. In the short term, graft and fraud enabled local farmers to exploit subsidy programs to their advantage. In the long run, though, the effect was to discredit local farmers' organizations and reduce the ability of farmers to resist EU policies.

In the absence of a coherent alternative to the present dominance of free markets, especially given the discrediting of leftist alternatives, what is considered to be "resistance" among rural Greeks has taken on an individualistic, opportunistic, and reactionary character. Households concentrate on defending themselves from the increasing regulation and surveillance of the state by resisting moves to "rationalize" agriculture and attempting to exploit weaknesses in the current system of subsidies. Most farmers focus on short-term gains while awaiting future opportunities. EU institutions and the Greek state have adapted well to such strategies, offering subsidies in exchange for surveillance and regulation and facilitating the supply of low-cost labor in exchange for low prices. Households have also reorganized and redeployed their labor in an effort to evade pressures from transnational commodity markets. The availability of cheap immigrant labor has allowed them to continue farming their small plots while at the same time searching for and exploiting other economic opportunities. Thus, the key tactic of "resistance" among the farmers of Argolida has been the exploitation of immigrant labor. This has been facilitated by state policies concerning immigration, as well as ideologies of national and ethnic difference that rationalize and legitimize the exploitation of immigrants.

Resistance and National Identity

The resistance of rural Greeks to transnational capitalism in the twentieth century has often been linked with the urban communist movement, but this relationship is complex. While certain rural areas have long supported the KKE in elections, rural and urban communists have often had different agendas and strategies. The civil war, for example, was largely initiated as a peasant uprising by ad hoc rural groups that in the beginning had only hesitant and ambivalent support from urban communist leaders. Indeed, "communism" has a somewhat distinct meaning for rural agriculturalists. In the villages, understandings of communism tend to idealistically reflect the communalism of peasant producers as they struggle against outside exploitation. When I asked villagers who were self-identified communists what communism meant to them, I received answers such as the following:

> Look, communism for us is a tradition, it is something handed down to us from our fathers, it is in our blood. We don't like foreigners telling us what to do and we don't like the rich, the bourgeoisie, exploiting us, making money from our sweat and blood.

Aside from a few local residents, mostly university educated, who in the past served as local party functionaries and officials, local communist ideologies are fairly undeveloped and often take the form of inchoate nationalist and ethnic sentiments.

Greeks think of themselves as a contentious, unruly people with a natural aversion to authority. This rebelliousness is enshrined in numerous popular rituals. Demonstrations of even the most mundane nature, such as neighborhood groups protesting against garbage dumps or school crossing guards demanding higher pay, both of which I witnessed in Athens during fieldwork, often result in street fighting with riot police. To the outsider, it often seems that Greeks are prepared to stage violent protests at the drop of a hat, and that the center of Athens is regularly closed down to allow for demonstrations.[5] Most Greeks are resigned to such inconveniences, which they see as a natural right, so much so that the image of the young anarchist fighting against the overpowering force of the state has become a vibrant element of civic mythology. Most towns have a major street named for "The Heroes of the Politechnic" to honor the student uprising against the dictatorship. These practices go beyond political confrontations.

Early in my fieldwork, when I was trying to unravel the regulations of the state agricultural policy, a local farmer told me, "Here everything is forbidden, and everything is allowed." Greeks tend to resist state authority at almost every level. Even traffic and parking regulations are generally not followed. In the town of Nauplio, near my fieldwork, a traffic light was installed at the busiest intersection, the first ever in this town of 15,000. It had to be removed a short time later because, as a local resident told me, "it caused too many accidents. Nobody stopped at the red light." Public meetings are invariably raucous, and most people freely argue with and even curse police officers and bureaucrats.

Even among the more docile villagers in the valley, the possibility of violent civil conflict is ever present. I often heard predictions that economic difficulties, if unresolved, would lead to violent conflict or civil war, and one young man, when I asked him who was to be blamed for his inability to make a living from his fields, said, "We are, because we don't take our guns into the streets." At times such armed threats come close to being fulfilled. One evening I saw the local game warden make a rare visit to a village square. Many Greek men are avid hunters and spend a lot of time discussing the locations of hares and comparing the skills of their hunting dogs. The game warden is a particularly hated authority figure because he often pursues and arrests those hunting out of season. As I sat with a group of men and the game warden, I noticed that he had refused to go inside the café and insisted on sitting with his back to the wall. He also made a quite obvious effort to show us that he was armed with a handgun. After half an hour he made a quick exit and left the village. The remaining men laughed and explained to me that another village man, whom the warden had recently arrested and who had sworn revenge, had just arrived. The warden was afraid that he would return with his hunting rifle to make good on the threat.

Resistance to authority is also enshrined in local rituals. Easter is one of the most important religious celebrations in Greece. The Saturday midnight church service is the culmination of Holy Week and is widely attended in the villages. At the services, crowds of boys and men invariably gather outside the churches to explode powerful firecrackers. At the service I attended in Gerbesi around thirty teenage boys and adult men remained outside the church throwing M-80 type firecrackers in the square

Figure 12. Hunting hares in the mountains above Midea

and onto the front porch of the church. The doors of the church were closed after one exploded near the entrance. At one point someone exploded a stick of dynamite near the wall of the church, provoking screams from inside. As people left the service, they had to use a side entrance to avoid the explosions. The nearby town of Asini has an Easter day tradition of shooting an effigy of Judas. After the midday feast, hundreds of drunken residents converge on a field where they spend an hour shooting the effigy with hunting rifles, finally blowing it up with dynamite. Even though it is technically illegal, the event is carried on the local news each year, and police are careful to stay away for fear of provoking the crowd.

Defying legal restrictions and flouting formal rules tends to increase social status in the villages, at least among males. The term *mangas*, used to denote a male who is defiant, tough, and ostentatious, is one of the highest compliments. Originally used by a marginal subculture of musicians and petty criminals among the Asia Minor refugees (Holst 1975: 14), the term is now used generally to denote someone who gains respect by flouting societal norms. Among villagers, *mangas* status can be attained through acts of conspicuous consumption at local festivals and parties. Men often compete to see who can spend the most money and destroy the most property, for which they will later be charged. One young man anticipating an upcoming village saint's day festival told me: "You don't know me well, I might go crazy. I could blow 1,000 euro at the festival. That's right. When I get in the mood, nothing can stop me. If I start drinking, look out! Last time I went all out. Whiskey? Whole bottles! Lined up on stage. Money to the orchestra? Tons of it! I'm a very good dancer, you can ask anyone, and once I get started, and if I'm drinking, forget about it! Once I emptied the whole freezer full of ice cream. On the floor! Cases of beer! Crash! On the floor. I smashed tables, chairs, everything I could find!" Such behavior elevates male status and provokes respect from other males who appreciate defiant aggression. Villagers also display a grudging respect for those among the rich who gained their wealth by challenging or swindling the existing order. Several villagers, for example, recounted for me the story of how Aristotle Onassis managed to rise from humble origins through various swindles to become one of the richest men in the world.

For many, rebellion is also enshrined in the very landscape, especially in the mountain villages with a rich history of partisan activity. During my fieldwork, as I traveled and worked with local residents, I was impressed by the frequency with which particular places or geographical features instigated historical narratives of resistance. The common terminology of place names in the area often referred to historical incidents or figures of the recent or distant past, but even where it did not, the places themselves gave rise to stories. Passing the church of St. John above the village of Gerbesi invariably elicited either the story of how St. John had sat down there on his travels or, alternately, how the people's court had met there during the occupation and civil war and decided the fate of those accused of collaboration. In the nearby town of Nauplio there is an area of the old town called "Arvanitia" for the Arvanites who were thrown to their deaths by Turkish soldiers during the Greek Revolution. When I accompanied several hunters into the mountains above Midea township, they provided an on-going narrative of the occupation and civil war as we passed cave hideouts and various sites of shootouts and executions. The ongoing narration of such stories reinforces a sense of rebellion and resistance among villagers. One young man from Gerbesi explained: "That's what makes us Greeks so manly, because we have a strong consciousness about our history. You hear all the stories, fighting the Turks and all the years of slavery, the civil war and occupation. It makes you tense, ready for action."

The conflation of resistance to the EU with the assertion of national identity has important implications for how that resistance is expressed. As the main discourse of resistance, nationalism serves to naturalize certain class characteristics of rural Greek landowners into perceptions of national identity. Greeks are "clever" (*poniri*), "lazy" (*tembeles*), and averse to following rules. Immigrants are hardworking, untrustworthy, and not very intelligent. Both views tend to naturalize the opportunities and strategies available to Greeks as landowners and immigrants as landless laborers. They also condition the ways that resistance is expressed and collusion is negotiated. By naturalizing the difference between Greek landowners and immigrant laborers, concepts of national identity also provide a strategy for evading the pressures of transnational markets through the increased exploitation of labor. In other words, nationalism and concepts of national identity provide a way of resolving the main contradiction of Greeks' involvement with EU institutions and markets, which is the spread of a liberal discourse of social equality and prosperity with a simultaneous devaluation of productive labor through the spread of "free" markets.

Despite the increasing Europeanization of the Greek state, and the concomitant tendency toward depoliticization, nationalism and ethnic identity continue to be strong forces in social relations in Midea township. Given the important role, historically, of the state in the production of Greek national culture, this persistence presents something of a puzzle. During my fieldwork, I found little evidence of a developing sense of European identity among Greeks. In fact, I witnessed only a handful of instances when people referred to themselves as Europeans. On the contrary, the category of European identity was almost exclusively used to denote either the economic core countries of Europe or the political-administrative structure of the EU Instead I found that national identity and ethnicity are still being actively produced, negotiated, and practiced among the Greeks in Midea township.

There has been a tendency to interpret the persistence, and in some cases re-emergence, of nationalism in Southeastern Europe as a result of the failure to adequately integrate into the globalized European economy. According to this view, contemporary nationalism could be seen as a popular reaction to the political-economic restructuring of the post-Cold War period. Optimistically, nationalism could then disappear as the neoliberal global economy extends its reach into the less developed areas of Eastern and Southern Europe. Indeed, there are some people in Argolida who hold this view. Much more common is the view of "Greekness" as a genetic condition capable of weathering the rise and fall of empires, with the EU being only the latest. In this sense national identity continues to be instrumental in European social organization. The contemporary nation, even as it is decoupled from the state, is not simply a holdover from a previous era of capitalist development but rather continues to be instrumental in the construction of social difference and solidarity, governing today a new complex of ethnic, class, gender, and kinship modes of the social reproduction of inequality.

In anthropology, ethnic differences have long been considered socially constructed categories whose importance lies in the boundaries they create rather than the characteristics they contain (Barth 1969; Vincent 1974). Ethnic differentiation thus tends to follow, and facilitate, processes of social stratification and class formation (Haaland 1969). In the anthropological literature the concepts ethnicity and nationality are theoretically slippery with overlapping definitions, and are sometimes used interchangeably. In Greek both concepts are conflated into the term *ethnikotita*. Greeks in Midea township, however, while at a loss to pinpoint the difference between the two, have strong feelings that they are distinctly separate. Arvanites, for example, strongly believe that they are Greek and not Albanian. They believe just as strongly that they are ethnically different from other Greeks. Thus people in Midea township draw upon several sources of identity when constructing social boundaries. National differences divide Greeks from Albanians, Bulgarians, Romanians, and others. Ethnic differences divide Arvanites from valley Greeks. Often these differences are legitimized in terms of genes. Today, as in the past, these differences have political implications. How and when they are cited by local residents invokes particular sets of social relations.

Greeks in Midea township maintain a strong sense of ethnic segmentation. For the Arvanites of Gerbesi, the experience of being Arvaniti comes not only from a notion of common descent, but from strong ties to local topography. For example, in Gerbesi I got the following explanation when I asked what Arvanites are:

> Look, our ancestors came down from Albania, from Illyria as it was called then. They were mercenaries, very good fighters, tall and strong. Then they settled here in the area. You can understand from the village names. There are villages in Epirus and Albania called Gerbesi, that was the name of a big family. The first village they settled was Limnes, that is the oldest Arvaniti village here. We are all descended from them, high up in the mountains. That's why so many of us are shepherds. But we also spread to other areas, like the Saronic islands, they are all Arvanites there, and even to southern Italy. Some people in southern Italy still speak Arvanitika!

Differences between Arvaniti villages are also prominent. Residents of Gerbesi, for example, consider themselves to be closely related to the Arvanites of Bardi, a small satellite village of Gerbesi that was traditionally a source of brides and was politically dependent on Gerbesi. They also claim kinship with the more distant and isolated village of Limnes, which they consider to be their ancestral village. In the common view of the village, the first settlers of Gerbesi descended from Limnes. Gerbesi, Bardi, and Limnes are all considered to be historically communist villages. On the other hand, the nearby villages of Arachneo and Prosimni, two Arvaniti villages that are larger than Gerbesi and whose lands border those of Gerbesi, are considered to be descended from separate lineages (*faroi*) and represent separate immigrations from Albania. Gerbesi has a long history of conflicts with these two villages arising from both land disputes and political differences. In addition, the valley villages of Agia Triada and even Manesi are considered by Arvanites to have been originally Arvaniti villages that were corrupted and came to be dominated by ethnic Greeks.

Arvaniti identity continues to be produced in the higher villages of Argolida, largely through the connection to topography and the claims on land. This is maintained in part by the increasing value of land in the upper elevations as irrigation networks are expanded and deep-well technology becomes more accessible. For residents of the valley, the strong ethnic identity of Arvanites is somewhat mystifying. They consider the Arvanites to be "wild" (*agrioi*) and unpredictable. Historically, Arvanites' identity has provided justification for political and economic domination by the valley "Greeks," but it has also been used by Arvanites themselves to define an arena of social autonomy in the face of this domination. The complex politics of domination and submission between and within valley and highland communities was largely conducted through the language of ethnicity. More recently, Albanian immigrants have been strictly excluded from Arvaniti identity, despite their historical affinities. Arvanites today are not only Arvanites; they also have a strong consciousness of being Greek, and sometimes claim to be more "Greek" than the valley Greeks, whom they consider to be "Turk-lickers" (*tourkogliftes*). In fact, Arvanites from Gerbesi often claim to be "original" (using the English term) Greeks. The fluidity of ethnic identities reflects the changing conditions under which they are produced.

In Midea township the assertion of "Greek" identity most often occurs in relation to either "Europeans" or "Albanians". Greek identity is invoked to subvert domination by European authority through the assertion and celebration of a "natural" rebelliousness. This ideology of rebelliousness and difference is used to organize patterns of resistance to the "rationality" of European neoliberalism. Greeks can count on each other to be Greeks and thus organize the manipulation and subversion of European policies and programs to their own benefit. In this sense Greek identity is a language of resistance to a transnational market economy that attempts to organize local communities as sites of production and consumption in accordance with market interests. At the same time, Greek identity is also invoked as a justification for the exploitation of immigrants.

In this context it acts to condition the exclusion of immigrants from the privileges of citizenship and naturalize the class relations that have evolved within the shifting political economy of "Europeanization." When Greek farmers speak of hiring day laborers, they often use the phrase "*na paro Alvano*" (I will take an Albanian). This phrase conflates ethnic and class identity, simultaneously defining subservience and exclusion in a way that crystallizes the social, economic, and political dimensions of the relations between farmers and the laborers on whom they depend. The generic usage of the term "Albanian" to indicate "laborer" is not only an effacement of identity among immigrants and a reflection of their "othering," but also a critical symptom of the new regime of inequality that has developed in the wake of European neoliberalism.

The production of Greek nationality is something that mountain and valley residents have in common, but like the production of ethnicity, its significance has changed. With the disarticulation of nation and state under the EU, the production of nationality is more and more framed as a site of resistance. As we have seen, the production of Greek national identity has historically been associated with an expansionary state. Today, the production of national identity is associated with resistance to a state that, no longer expansionary, increasingly falls under the direct control of transnational political and economic forces. As the state has become depoliticized under the neoliberal EU regime, the production of national identity has become more politicized. In short, there has occurred a fundamental reversal of roles between the nation and the state. Whereas in the early history of nationalism, national identity was generally an "anti-politics machine," obscuring class differences in the development of capitalist markets, today it is the state that fulfills that role. National identity has become the primary site for the production of class differences through the exploitation of an immigrant working class, while the state works to obscure the contradictions this production engenders. Paradoxically, it is nationalism, as a site of resistance, that facilitates the development of the class relations necessary to the transnational European political economy.

Notes

1. As Martinez has pointed out for Haitian "braceros," they are "neither slave nor free" (1996: 22). That is, the lack of freedom faced by immigrants is tempered by the dire economic conditions from which they emigrated. Haitian braceros are probably in a more desperate situation than that faced by most Eastern European migrants, but the logic of their acceptance of conditions in the host country is similar.
2. The vast majority of immigrants are not unionized, and because they are concentrated in agriculture and the informal sector, they have little contact with the unions. The one exception is the construction trades, where some immigrants have been unionized. The vice-president of the communist-controlled construction trade union federation is an immigrant from Albania.
3. Frank (1997) has argued that the "rebellion" of youth culture has in actuality strengthened capitalism and reinforced capitalist social relations through its emphasis on consumption as a mode of rebellion, a tactic easily co-opted by marketers and advertisers.
4. The most common illegal drug in Midea township during my fieldwork was marijuana. Other drugs, such as the heroin and hashish that are also common in urban areas, were rare. I heard reports of heroin use among a few young men in their twenties, but in each case they had reportedly become users while living in Athens or in the nearby town of Nauplio.
5. Militant demonstrations by farmers have occurred in some parts of Greece. The most serious have occurred in the cotton producing region of Thessaly in Central Greece, where in 1996 farmers used tractors to block the main north-south roads for 25 days. The farmers were upset over the compensation offered for crop damage from heavy rains, among other issues. The protest paralyzed Greece's transportation system and provoked a national crisis (Louloudis and Maraveyas 1997).

— *Chapter VII* —

NATIONALISM IN A GLOBALIZING ECONOMY

In 1981 Greece formally joined the European Community (later European Union), ushering in a new chapter in the modern history of the country. Since then, virtually all parts of Greek society have undergone enormous changes. The process of social transformation has been complex and largely unpredictable. When Greece entered the European Community, some residents expected that a new era of prosperity and democratization would ensue, leaving behind the legacy of dictatorship and class polarization that characterized Greece for much of the twentieth century. Others expected economic catastrophe and the reversal of the few gains made by the working and middle classes in the postwar era. Now, looking back after twenty five years, it is clear that neither of these predictions was completely accurate. While internal markets have been liberalized to a great extent and opened to the pressures and regulatory mechanisms of transnational capital, other, unforeseen developments have occurred to alter the dynamic of Greek society. One of the most prominent has been the institutionalization of illegal immigrant labor markets.

EU integration has been shaped by a distinctive, neoliberal political and economic discourse that has given rise to a novel set of social problems. The EU project has been characterized by a fundamental contradiction between the spread of a liberal discourse of social equality and a simultaneous devaluation of productive labor through the spread of free markets. One of the most important effects on rural Greek society has been to undercut its ability to reproduce exploitable labor, which in the past has largely come from the household. The labor crisis in rural Greece has been partially resolved through the widespread use of illegal immigrant labor, which has effectively subsidized the "Europeanization" of Greece. At the same time, however, the dependence on immigrant labor has also created a new set of class relations. Eastern European immigrants, primarily from Albania, now constitute a class of agricultural wage laborers. Immigrants, while essential to economic production, are at the same time politically and socially marginalized. Their economic incorporation and simultaneous political and social exclusion has been conditioned by a resurgence of xenophobia, ethnic nationalism, and racist discourse among native Greeks. Despite the profound changes the Greek nation-state has undergone, the production of national identity continues to be instrumental for the reproduction of social inequality. Paradoxically, the integration of Greece into a multicultural and liberal Europe has been accompanied by new, and arguably more brutal, forms of exploitation in agricultural production, along with a hardening of class divisions along ethnic lines.

The production of national identity has been a hallmark of capitalist social relations under the nation-state system. Today, though, it operates within a different context. Insofar as the EU has transcended the old European nation-states and represents a novel form of transnational state-like organization, the bonds between nation and state have shifted. The state, in a sense, has gotten out of the business of nation building, or perhaps more accurately, has subcontracted that role to various corporate interests and civil institutions. Instead, the state has been reoriented as a liaison between transnational and global markets on the one hand and the local communities that serve as centers of production and consumption on the other. In this sense the relationship between nation and state has been rearticulated to accommodate new transnational and global markets. Nation and state still act to produce and regulate social inequalities, but they do so in a new way. To understand this new regime of inequality in Europe, it is necessary to understand the relationships between new patterns of labor migration, the contemporary state, and the production of national identity within the context of globalizing local economies.

The social inequalities embodied in transnational and global economies have long been a concern of anthropological research, particularly among anthropologists following a political-economy perspective (Mintz 1998). More recently, fundamental changes in the world economy have refocused attention on the global dimensions of inequality. In the 1980s and 1990s, "globalization" became an important keyword in the anthropological lexicon as anthropologists representing many different theoretical approaches tried to come to grips with the seemingly ubiquitous spread of capitalist commodity markets and relations of production, especially after the fall of the Soviet bloc (Kearny 1995). Among social theorists, and in popular discourse as well, there are two basic tendencies in the interpretation of "globalization": to interpret new forms of global capitalist organization as a fundamental rupture with, and transcendence of, the past (Appadurai 1990; Castells 1996), and to see recent changes as the extension and re-invigoration of basic capitalist forms (Harvey 1990). However, one of the enduring lessons of anthropology is that often such analyses of global phenomena are stymied at the micro-level. In other words, it is one thing to understand capitalism at a global, and therefore necessarily abstract, level, and quite another to understand how capitalism is created and reproduced in the immediacy of daily life. As a result, anthropologists have paid increasing attention to "bottom-up" views of globalization grounded in ethnographic methodologies (Burawoy 2001). There has also been renewed attention focused on the uneven and variable nature of capitalist development (Blim 2000; Coronil 2000). In the preceding chapters I presented a "bottom-up" view of globalization that illustrates the incomplete and uneven reach of global forces into a particular locality. The intrusion of global forces is incomplete in the sense that it creates fundamental contradictions that must be addressed at the local level by practical and immediate means. Specifically, I argued that the process of restructuring markets while infusing neoliberal practices of citizenship that has characterized the reach of global capitalism into rural Greece has been facilitated though the exploitation of "illegal" labor and a resurgence of ethnic nationalism. Thus the globalization of the rural Greek economy has worked in a curious way to revitalize some of the organizational techniques of the nation-state, albeit in a new context.

Processes of globalization are much broader than a simple widening of the transnational circulation of capital or the transnationalization of commodity production. In social terms, the dynamics of contemporary globalization can be understood historically as a shift in relations between the main constituents of the modern world system: states, nations, and relations of production. The tensions and contradictions between and within these elements provide the impetus for historical development. From this perspective, any analysis of contemporary processes of globalization must take into account the dynamic quality of resistance encountered by the global patterns of capitalist production. Terence Turner has argued that much of globalization theory has obscured the crucial issue of "the relation between the inner contradictions of globalization and the rise of political and ideological movements directly or indirectly opposed to global capital and the neoliberal ideology and policies that have served as its ideological and political auxiliaries" (2003: 37-38). The experience of rural Greek agriculturalists helps to shed light on this relationship between global interests and local opposition. Greeks "resist" globalization in a variety of ways. As Turner suggests, it is misleading to interpret resistance to globalization as a simple oppositional dialectic. In fact opposition is much more complexly situated. As we have seen, some of the most prominent and self-conscious forms of resistance in Argolida more accurately serve to (perhaps partially) resolve and deflect the contradictions of globalization. In the process, they actively contribute to the formation of new social relations.

New Dynamics of Immigration

For the countries on the Mediterranean periphery of Europe, such as Greece, new patterns of immigration represent a fundamental shift from their former roles as labor exporters and are part of a complex set of social changes, including a dramatic drop in fertility rates and changes in the deployment of women's labor. The task facing Mediterranean anthropology at the dawn of the twenty-first century is to understand these changes and their effects on social relations. The data presented here suggest that the shifting mode of reproducing labor in Greece is directly related to the trajectory of modernization inherent in the EU project.

The incorporation of illegal migrant labor into local economies is a problem of global scope (Herod 1997; Koser and Lutz 1998; Miles 1993; Richmond 1994; Sassen 1983, 1998). Modern capitalist economies have always been characterized by patterns of transnational labor migration. With the advent of globalization, these patterns have widely taken on an illegal character as more and more migrants travel without official papers or permits. In contemporary political discourse the "problem" of immigration is often framed in terms of its illegality. Under such conditions immigrants are outside the scope of state regulation and surveillance, giving rise to popular fears of social disorder, criminality, and epidemics. Given that immigrants fill a necessary role in the economies of developed countries, how are we to explain their pervasive illegality? By now it is clear that the illegality of immigrants has the effect of producing an extremely vulnerable workforce with few of the protections offered legal workers and citizens (Bales 1999; Harris 1995). From this perspective illegality is clearly an advantage for business owners and others who seek to profit from their labor. There are other implications as well. Immigrants today are increasingly replacing much of the household labor previously performed by women (Hochschild 2002). As in rural Greece, immigrant labor around the world tends to be concentrated in "informal" and "irregular" sectors of economies (Castells 1989; Kloosterman et al. 1998; Wilpert 1998). In many parts of the world, migration flows have been gendered and single females are moving in greater numbers (Anthias 2000). From this perspective, the illegality of immigrants is analogous to the political marginalization of the women and other domestic workers they have replaced.

The vast majority of immigrants enter the Greek economy with an illegal status. Greece was one of the last European countries to regulate immigration. A comprehensive system of temporary working permits was not instituted until 1997. By then over half a million illegal immigrants had already entered the Greek economy. Since the beginning of the 1980s, the position of the Greek state vis-à-vis immigration has been marked by contradictory policies. While immigrants entered and remained in Greece illegally, the state often turned a blind eye to their existence. Periodic police sweeps and mass deportations occurred in response to public outcries, but there was a tacit understanding that low-cost immigrant labor was a boon to employers. In rural areas, for example, police sweeps were generally limited to the months after harvest season. Publicly, officials claimed that Greece's mountainous borders were too porous to adequately control. However, given that these same borders were considered part of the "iron curtain" that two decades before had walled off Albanians and other Eastern Europeans against their will, these claims seem disingenuous.

The illegal status of immigrants seems paradoxical, given the important and necessary role that immigrants now play in the Greek economy, until we consider how illegality serves to construct immigrants as an extremely vulnerable and flexible source of labor. Being illegal enforces a marginal social position. Immigrants have little choice but to accept lower wages and are not eligible for benefits provided to Greek workers. Immigrants are often controlled by brutal mafias, sometimes working in collusion with local police, and have little recourse to state protections. Sex trafficking rings are the most brutal example of these types of organizations (Psimmenos 2000). The need for immigrants in the rural economy has been created by the displacement of other sources of highly vulnerable labor. In Greek agriculture, immigrants do not fill new positions but rather replace the now-scarce labor of women, children, land-poor peasants, and minorities such as Roma. In this sense immigration is linked to other social developments such as the expansion of citizenship rights, growing female employment in the formal economy, declining birthrates, and the economic position of children as primarily consumers rather than producers.

In the villages, immigrants have taken on the bulk of seasonal agricultural labor, replacing women, children, and land-poor peasants and allowing family members to be economically "pluriactive" and increase their incomes. Because they are illegal and temporary, immigrants are low-cost and help to ease the economic pressures created by flat market prices and rising consumption demands that Greek farmers face. They also help to free up family members so they can participate in wage and salary labor in order to supplement household incomes. In short, illegality serves to structure the economic integration of immigrants in ways that in turn subsidize the integration of rural households into the transnational markets of the EU.

In Greece, as in other parts of the world, state policies and practices have been instrumental in conditioning the exploitation of immigrant labor. The role of the state in shaping patterns of immigration has been characterized by some as "ambivalent" because of the lack of legal regulations (Cornelius 1994; Morris 1997), but in fact the ambivalent posture of the state has worked to produce vulnerability and reflects a transformation of state practices. The state, both EU and national, has been active in promoting a liberal conception of citizenship and extending social rights to previously excluded people like women and children. The expansion of consumer markets has been facilitated by state policies. The state has also tried to soften some of the contradictions rural agriculturalists experience by participating in global markets through the disbursement of subsidies and the policing of an "illegal" labor market. But state policies have also had a contradictory effect on rural communities. The liberalization of social policy and expansion of consumerism have contributed to a labor crisis gripping small towns and villages. Excluding immigrants from state protections while at the same time tacitly accepting their presence is one way this labor crisis has been resolved. The ambivalence of the state in the face of massive illegal immigration has the effect of delivering a vulnerable workforce to employers while keeping their hands clean of the dirty work necessary for producing that vulnerability.

While the contemporary state in Europe appears more liberal, in the sense that markets and arenas of civil society have been granted more freedom, in reality this is something of a shell game. If we take into account noncitizens and temporary residents—those excluded from the body of contemporary nations—a significant proportion of the population still lives under conditions of political and social oppression. Thus, perceptions of social improvement are dependent, in part at least, on changes in identity. As previously excluded groups, such as women, children, peasants, and others, have taken on the identity of citizens in the new Europe, the bottom rungs of the working class have been filled by groups whose identity as noncitizens naturalizes their exploitation and makes them invisible. Being social and political outsiders, immigrants do not count as part of the "we" of national discourse. Nor can they lay claim to the social benefits of participating in the transnational world of the EU. Instead, immigrants must bear the burden of EU prosperity through their cheap labor, a burden that is lightened only by the favorable exchange rates of their remittances as they climb the class ladder in their home countries.

The EU, with its particular brand of neoliberal globalization, plays an important role in this reorganization of national identity. The EU represents a sort of supranational state, an innovative transnational form of economic, political, and social integration intended to globally project the economic power and competitiveness of Europe (Verdun 2002). Within the EU there is a high degree of mobility of capital, commodities, and labor, while at the same time external borders have been kept relatively strong. At the same time, the EU operates both above and through existing nation-states. The development of transnational institutions and policies in the EU has followed a principle of "subsidiarity" (Holmes 2000), which involves the selective centralization of decision-making powers, state functions, and market organization and has resulted in a largely technocratic and depoliticized regime (G. Smith 2003; Tsoukalis 1997) managed by an elite of appointed officials and interest-group representatives (Bellier 2000). Nation-states continue to be important sites for implementation of, and resistance to, EU policies, but they are constrained by transnational authority and markets.

Under the EU, many aspects of society that were previously regulated, at least in part, by the state have been rescaled or reorganized in a more opaque fashion. The production of national identity, once an important technique of state power, has been largely placed in the hands of corporate interests who see identity as primarily a marketing tool. In the era of "universal rights," the production of social inequality has largely been outsourced to local communities, where immigrant "others" can be useful scapegoats in the contradiction between people's expectations of prosperity and the realities of capitalist markets. While the state continues to participate in both of these processes, it does so largely indirectly, through, for example, the sale of broadcasting rights or the exclusion of immigrants (who now constitute a *class* of labor) from citizenship. The contemporary state maintains a front of equal rights, leaving the work of producing vulnerable labor largely to the privatized mass media and the informal violence of local communities.

One of the core problems of the EU project has been that it encompasses two often contradictory goals (Bellier and Wilson 2000). The first is the consolidation and expansion of capitalist production and markets in the face of global competition. The second is the promotion of social stability and cohesion through the construction and projection of a "European" model of common social structures and cultural affinities, a process often described as "Europeanization" (Borneman and Fowler 1997; Featherstone 2003). The basic contradiction between these two goals is that the first necessarily involves the production of new inequalities while the second seeks to erase the older inequalities. This contradiction has been partly resolved through the development of an elaborate system of state subsidies, ostensibly to ease the transition to free markets. However, to a large extent the resolution has also been "off-shored." That is, the problem of the creation of new inequalities has been resolved, or rather partly resolved, through the creation of a new class of labor that is explicitly *not* "European": immigrants.

Within this context, "resistance" in the form of a resurgent nationalism has emerged among Greek farmers as a way of resolving the contradictions of their integration into the transnational political economy of the EU. In the face of tensions between the promises of neoliberal prosperity and freedom and the reality of an increasingly problematic economic base, farmers assert their national identity both as a way of framing opposition to the neoliberal ideology of the state and as a way of naturalizing the exploitation of immigrant laborers. Local opposition to the state seeks to subvert neoliberal ideology and policies, but its expression generally reaffirms the basic principles of the capitalist market through a reliance on claims to neoliberal rights and social markers generated by commodity consumption. The focus on national identity as a basis for claim-making also reinforces the marginalization of immigrant laborers. The exploitation of immigrant laborers ultimately subsidizes the participation of Greek farmers in the transnational markets of the EU as both producers and consumers. Resistance is thus safely deflected into forms that ultimately strengthen the expansion of European capitalism.

The Rebirth of the Nation

Along with the increased transnational mobility of capital that has been achieved through technological means, the rearticulation of the relationship between nation and state is an important element in "globalization." The role of the state has shifted in significant ways from the Fordist and social democratic models of interclass mediation. In the EU, some state functions, such as monetary regulation, have been reorganized into transnational economies of scale, while others have been "privatized," or opened up to direct exploitation by capital markets. The production of national identity is one area in Europe that has been largely privatized but has generally resisted rescaling, despite the apparent economy of scale offered by pan-European markets. That is, in economic terms, there continues to be a "market" for Greek identity. Often this is assumed to be a form of resistance, or reaction, to the globalizing pressures of the EU, a positioning of nation against state, which in itself would be a somewhat novel arrangement. However, as we have seen, the production of national identity continues to be crucial to resolving the contradictions entailed in integrating household economies into the EU. Despite their apparent de-linking, state and nation in Argolida continue to work together at a fundamental level even though their formal links have been severed, or at least made tenuous, by the pervasive liberalism of the state apparatus.

In some of the literature on globalization there is a common assumption that forces of globalization are antithetical to the forces that for the last several centuries have driven the formation of national identity and the consolidation of the modern nation-state. As finance capital, industrial production, and commodity consumption have become increasingly organized into transnational or global networks, the nation-state, or so it is thought, has lost its relevance and begun a long slow slide into insignificance (for example, Lukacs 1993). Capitalism, in short, is thought to have lost its moorings in the social and political relations nurtured by the global expansion of nation-states that accompanied the Industrial Revolution. As the state has become increasingly constrained in its ability to foster and regulate the social relations necessary for capitalist production, the value of nationalism, and of the formation of national identities, is also thought to have declined, becoming a historical vestige of an earlier era of capitalist development and something of a loose cannon on the decks as capitalism sails into its global future. Even those who, like Swyngedouw, argue that a "hollowed out" state continues to be a contested arena for sociopolitical interests see nationalism as a form of "militant particularism in which local loyalties, identity politics, and celebrating the different other(s) attest to an impotence when faced with the call to embrace an emancipatory and empowering politics of scale" (1989: 160).

Others are equally pessimistic about the future of nationalism. Sociologist Mark Juergensmeyer, for example, suggests that ethnic and religious nationalisms face three possible futures: "one where religious and ethnic politics ignore globalization, another where they rail against it, and yet another where they envision their own transnational futures" (2002: 13). Nationalism—and national identities, it is thought—have lost their purpose in the new global order and serve only as a reaction, a doomed rear-guard defense that has mutated into virulent new forms of racism and social exclusion on the part of particular social groups, classes, or class fractions most threatened by the new world order. In rural Greece, however, there is little evidence of such a development. Instead, nationalism and concepts of national identity continue to be instrumental to the reproduction of relations of production in the new political-economic environment of globalization. Paradoxically, while ideologies and practices of cultural differentiation continue to be instrumental, they tend to be thought of by theorists and participants alike as forms of resistance, in so much as they threaten the hegemony of global capitalism. The implications of both the instrumentality of national identities in rural Greece and their perceived role as sites of resistance have yet to be fully understood.

The withering of the nation-state breathlessly predicted by some early studies of globalization has, of course, not come to pass, at least not yet. More recent assessments have tended toward the sober view that the national state, while its role and function are changing, is in no danger of disappearing (Comaroff and Comaroff; 2000 Sassen 1996). While the ability of states to set economic policies, and to a lesser extent social and political policies, has been undermined with the growth and expansion of transnational regulatory institutions such as the International Monetary Fund and the World Bank, states are still crucial instruments both for facilitating the circulation of capital and the extraction of surplus labor and for resolving or mitigating the contradictions arising from capitalist relations of production. Capital itself has only partially transcended state boundaries and is still highly dependent on the protection of state and parastate institutions. In addition, labor and commodity markets tend to remain segmented by national economies (Mair 1997). Labor does circulate, as we can see from the global flows of migrant workers, but is prevented by state regulations from circulating with the same freedom as capital. This can be seen in the EU, where even as internal European frontiers have been dismantled, external frontiers have been strengthened, and even as social-democratic welfare systems are being weakened, states continue to be called upon to resolve the contradictions emerging from neoliberal capitalism by mitigating the social inequalities and poverty wrought in its wake.

Many early anthropological studies of globalization described the tendency of globalized networks of production and exchange to shape cultural processes of identity formation. Appadurai (1990) argued that identities were becoming transnationalized through processes of hybridity that were giving rise to new forms, mediated through global networks of social relations. In a similar vein, Castells (1996) argued that developments in information technology and the dispersal of production had profound effects on social relations, bypassing older techniques of the nation-state. In retrospect, such pronouncements seem exaggerated. More recent analyses have pointed out that globalization is not fostering a new era of cultural hybridization as much as stimulating increasing social polarization (Friedman 2003). Much of the early work has been criticized for ignoring or obscuring class differences in the development of global identities (Turner 2003). While certain economic and political elites, as well as diaspora communities of labor migrants, have certainly experienced a process of deterritorialization and hybridity, the vast majority of people who do not belong to these two groups have experienced these processes to a much lesser degree. Indeed, the qualitative social and cultural changes that globalization was thought to represent in early analyses has been tempered by more recent assessments that consider the similarities between the contemporary era of globalism and early periods of capitalist expansion.

What most analyses of globalization share, however, is an assumption that under current political and economic conditions nationalism is in a state of decline. Friedman, for example, argues that in addition to increasing "vertical," or class, polarization, global economic forces have spurred increasing "horizontal" fragmentation. National identity has become increasingly fragmented and "ethnified" (2003: 8) as ethnic groups compete for social resources. Terence Turner has argued that the weakening of the nation-state has led to its "de-hyphenation" and a "crisis of sovereignty" as national identity has lost its instrumentality for the projection of class hegemony (2003: 50-51). Such views seem to be based not on empirical evidence, but rather on assumptions about the relationship between nationalism on the one hand and the modern nation-state on the other. As the traditional role of the state has shifted and its sovereignty and range of movement narrowed, national identity has become less important for the projection of class power and reproduction of class relations. By such logic, the "persistence" of nationalism is a defensive reaction against the contradictions engendered by the new globalism and an expression of rage on the part of the downwardly mobile classes and class fractions that make up the losers in the new economy. In this sense nationalism is linked to ethnic violence accompanying the disintegration of some states. Others have described it as an attempt to reestablish the purity of social categories (and, by extension, class privileges) disrupted by the hybridity of globalization (Appadurai 1998).

Such analyses are of little use in understanding contemporary rural Greece. As we have seen, in Argolida a strong and vibrant discourse of nationalism and national identity has developed alongside the incorporation of the Greek state into the EU. Expressions of nationalism are especially associated with a strong and pervasive xenophobia and racism directed toward labor immigrants from Eastern Europe. The resurgence of a virulent xenophobic nationalism has been documented in many areas of Europe and is usually explained as a defensive reaction against the loss of protection of the old nation-state structure in the new globalized political economy through a scapegoating of immigrants (Balibar 1991; Pred 2000; Stolke 1995). Given the weakening of the autonomy of the Greek state in the context of the EU suprastate, we would expect that expressions of nationalism would be associated with demands among down-wardly mobile classes for declining state resources. Indeed, the perception among most rural Greeks is that ethnic nationalism and anti-EU sentiment is a reaction to the threat that EU markets and institutions pose to their livelihood. At the same time, most people will also readily acknowledge that standards of living and social conditions in rural areas have generally improved under the EU. Thus, in Argolida we have seen that such expressions of this "bottom-up" nationalism are most common among those who have objectively benefited from EU integration, i.e., the Greek farmers, rather than those who are most exploited, i.e., the immigrant laborers. Indeed, the strategy of most immigrant laborers is to minimize their ethnic difference and assimilate into Greek society. What are we to make of this contradiction? The evidence from Argolida casts doubt on the hypothesis that nationalism in Europe is in a state of decline and that its resurgence is a last-ditch resistance to the predations of global capitalism. Instead, I argue that nationalism is a response to the conditions of globalization that undercut the ability of rural Greek households to reproduce exploitable labor. Under these conditions, nationalism and concepts of national identity have taken on a new importance as they serve to organize the new relations of agricultural production and facilitate the incorporation of the region into EU markets.

Reports of the demise of nationalism, like the state, have certainly been premature. Part of the problem arises from our understanding of the nature of the nationalism. Perhaps due to nostalgia, there has been a tendency to idealize the old European nationalisms into coherent institutions of social solidarity rather than the chaotic processes of social differentiation they more accurately represent. The endless variability and basic incoherence and irrationality of nationalism documented by Hobsbawm (1990) have long presented problems for the generalization of nationalism as a social phenomenon. Nationalism and the construction of national identities make up a multidimensional and often contradictory process. On the one hand, the emergence of modern nations in Europe has been strongly linked to the emergence of modern states in the context of the development and expansion of capitalism. In this process nationalism is seen as a form of social solidarity that provides both ballast against the class polarization inherent in capitalist development and an economy of scale for the development of capitalist markets. On the other hand, nationalism has been seen as a form of political organization associated with the modern state's need to exercise a greater degree of centralized, direct rule and mobilize larger armies (Tilly 2002: 161-169). It is this link between nationalism and the emergence of strong European states that underpins the assumption that as states weaken so will nationalism, or as Tilly (2002: 162) suggests, "what we loosely call nationalism waxes and wanes with the manifest value and feasibility of ruling your own state."

The assumption that European states have weakened is problematic. To be sure, various global institutions and forces have reduced the ability of states to set policies and prescribed a host of economic measures that have narrowed or constrained national political options. Many have argued that processes of globalization have diminished state powers and that "in fact most states in the world system are apparent states that maintain the apparatus of sovereignty but are stripped of the ability to develop economic structures and activities that provide for the needs of the majority of their people" (Glick-Schiller and Fouron 2003: 205). But is this really a new development, or are we merely idealizing the old nation-state system? In reality, modern states have always been politically constrained by the economic imperatives of the capitalist economic system. The assumption that before the current era of globalization states were able to exercise political autonomy in the world system is misleading. Given the history of foreign domination and authoritarian regimes in Greece, for example, it is difficult to argue that the Greek state has lost sovereignty or been stripped of its autonomy under the EU regime. In fact, we could more easily argue that in many ways, the Greek state has been strengthened by recent changes in the global political economy. State powers of regulation, surveillance, and policing are increasingly robust. Under the current subsidy programs, state regulation of agricultural production and marketing in Argolida is at historically unprecedented levels, despite the rampant opportunism and petty graft pervasive in the countryside. As we have seen, the state is also crucial for the creation of a class of flexible, low-wage agricultural workers through the development of a work permit system that encourages a paternalistic relationship between immigrant workers and native employers. The result has been to create a two-tiered system of citizenship where "temporary" immigrants hold an official second-class status and are excluded from full political, economic, and social rights. The fact that the Greek state now operates in the context of EU instead of US domination has done little to diminish its exercise of power through the construction and management of exploitable labor.

The apparent de-linking of the state and nation under the transnational EU regime is also problematic. While it is true that formal state institutions no longer play a leading role in the reproduction of national identity through the traditional means of public education, state-controlled media, and the old church-state alliance, it would be misleading to say that the state has gotten out of the business of nation-building altogether. The fact that some state functions have been "privatized" does not necessarily mean they have no links. Indeed, national identity itself has not been measurably weakened by the neoliberal tendencies of the contemporary state. The privatized television stations that have taken up the slack in national identity production are not part of a popular, democratic "public arena" or "civil society." On the contrary, privatization has led to the centralization, regulation, and monopolization of mass media at an unprecedented level. At a functional level, television, while formally independent, in reality serves as an appendage of the state, simultaneously representing the state to its citizens and the citizens to the state.[1] Rather than a withering away of the nation-state, or a denationalization of the state, it is more accurate to speak of its reorganization and the rearticulation of the relationship between nation and state. Just as the state continues to be necessary to the system of global capitalism, so does the nation.

The symbiosis of state and privatized national media has formed a "mediacracy" that continues to stimulate the formation and exercise of national identities as a means of shaping social relations of production in the present context of globalized capitalism. Ethnographic evidence from around the world suggests that mass media condition the construction of national cultures in several important ways. As a discursive formation, mass media, and in particular television, have become one of the primary means by which individuals participate in nations. Today in most parts of the world it is primarily through television that nationalist narratives are disseminated, in the form of news and fictional drama, and their shared discursive features tend to articulate and reinforce contemporary notions of nation and nationalism (Mankekar 2002; Hamilton 2002)). Some researchers have argued that the shift to television has also entailed qualitative changes in the way nations are experienced. For Egyptians, Abu-Lughod (2002) has argued, television has been an important agent for constructing "modern sensibilities." Studying televised serial dramas, she argues that the modernist project is being promoted "through disseminating in their story lines moral messages inflected by local and national political ideologies, thus attempting to set the terms of social and political debate; but also more subtly through popularizing a distinctive configuration of narrative, emotion, and subjectivity" (Abu-Lughod 2002: 116). In Foucaldian terms, television has become a technology for the production of new kinds of selves.

Besides the narrative, or textual, content of its programming, television has conditioned national consciousness in other ways. Wilk (2002) argues that in Belize, the arrival of advanced television technologies and widespread access has altered national conceptions of social difference. The development of more sophisticated television technologies has broken the link between geographic periphery and cultural lag, negating the perception of national and regional difference through the metaphor of time, with peripheries seen as "stuck in time" and "backward." Instead, social differences at the national and regional level are increasingly seen in cultural or political terms. Modernization is no longer perceived as a function of economic development over time in which national elites are legitimized through their role as a conduit of progress and fashion. Rather, social relations have come to be more spatially constructed, with difference and inequality legitimized through notions of cultural and national difference. As a result, Wilk speculates that "television imperialism may do more to create a national culture and national consciousness in Belize than forty years of nationalist politics and nine years of independence" (2002: 184). It seems clear that television has taken up a role as a primary instrument of nationalism and, at the same time, altered the techniques by which nationalism and national identities are constructed.

In rural Greece, television connects people to the nation in ways that previous institutions and technologies did not. Political parties, public schools, and the military draft, all once primary conduits of nationalism, have lost their instrumentality and withered under state privatization programs. The media, on the other hand, and in particular television, continue to be a potent force in the production of national identity. This has proved to be especially conducive to the governmentality of neoliberalism. Its ability to ideologically frame national identity in terms of consumption, the citizen as consumer, and its ability to naturalize capitalist markets while at the same time delegitimizing the state have proven useful to the transnationalized EU economy. The media occupy an increasingly central role in constructing processes of "democracy," through for example the construction of "public opinion" and the managing of elections, while at the same time destroying or co-opting popular movements. Structurally, television media represent a quite novel way of constructing citizens and linking them to the state. In Argolida television has tended to replace older institutions such as schools and political parties. These institutions allowed individuals to participate as groups, promoting forms of social solidarity that were also bases for resistance and negotiation. Television, on the other hand, is an individualistic experience that replaces the immediate social relations of groups with an imagined community of fellow viewers. The solidarity of viewers is precluded, except insofar as it is represented by the media itself—that is, as an ethereal, and corporately owned, "public" easily shaped by market interests or "viewer demographics." As television programming tends to set the terms of debate and shapes public discourse, the agency of viewers is reduced to choosing from among a relatively narrow, preselected set of options.

As the media have become more significant for the production of nationalism, they have also moved into an ostensible opposition vis-à-vis the state. Independent media organizations have become the main channels of communication between local communities, the nation, and the state. The representation of the nation embodied in national media organizations is necessary for their legitimacy and powerfully instrumental in the reproduction of national identity. Claiming to represent both the nation and local communities, the media generally maintain a cynical stance toward the state while at the same time demanding its strengthening. The opposition of the national media and their cynical interpretation of the state constitute a sort of resistance to the state and global capitalism in general. However, it is a form of resistance that is profoundly ambivalent. The media contain strong expressions of nationalism but maintain a fundamentally symbiotic relationship with the state and other forces of EU integration. In fact, despite the *vox populi* image of many talk shows and new programs, media outlets are being increasingly consolidated under the ownership of powerful capitalists (such as Berlusconi in Italy and Murdock in Britain) or corporations (such as Disney, General Electric, and Time-Warner in the U.S.). These owners clearly have a strong interest in both state power and global financial networks.

Nationalism continues to be useful because of its ability to define social difference and construct social relations of inequality. Nationalism was never solely an inclusionary force of social solidarity. It was at the same time an exclusionary force that served to define and reproduce social differences necessary for relations of production. In Greece, concepts of national identity have always been gendered and provided the ideological basis for a gendered division of labor, in household production as well as the formal economy. Concepts of national identity also facilitated the subordination of internal ethnic minorities and class formation under capitalist development. Arvanites and other internal minorities, for example, were included in the Greek national identity but were also simultaneously subordinated to urban elites through their lack of access to the literacy and education that conferred the trappings of legitimacy on their national bourgeois patrons. In other words, nationalism has served to resolve the contradictions inherent in capitalist society not only by mitigating the social effects arising from the extraction of surplus labor, but also by creating the ideologies of social difference that make the extraction, or exploitation, possible. Nation and state are still called upon today to resolve the contradictions of capitalist production, but the particulars of their arrangement have changed. One of the most important changes has been a repositioning, or rearticulation, of the nation as resistant to the transnationalizing state. This resistance, however, is paradoxical in the sense that its expression, rather than threatening the transnational project of the state, in fact strengthens it.

The Paradox of Resistance

If indeed what has been described as global capitalism constitutes a transformation of the world capitalist system and the beginning of a new systemic regime of accumulation, one of the more curious aspects of its development has been the relative ease with which it has established hegemony. Apart from certain notable exceptions such as the Middle East, its ascendance has been accompanied not by bangs but by a series of whimpers. In both the social democratic states of Western Europe and the communist regimes of Eastern Europe and the Soviet Union, the reorganization of national economies under the dominance of globalized capital has been accomplished with surprisingly little violence or organized resistance.[2] In Greece, the incorporation into successive world systems has generally been characterized by widespread violent conflict, first in the War of Independence that brought Greece into the orbit of the British Empire and then during the civil wars of the 1940s that established American dominance. In contrast, the events of the last several decades have been notable for their lack of violent resistance. Despite the opposition of a sizable percentage of the population, the incorporation of Greece into the EU and submission to the discipline of transnational markets has never been in doubt. In Argolida, many people see the lack of organized resistance as a weakness that has facilitated their subordination.

Of course, as we have seen, there are patterns of resistance that can be discerned in the villages and towns of Argolida. Farmers have resisted the goals of EU policy in a myriad of ways. Farmers actively resist the surveillance and regulation of the EU through the defrauding of subsidy programs. They regularly overreport production in order to secure larger subsidy payments, and they constantly search for ways to take various grant monies without following through on the commitments entailed. Farmers also passively resist the capitalist rationalization of agriculture through the maintenance of the symbolic value of land. Their refusal to sell land and avoidance of using land as collateral have kept land prices high and plot sizes small, and have stymied the introduction of industrial agriculture. In addition, farmers have been able to resist the rationalization of agriculture through the squeezing of labor costs. By taking advantage of immigrant labor, they have been able to resist market pressures, at least temporarily, in effect playing off one "force" of globalization, the transnationalization of labor markets, against another. The use of the term "resistance" to describe these efforts may be somewhat misleading. They may just as well be described as reaction or accommodation to the implementation of EU policies and global markets. However, what is important here is that, in general, the residents of Argolida perceive these actions to be forms of resistance (*antistasi*). This perception, confirmed for them by media images of the rebellious and noncompliant Greek character, is crucial to understanding the mechanism by which Argolida has become incorporated into the world system of contemporary capitalism.

The residents of Argolida see these tactics as defensive measures. They generally feel that, faced with the overwhelming force of global markets, the best they can do is to try and blunt the offensive through various forms of sabotage and noncompliance, and in the process negotiate greater autonomy. In some ways this has been highly effective: the Common Agricultural Policy of the EU is largely seen today as a failing project and a huge drain on EU resources. In this sense, the farmers of Argolida perceive themselves to be involved in a class struggle with a European bourgeoisie. Their view is based on a consciousness of themselves as a class, either "farmers" (*agrotes*) or "middle-class" (*mikro-mesai*) whose interests are diametrically opposed to the "rich" (*plousi*) or "bosses" (*afentika*) that control the global economy. In class terms such an analysis generally follows Gramsci's (1971) concept of a "war of position," a form of trench warfare between dominant and subordinate classes. For Gramsci a war of position ensues in historical periods when direct frontal attacks ("wars of maneuver") are untenable. In the war of position, subordinate classes assume a largely defensive position of resistance, contesting the hegemony of the dominant class on the battleground of civil society and the state. For the dominant class, "an unprecedented concentration of hegemony is necessary and hence a more 'interventionist' government, which will take the offensive more openly against the oppositionists and organize permanently the 'impossibility' of internal disintegration with controls of every kind, political, administrative, etc, reinforcement of the hegemonic 'positions' of the dominant group, etc." (Gramsci 1971: 238-239). Many of the farmers of Argolida would see in Gramsci's description their own predicament.

Several problems arise with applying Gramscian analysis to the situation in Argolida. First, of course, as a class the farmers of Argolida in many ways have come to resemble a parasitic class of rural petty bourgeoisie living on rents and pensions more than a dynamic urban working class engaged in a "war of position." That is, despite the self-consciousness of farmers in Argolida as an exploited class of labor, in reality it is the immigrants who do the bulk of the work. The farmers themselves essentially live off a form a rent on the one hand, and the subsidies that the EU pays in order to keep them quiet while the work of economic restructuring takes place on the other. Leaving aside the problem of class, though, there is also the problem of the character of the resistance itself. In much of the literature on globalization, resistance is taken as a somewhat unproblematic category. Even those theorists sensitive to the importance of class in the analysis of forces of globalization tend to posit forces and acts of resistance as a more or less dialectical reaction to the action of capital. In the case of Argolida, tactics that are cast as acts of resistance to forces of globalization have a complex and sometimes contradictory relation to the forces that ostensibly provoke them.

As we have seen, the active defrauding of subsidy programs has had the effect of reinforcing the surveillance and regulatory power of EU institutions while at the same time weakening the local farmers' organizations. The process by which this has occurred is similar to that documented by Ferguson (1990) for development schemes in Lesotho, where the "failure" of development programs was nevertheless successful in both strengthening the Lesotho state, along with a transnational regime of surveillance and regulation, and depoliticizing development policy and local administration. In the case of Argolida, it is not simply a matter of development "experts" reifying and misreading local cultures for their own bureaucratic needs, but also a resistance among the farmers that serves to derail programs aimed at economic restructuring. The fact that this resistance is widely attributed to a Greek "culture" of noncompliance and anti-authoritarianism helps to depoliticize the entire process. "Resistance" becomes deflected and ultimately harnessed to the interests of European capital.

The general lack of resistance to the spread of neoliberal capitalism, despite its effect of greater income inequality, has been widely noted in many parts of the world. Storper (2000) argues that this lack of resistance can be explained in terms of "positionality." In Storper's argument a growing consumer surplus, in the form of cheaper goods, and a broad tendency to redefine identity and status in terms of consumption has altered the "lived experience" of inequality under postmodern capitalism (see also Baudrillard 1998). Following Storper, we could explain the lack of active resistance on the part of Albanian workers in terms of their increased contact with home communities through the technological construction of a diaspora as well as the higher status immigrants gain in their country of origin through their access to consumer goods and capital, i.e., their advantageous social position. Likewise, for Greek farmers, the dramatic increase in access to consumer goods over the last several decades through participation in global markets has offset the economic pain they have endured through the same process of global economic restructuring. Indeed, Greek farmers themselves often give such an analysis to explain their predicament.

Further, Storper calls on the metaphor of the "prisoner's dilemma" (2000:399) to explain why the pervasive dissatisfaction and skepticism surrounding this process of consumer entanglement does not lead to active or organized resistance. The prisoner's dilemma alludes to the common police tactic of interrogating suspects separately. Despite the possibility that they will go free if they refuse to cooperate, suspects will often confess and agree to testify against the others because they doubt the others' loyalty. In this sense the destruction of class-based organizations and solidarity and the elevation of consumer identities, especially as constructed through the individualistic experience of television, preclude resistance because individuals doubt that others will do the same.

The elevation of a consumerist logic among contemporary capitalist societies as an explanation of recent social transformations in Storper's analysis is similar to Collier's description of the ascendancy of "desire" as a disciplinary technique in rural Spanish communities. The growing predominance of a discourse of consumption as a framework for the construction of identity also has implications for processes of resistance, negotiation, and accommodation in social relations under global neoliberal capitalism. Put simply, the resistance of the *consumer* seems to be qualitatively different from the resistance of the *producer*. In the growing body of literature related to the anthropology of consumption there are two main theoretical tendencies regarding the interpretation of consumer resistance. Drawing on the work of both Walter Benjamin and Bourdieu, some theorists, such as De Certeau (1984) and Miller (1995), view consumption as a process of negotiation where the subaltern agency of the consumer is able to deflect and resist the imposition and regulation of behavior from above and in the process challenge the hegemony of capitalist markets. Such an approach celebrates the rebellious *flaneurs* who carry on the struggle against capitalist exploitation as a new and self-conscious proletariat. Others, such as Frank (1997) and Klein (1999), argue that consumer resistance has become institutionalized and commercialized under postmodern capitalism. Frank, citing the widespread use of revolutionary and subaltern symbolism in modern advertising, suggests that "[t]he countercultural idea has become capitalist orthodoxy, its hunger for transgression upon transgression now perfectly suited to an economic-cultural regime that runs on ever-faster cyclings of the new" (Frank 1997: 34). From this perspective, consumer agency is more accurately seen as a manifestation of the neoliberal technique of reproducing disciplinary regimes within the individual consumer.

Consumerism has indeed become a major arena for challenging social hierarchy in Argolida. Villagers today often pride themselves on their familiarity with the latest fashions and their access to the latest consumer goods. This has certainly contributed to a disruption of the traditional domination by urban elites. In addition, local residents prize their own ability to produce a sort of "creolized" consumer culture whereby commodities are incorporated into village society in ways that bolster a sense of local, village identity. Early examples of this, as we have seen, were the music and fashion commodities that stimulated a local youth movement in the early 1970s that was largely a pirated form of a global urban phenomenon. It is important to note, however, that the effects of consumerism have been experienced differently by different segments of the population. In Argolida, the contradictions of consumer resistance are felt most acutely by older males, precisely those who benefited the most from earlier forms of class-based organized resistance. Women and youth, on the other hand, tend to experience the new form of consumerism as empowering, enabling them to escape earlier forms of kinship and gender exploitation. There is little doubt that consumerism has had a great effect by disrupting local inequalities, both between and within villages. At the same time, growing commodity consumption has entangled local communities into new webs of domination and exploitation, particularly as it has brought the villages and households into more direct relations with transnational markets.

Most theories of consumption center their analysis on the consumer and the point of consumption. It seems clear, though, that whatever the importance of consumer agency in deflecting and/or resisting the hegemony of capitalism, consumption also carries with it unseen transnational relations of production. In early capitalism, for example, the consumption of commodities such as sugar (Mintz 1985) and calico (Mukerjee 1983) by the working classes of industrial nations was an important factor in the shift to capitalist social relations in both the national and global arenas. In the contemporary world the exploitation entailed in chains of commodity production and consumption are difficult to discern, given the scale of global trade and the demise of formal colonial systems. As Roseberry (1996) has shown in the case of specialty coffee consumption, however, these relations persist. In Argolida such relations are easy to spot. The increased commodity consumption of rural Greeks is subsidized by, and legitimizes, the exploitation of immigrant labor.

In Argolida, national identity is often expressed in terms of the rights and privileges of consumption. Greeks and immigrants occupy different positions in the relations of agricultural production. These differences are often justified in terms of what each group can appropriately consume. Greeks and immigrants are thought to "need" different things. Consumer goods such as cell phones, automobiles, household appliances and fashionable clothing are the material effects of Greece's participation in the transnational markets of the EU, and have become important symbols of the rights of European citizenship. However, their new status as "necessities" has also put economic pressures on households, especially since the expansion of consumer markets has largely come at the expense of productive labor. EU membership has been a double-edged sword for Greeks, bringing lower-cost consumer goods but at the same time effectively devaluing agricultural labor. For rural Greeks, the assertion of their rights to consumption, and therefore their rights to equal citizenship, has become a hallmark of resistance against what they perceive to be an exploitative economic and political system. To consume without being subjected to the rationality of capitalist production is for them a defiant act that reaffirms their indomitable nature. In practical terms, however, this defiance is being carried on the backs of their immigrant laborers. Immigrants, those noncitizens whose status is confirmed by a lack of consumption, have become the means by which Greeks are able to resist the encroachments of European capital. The social exclusion of immigrants and the denial of both citizenship and consumption rights makes the exploitation of immigrants possible. Rural Greeks, in order to underwrite their own survival, enforce this exclusion through a discourse of national identity.

What can be framed as "resistance" to globalization in Argolida thus contains a contradictory dynamic. The nationalism and concepts of national identity that provide the discourse for resistance against the transnational forces of globalization at the same time facilitate the integration of local economies into the global. The successful co-optation of local forms of resistance in this manner presents a stark difference from earlier periods when global economies relied on military force, in addition to economic and cultural exchanges, to carry out their objectives. Within this difference we can discern the novelty of neoliberal forms of government and their value in the construction of the new global political economy. An important element in the success of neoliberal forms of government is the ability to produce disciplinary techniques within subjects, rather than to simply impose them from outside. In other words, it is resistance itself that is instrumental to the hegemony of global capitalism and a major technique by which local communities have become integrated into transnational markets.

The emergence of global capitalism at the end of the twentieth century in some ways marks a shift in the political economy of capitalist world systems. Capital flows and commodity production and consumption have changed their relationship to the structure and processes of the nation-state. Under the neoliberal form of contemporary capitalism that has emerged as a result of a rearticulation of the nation-state, capitalist markets have become consolidated through a discourse of market rationality in which the market stands for society itself. This discourse of neoliberal governmentality, even without the complete implementation of neoliberal forms of governance, has been very effective in depoliticizing the state and creating an aura of inevitability about the spread and utility of the capitalist market. However, the spread of capitalist markets also creates intense contradictions that in the past were partly resolved through the nation-state and the production of national identity. Put simply, the "free" markets of neoliberal capitalism still require the production of "unfree" or fettered labor. The capitalist system, no matter how much ideological dressing is applied, still requires the reproduction of social inequality as the basis for the extraction of surplus labor. This inequality is being enforced not just through the fetters of social identity, but also by a fundamentally different relation to the state through practices of citizenship and national identity. Today, consumers' demand for an ever wider range of goods at accessible prices has intensified this requirement and diffused its enforcement throughout social classes. Global capitalism has managed to "outsource" much of the reproduction of social inequality to the subjects of global domination. Thus, the dark underside of the liberalization of the Greek countryside is the development and spread of a racist nationalism, a privatized production of social inequality that serves to construct new, and arguably more heavily exploited, working classes in the empty nest of the old.

Notes

1. In the past this role was largely filled by political parties and patronage networks. Today, most people get information on state policies through television and newspapers. For example, election campaigns are largely run through the medium of television. In addition television, through various talk shows, news reporting, and surveys, has become the main medium for transmitting the views and opinions of the populace to politicians and political leaders.
2. Latin America may be another exception to this, particularly in the cases of Venezuela and Cuba, which both continue to directly oppose US policies. In addition, other states such as Brazil, Bolivia, Argentina, and Uruguay have begun to challenge US hegemony in the region with the election of center-left regimes. However, their ability to seriously challenge the institutions and practices of international capital remain to be seen.

BIBLIOGRAPHY

Abu-Lughod, Lila. 2002. "Egyptian Melodrama: Technology of the Modern Subject?" In *Media Worlds*, ed. F. Ginsburg, L. Abu-Lughod, and B. Larkin. Berkeley: University of California Press.

Anderson, Benedict. 1983. *Imagined Communities: Reflections on the Origin and Spread of Nationalism.* London: Verso.

Anderson, James. 1996. "The Shifting Stage of Politics: New Medieval and Postmodern Territorialities?" *Environment and Planning D: Society and Space* 14, no. 2: 133-153.

Antonakatou, Diana. 1973. *Argolidos Periigisis.* Nauplio: Nomarchia Argolidos.

Andromedas, John. 1976. "Maniat Folk Culture and the Ethnic Mosaic in the Southeast Peloponnese." In *Regional Variation in Modern Greece and Cyprus*, ed. M. Dimen and E. Friedl. New York: New York Academy of Sciences.

Anthias, Floya. 1998. "Evaluating 'Diaspora': Beyond Ethnicity?" *Sociology* 32, no. 3: 557-580.

_____. 2000. "Metaphors of Home: Gendering New Migrations to Southern Europe." In *Gender and Migration in Southern Europe*, ed. F. Anthias and G. Lazaridis. New York: Berg.

Anthias, Floya, and Gabriella Lazaridis. 2000. "Introduction: Women on the Move in Southern Europe." In *Gender and Migration in Southern Europe*, ed. F. Anthias and G. Lazaridis. New York: Berg.

Appadurai, Arjun. 1990. "Disjuncture and Difference in the Global Cultural Economy." *Public Culture* 2, no. 1: 1-24.

_____. 1998. "Dead Certainty: Ethnic Violence in the Era of Globalization." *Public Culture* 10, no. 2: 225-248.

Arrighi, Giovanni. 1994. *The Long Twentieth Century.* London: Verso.

Aschenbrenner, Stanley. 1987. "The Civil War from the Perspective of a Messenian Village." In *Studies in the History of the Greek Civil War, 1945-1949*, ed. L. Baerentzen, J. Iatrides, and O. Smith. Copenhagen: Museum Tuculanum Press.

Athanasopoulou, Angeliki. 2002. *Arvanites kai Alvanoi Metanastes: Diapragmatefsi tis Sillogikis Taftotitas se mia Agrotiki Koinotita tou Nomou Argolidas.* Unpublished PhD dissertation. University of the Aegean, Mitilini.

Augustinos, Gerasimos. 1992. *The Greeks of Asia Minor*. Kent, OH: Kent State University Press.

Averoff-Tossizza, Evangelos. 1978. *By Fire and Axe: The Communist Party and the Civil War in Greece, 1944-1949*. New Rochelle, NY: Caratzas Bros.

Baldwin-Edwards, Martin, and Constantina Safilios-Rothschild. 1999. "Immigration and Unemployment in Greece: Perceptions and Realities." *South European Society and Politics* 4, no. 3: 206-221.

Bales, Kevin. 1999. *Disposable People: New Slavery in the Global Economy*. Berkeley: University of California Press.

Balibar, Etienne. 1991. "Is There a "Neo-Racism?" In *Race, Nation, Class: Ambiguous Identities*, ed. E. Balibar and I. Wallerstein. New York: Verso.

Banfield, Edward. 1958. The *Moral Basis of a Backward Society*. New York: The Free Press.

Barth, Frederik. 1969. "Introduction." In *Ethnic Groups and Boundaries*, ed. F. Barth. Boston: Little, Brown.

Baudrillard, Jean. 1998 [1970]. *The Consumer Society: Myths and Structures*. Thousand Oaks, CA: Sage.

Bellier, Irene. 2000. "The European Union, Identity Politics and the Logic of Interests' Representation." In *An Anthropology of the European Union: Building, Imagining and Experiencing the New Europe*, ed. I. Bellier and T. M. Wilson. New York: Berg.

Bellier, Irene, and Thomas M. Wilson. 2000. "Building, Imagining and Experiencing Europe: Institutions and Identities in the European Union." In *An Anthropology of the European Union*, ed. I. Bellier and T. M. Wilson. New York: Berg.

Berger, John. 1975. *A Seventh Man: Migrant Workers in Europe*. New York: Viking.

Blim, Michael. 1992. "The Emerging Global Factory and Anthropology." In *Anthropology and the Global Factory*, ed. M. Blim and F. Rothstein. New York: Bergin and Garvey.

_____. 2000. "Capitalisms in Late Modernity." *Annual Review of Anthroplogy* 29: 25-38.

Blok, Anton. 1974. *The Mafia of a Sicilian Village, 1860-1960*. Prospect Heights, IL: Waveland.

Borneman, John, and Nick Fowler. 1997. "'Europeanization,'" *Annual Review of Anthropology* 26: 487-514.

Brandes, Stanley. 1980. *Metaphors of Masculinity: Sex and Status in Andalusian Folklore*. Philadelphia: University of Pennsylvania Press.

Buckingham, David. 1997. "News Media, Political Socialization and Popular Citizenship: Towards a New Agenda." *Critical Studies in Mass Communication* 14, no. 3: 344-366.

Burawoy, Michael. 2001. "Manufacturing the Global." *Ethnography* 2, no. 2: 147-159.

Burchell, Graham. 1996. "Liberal Government and Techniques of the Self." In *Foucault and Political Reason*, ed. A. Barry, T. Osborne, and N. Rose. Chicago: University of Chicago Press.

Calleo, David. 2001. *Rethinking Europe's Future*. Princeton: Princeton University Press.

Campbell, John K. 1964. *Honour, Family and Patronage*. New York: Oxford University Press.

Canclini, Nestor Garcia. 2001. *Consumers and Citizens: Globalized and Multicultural Conflicts*. Minneapolis: University of Minnesota Press.

Castells, Manuel. 1989. "World Underneath: The Origins, Dynamics, and Effects of the Informal Economy." In *The Informal Economy*, ed. A. Portes, M. Castells, and L. Benton. Baltimore: Johns Hopkins University Press.

_____. 1996. "The Net and the Self: Working Notes for a Critical Theory of the Informational Society." *Critique of Anthropology* 16, no. 1: 9-38.

Castles, Stephen, and Godula Kosack. 1973. *Immigrant Workers and Class Structure in Western Europe*. London: Oxford University Press.

Cerny, Philip. 1995. "Globalisation and the Changing Logic of Collective Action." *International Organization* 49, no. 4: 595-625.

Clifford, James. 1994. "Diasporas." *Cultural Anthropology* 9, no. 3: 302-338.

Clogg, Richard. 1992. *A Concise History of Greece*. New York: Cambridge University Press.

Cohen, Stanley. 1980. *Folk Devils and Moral Panics*. New York: St. Martin's Press.

Cole, Jeffrey. 1997. *The New Racism in Europe: A Sicilian Ethnography*. Cambridge: Cambridge University Press.

Collier, Jane. 1997. *From Duty to Desire: Remaking Families in a Spanish Village*. Princeton: Princeton University Press.

Comaroff, Jean, and John Comaroff. 2000. "Millenial Capitalism: First Thoughts on a Second Coming." *Public Culture* 12, no. 2: 291-343.

Cornelius, Wayne. 1994. "The Ambivalent Quest for Immigration Control." In *Controlling Immigration: A Global Perspective*, ed. W. Cornelius, P. Martin, and J. Hollifield. Stanford: Stanford University Press.

Coronil, Fernando. 2000. "Towards a Critique of Globalcentrism: Speculations on Capitalism's Nature." *Public Culture* 12, no. 2: 351-374.

Couloumbis, Theodore, John Petropulos, and Harry Psomiades. 1976. *Foreign Interference in Greek Politics*. New York: Pella.

Cowan, Jane. 1991. "Going Out for Coffee? Contesting the Grounds of Gendered Pleasure in Everyday Sociality." In *Contested Identities*, ed. P. Loizos and E. Papataxiarchis. Princeton: Princeton University Press.

Crouch, Colin. 1999. *Social Change in Western Europe*. New York: Oxford.

Crouch, Colin, and Wolfgang Streek. 1997. "The Future of Capitalist Diversity." In *Political Economy of Modern Capitalism: Mapping Convergence and Diversity*, ed. C. Crouch and W. Streek. Thousand Oaks, CA: Sage.

Damianakos, Stathis. 1997. "The Ongoing Quest for a Model of Greek Agriculture." *Sociologica Ruralis* 37, no. 2: 190-207.

Damianos, Dimitris, and Katerina Hassapoyannes. 1997. "Greece and the Enlargement of the European Union." *Sociologia Ruralis* 37, no. 2: 302-312.

Debord, Guy. 1995. *The Society of the Spectacle*. New York: Zone Books.

De Certeau, Michel. 1984. *The Practice of Everyday Life.* Berkeley: University of California Press.

DeGenova, Nicholas. 2002. "Migrant 'Illegality' and Deportability in Everyday Life." *Annual Review of Anthroplogy* 32: 419-447.

Dimen, Muriel. 1986. "Servants and Sentries: Women, Power, and Social Reproduction in Kriovrisi." In *Gender and Power in Rural Greece*, ed. J. Dubisch. Princeton: Princeton University Press.

Dinan, Desmond. 1999. *Ever Closer Union: An Introduction to European Integration.* Boulder, CO: Lynne Rienner Publishers.

_____. 2004. *Europe Recast: A History of the European Union.* Boulder, CO: Lynne Rienner Publishers.

Droukas, Eugenia. 1998. "Albanians in the Greek Informal Economy." *Journal of Ethnic and Migration Studies* 24, no. 2: 347-365.

Dubisch, Jill. 1986. "Culture Enters Through the Kitchen: Women, Food and Cultural Boundaries in Rural Greece." In *Gender and Power in Rural Greece*, ed. J. Dubisch. Princeton: Princeton University Press.

Du Boulay, Juliet. 1974. *Portrait of a Greek Mountain Village.* Oxford: Clarendon Press.

Eleutherotipia (n.a.). 2004. "Ta Metallia tis Egklimatikotitas." 27 July: 54.

Ettema, James. 1997. "Press Rites and Race Relations: A Study of Mass Mediated Ritual." In *Social Meaning of News*, ed. D. Berkowitz. Thousand Oaks, CA: Sage.

Eudes, Dominique. 1972. *The Kapitanios: Partisans and Civil War in Greece 1943-1949.* London: NLB Press.

Fakiolas, Rossetos. 2000. "Migration and Unregistered Labour in the Greek Economy." In *Eldorado or Fortress? Migration in Southern Europe*, ed. R. King, G. Lazaridis, and C. Tsardanidis. New York: St. Martin's Press.

Featherstone, Kevin. 2003. "Introduction: In the Name of Europe." In *The Politics of Europeanization*, ed. K. Featherstone and C. Radaelli. Oxford: Oxford University Press.

Ferguson, James. 1990. *The Anti-Politics Machine: "Development", Depoliticization, and Bureaucratic Power in Lesotho.* Cambridge: Cambridge University Press.

Foucault, Michel. 1991. "Governmentality." In *The Foucault Effect: Studies in Governmentality*, ed. G. Burchell, C. Gordon, and P. Miller. Chicago: University of Chicago Press.

Fouskas, Vassilis. 1997. "The Left and the Crisis of the Third Hellenic Republic, 1989-97." In *Looking Left: Socialism in Europe after the Cold War*, ed. D. Sassoon. New York: New Press.

Frangakis, Nikos, and Antonios D. Papayannides. 2003. "Greece: A Never-Ending Story of Mutual Attraction and Estrangement." In *Fifteen into One? The European Union and its Member States*, ed. W. Wessels, A. Maurer, and J. Mittag. New York: Manchester University Press.

Frank, Thomas. 1997. "Why Johnny Can't Dissent." In *Commodify Your Dissent*, ed. T. Frank and M. Wieland. New York: Norton.

Friedl, Ernestine. 1962. *Vasilika.* New York: Holt, Rinehart and Winston.

_____. 1986. "The Position of Women: Appearance and Reality." In *Gender and Power in Rural Greece*, ed. J. Dubisch. Princeton: Princeton University Press.

Friedman, Jonathan. 2003. "Globalization, Dis-integration, Re-organization: The Transformations of Violence." In *Globalization, the State, and Violence*, ed. J. Friedman. Walnut Creek, CA: AltaMira.

Galanopoulou, Antoni. 2003. "'Apomonosi' gia Metanastes, Tsigganous." *Eleutherotipia* 21 February: 18.

Gefou-Madianou, Dimitra. 1999. "Cultural Polyphony and Identity Formation: Negotiating Tradition in Attica." *American Ethnologist* 26, no. 2: 412-439.

Gellner, Ernest. 1983. *Nations and Nationalism*. Ithaca, NY: Cornell University Press.

_____. 1995. "The Importance of Being Modular." In *Civil Society: Theory, History, Comparison*, ed. J. A. Hall. Cambridge: Polity Press.

Giannitsis, Tassos. 1994. "Trade Effects, the Balance of Payments and Implications for the Productive System." In *Greece and E.C. Membership Evaluated*, ed. P. Kazakos and P. C. Ioakimidis. New York: St. Martin's Press.

Giannuli, Dimitra. 1995. "Greeks or 'Strangers at Home': The Experience of Ottoman Greek Refugees During their Exodus to Greece, 1922-1923." *Journal of Modern Greek Studies* 13, no. 2: 271-287.

Gilmore, M., and D. Gilmore. 1979. "Machismo: A Psychodynamic Approach." *Journal of Psychological Anthropology* 2, no. 2: 281-300.

Gilroy, Paul. 1993. *The Black Atlantic*. London: Verso.

Glick-Schiller, Nina, and Georges Fouron. 2003. "Killing Me Softly: Violence, Globalization and the Apparent State." In *Globalization, the State, and Violence*, ed. J. Friedman. Walnut Creek, CA: AltaMira.

Goode, Erich, and Nachman Ben-Yahouda. 1994. "Moral Panics: Culture, Politics and Social Construction." *Annual Review of Sociology* 20: 149-202.

Gordon, Colin. 1991. "Governmental Rationality: An Introduction." In *The Foucault Effect: Studies in Governmentality*, ed. G. Burchell, C. Gordon, and P. Miller. Chicago: University of Chicago Press.

Gramsci, Antonio. 1971. *Selections from the Prison Notebooks*. New York: International Publishers.

Gray, John. 2000. "The Common Agricultural Policy and the Re-invention of the Rural in the European Community." *Sociologia Ruralis* 40, no. 1: 30-52.

Haaland, Gunnar. 1969. "Economic Determinants in Ethnic Processes." In *Ethnic Groups and Boundaries*, ed. F. Barth. Boston: Little, Brown.

Hadjimichalis, C., and D. Vaiou. 1987. "Changing Patterns of Uneven Regional Development and Forms of Social Reproduction in Greece." *Environment and Planning D: Society and Space* 5, no. 1: 19-33.

Hall, John A. 1995. "In Search of Civil Society." In *Civil Society: Theory, History, Comparison*, ed. J. A. Hall. Cambridge: Polity Press.

Hall, Stuart. 1978. *Policing the Crisis*. New York: Holmes and Meier.

_____. 1990. "Cultural Identity and Diaspora." In *Identity: Community, Culture, Difference*, ed. J. Rutherford. London: Lawrence and Wishart.

Hamann, Kerstin, and Bruce Wilson. 2001. "Surviving the Political Consequences of Neoliberal Policies." *Contemporary Politics* 7, no. 2: 129-147.

Hamilton, Annette. 2002. "The National Picture: Thai Media and Cultural Identity." In *Media Worlds*, ed. F. Ginsburg, L. Abu-Lughod, and B. Larkin. Berkeley: University of California Press.

Hann, Chris. 1995. "Philosopher's Models on the Carpathian Lowlands." In *Civil Society: Theory, History, Comparison*, ed. J. A. Hall. Cambridge: Polity Press.

Harris, Nigel. 1995. *The New Untouchables: Immigration and the New World Order*. New York: I.B. Tauris.

Hart, Janet. 1996. *New Voices in the Nation: Women and the Greek Resistance 1941-1964*. Ithaca, NY: Cornell University Press.

Harvey, David. 1990. *The Condition of Postmodernity*. Malden, MA: Blackwell.

_____. 2005. *A Brief History of Neoliberalism*. New York: Oxford University Press.

Hatton, Timothy, and Jeffrey Williamson. 1998. *The Age of Mass Migration*. New York: Oxford University Press.

Herod, Andrew. 1997. "Labor as an Agent of Globalization and as a Global Agent." In *Spaces of Globalization*, ed. K. Cox. New York: Guilford.

Herzfeld, Michael. 1982. *Ours Once More: Folklore, Ideology and the Making of Modern Greece*. Austin: University of Texas Press.

_____. 1985. *The Poetics of Manhood: Contest and Identity in a Cretan Mountain Village*. Princeton: Princeton University Press.

_____. 1986. "Within and Without: The Category of 'Female' in the Ethnography of Rural Greece." In *Gender and Power in Rural Greece*, ed. J. Dubisch. Princeton: Princeton University Press.

Hirschon, Renee. 1989. *Heirs of the Greek Catastrophe: The Social Life of Asia Minor Refugees in Piraeus*. Oxford: Clarendon.

Hobsbawm, E. J. 1990. *Nations and Nationalism since 1789: Programme, Myth, Reality*. Cambridge: Cambridge University Press.

Hochschild, Arlie Russell. 2002. "Love and Gold." In *Global Woman: Nannies, Maids and Sex Workers in the New Economy*, ed. B. Ehrenreich and A. Hochschild. New York: Henry Holt and Co.

Hoggart, Keith, and Cristobal Mendoza. 1999. "African Immigrant Workers in Spanish Agriculture." *Sociologia Ruralis* 39, no. 4: 538-559.

Holmes, Douglas. 2000. "Surrogate Discourses of Power: The European Union and the Problem of Society." In *An Anthropology of the European Union: Building, Imagining and Experiencing the New Europe*, ed. I. Bellier and T. M. Wilson. New York: Berg.

Holst, Gail. 1975. *Road to Rembetika*. Athens: Anglo-Hellenic Publishing.

Iatrides, John O. 1972. *Revolt in Athens*. Princeton: Princeton University Press.

Ioakimidis, P. C. 2000. "The Europeanization of Greece: An Overall Assessment." *South European Society and Politics* 5, no. 2: 73-94.

Jessop, Bob. 2002. "Liberalism, Neoliberalism and Urban Governance: A State-Theoretical Perspective." *Antipode* 34, no. 3: 452-472.

Juergensmeyer, Mark. 2002. "The Paradox of Nationalism in a Global World." In *The Postnational Self: Belonging and Identity*, ed. U. Hedetoft and M. Hjort. Minneapolis: University of Minnesota Press.

Kalantaridis, Christos, and Lois Labrianidis. 1999. "Family Production and the Global Market: Rural Industrial Growth in Greece." *Sociologia Ruralis* 39, no. 2: 146-164.

Kalivas, Stathis. 2002. "Morfes, Diastaseis kai Praktikes tis Vias ston Emfilio (1943-1949): Mia Proti Prosengisi." In *O Emfilios Polemos*, ed. I. Nikolakopoulos, A. Rigos, and G. Psallidas. Athens: Themelio.

Karakasidou, Anastasia. 1993. "Politicizing Culture: Negating Ethnic Identity in Greek Macedonia." *Journal of Modern Greek Studies* 11, no. 1: 1-29.

_____. 1997. *Fields of Wheat, Hills of Blood: Passages to Nationhood in Greek Macedonia 1870-1990*. Chicago: University of Chicago Press.

Karpat, Kemal. 1973. *An Inquiry into the Social Foundations of Nationalism in the Ottoman State*. Princeton: Center of International Studies.

Kasimis, Charalambros, and Apostolos Papadopoulos. 1997. "Family Farming and Capitalist Development in Greek Agriculture: A Critical Review of the Literature." *Sociologica Ruralis* 37, no. 2: 209-227.

_____. 2005. "The Multifunctional Role of Migrants in the Greek Countryside." *Journal of Ethnic and Migration Studies* 31, no. 1: 99-127.

Kasimis, Charalambos, Apostolos Papadopoulos, and Ersi Zacopoulou. 2003. "Migrants in Rural Greece." *Sociologia Ruralis* 43, no. 2: 167-184.

Kazakos, Panos. 2004. "Europeanization, Public Goals and Group Interests: Convergence Policy in Greece, 1990-2003." *West European Politics* 27, no. 5: 901-918.

Kazakos, Panos, and P. C. Ioakimidis. 1994. "Greece and E.C.: Historical Review." In *Greece and E.C. Membership Evaluated*, ed. P. Kazakos and P. C. Ioakimidis. New York: St. Martin's Press.

Keane, John. 1998. *Civil Society: Old Images, New Visions*. Stanford: Stanford University Press.

Kearny, Michael. 1995. "The Local and the Global: The Anthropology of Globalization and Transnationalism." *Annual Review of Anthropology* 24: 547-565.

Ketsetzopoulou, Maria. 2002. "Ginaikeia Apasholisi." In *To Koinoniko Portraito tis Elladas 2001*, ed. A. Mouriki, M. Naoumi, and G. Papapetrou. Athens: National Centre for Social Research.

King, Russell. 2000. "Southern Europe in the Changing Global Map of Migration." In *Eldorado or Fortress? Migration in Southern Europe*, ed. R. King, G. Lazaridis, and C. Tsardanidis. New York: St. Martin's Press.

King, Russell, Theodoros Iosifides, and Lenio Myrivili. 1998. "A Migrant's Story: From Albania to Athens." *Journal of Ethnic and Migration Studies* 24, no.1: 159-175.

Klein, Naomi. 1999. *No Logo: Taking Aim at the Brand Bullies*. New York: Picador.

Kloosterman, Robert, Joanne van der Leun, and Jan Roth. 1998. "Across the Border: Immigrants' Economic Opportunities, Social Capital and Informal Business Activities." *Journal of Ethnic and Migration Studies* 24, no. 2: 249-268.

Kourtovik, Ioanna. 2001. "Metanastes: Anamesa sto Dikaio kai sti Nomimotita." In *Metanastes stin Ellada*, ed. A. Marvakis, D. Parsanoglou, and M. Pavlou. Athens: Ellinika Grammata.

Koser, Khalid, and Helma Lutz. 1998. *The New Migration in Europe: Social Constructions and Social Realities*. New York: St. Martin's Press.

Kottis, Athena. 1990. "Shifts over Time and Regional Variation in Women's Labor Force Participation Rates in a Developing Economy: The Case of Greece." *Journal of Development Economics* 33, no. 1: 117-132.

Kwong, Peter. 1997. *Forbidden Workers: Illegal Chinese Immigrants and American Labor*. New York: New Press.

Ladas, Stephen. 1932. *The Exchange of Minorities: Bulgaria, Greece and Turkey*. New York: Macmillan.

Laffan, Brigid. 1998. "The European Union: A Distinctive Model of Internationalization." *Journal of European Public Policy* 5, no. 2: 235-253.

Lampiri-Dimaki, Ioanna. 1990. "I Koinoniki Erevna ston Elliniko Agrotiko Horo." In *Koinotita, Koinonia, kai Ideologia*, ed. M. Komninou and E. Papataxiarchis. Athens: Papazisi.

Lamprinidou, Mihail. 1950. *I Nauplia*. Athens: Kleisiouni.

Lazaridis, Gabriella, and Johanna Poyago-Theotoky. 1999. "Undocumented Migrants in Greece: Issues of Regularization." *International Migration* 37, no. 4: 715-737.

Lazaridis, Gabriella, and Iordanis Psimmenos. 2000. "Migrant Flow from Albania to Greece: Economic, Social and Spatial Exclusion." In *Eldorado or Fortress? Migration in Southern Europe*, ed. R. King, G. Lazaridis, and C. Tsardanidis. New York: St. Martin's Press.

Lianos, Theodore. 2001. "Illegal Migrants to Greece and their Choice of Destination." *International Migration* 39, no. 2: 5-25.

Loizos, Peter. 1975. *The Greek Gift: Politics in a Cypriot Village*. New York: St. Martin's Press.

Louloudis, Leonidis, and Napoleon Maraveyas. 1997. "Farmers and Agricultural Policy in Greece since the Accession to the European Union." *Sociologica Ruralis* 37, no. 2: 270-286.

Lukacs, John. 1993. *The End of the Twentieth Century and the End of the Modern Age*. New York: Ticknor and Fields.

Mair, Andrew. 1997. "Strategic Localization: The Myth of the Postnational Enterprise." In *Spaces of Globalization*, ed. K. Cox. New York: Guilford Press.

Mankekar, Parnima. 2002. "Epic Contests: Television and Religious Identity in India." In *Media Worlds*, ed. F. Ginsburg, L. Abu-Lughod, and B. Larkin. Berkeley: University of California Press.

Maraveyas, Nikos. 1994. "The Common Agricultural Policy and Greek Agriculture." In *Greece and E.C. Membership Evaluated*, ed. P. Kazakos and P. C. Ioakimidis. New York: St. Martin's Press.

Marsden, Terry. 1999. "Rural Futures: The Consumption Countryside and Its Regulation." *Sociologia Ruralis* 39, no. 4: 501-520.

Martinez, Samuel. 1996. "Indifference within Indignation: Anthropology, Human Rights, and the Haitian Bracero." *American Anthropologist* 98, no. 1: 17-25.

Mather, Charles, and Stephen Greenberg. 2003. "Market Liberalization in Post-Apartheid South Africa: The Restructuring of Citrus Exports after 'Deregulation.'" *Journal of Southern African Studies* 29, no. 2: 393-413.

Mauros, Takis. 1980. "Toponimiko tis Argolidas." *Ethnographica* 2, no. 1: 23-35.

Medick, Hans. 1981. "The Proto Industrial Family." In *Industrialization before Industrialization: Rural Industry in the Genesis of Capitalism*, ed. P. Kriedte, H. Medick, and J. Schlumbohn. Cambridge: Cambridge University Press.

Miles, Robert. 1982. *Racism and Migrant Labor*. Boston: Routledge.

_____. 1987. *Capitalism and Unfree Labour*. New York: Tavistock.

_____. 1993. "Europe 1993: The Significance of Changing Patterns of Migration." *Ethnic and Racial Studies* 16, no. 3: 459-466.

Miller, Daniel. 1995. "Consumption Studies as the Transformation of Anthropology." In *Acknowledging Consumption: A Review of New Studies*, ed. D. Miller. New York: Routledge.

Mintz, Sidney. 1985. *Sweetness and Power: The Place of Sugar in Modern History*. New York: Viking.

_____. 1998. "The Localization of Anthropological Practice: From Area Studies to Transnationalism." *Critique of Anthropology* 18, no. 2: 117-133.

Molle, Willem. 1994. *The Economics of European Integration*, 2nd ed. Brookfield, NH: Dartmouth Press.

Morley, David, and Kevin Robins. 1995. *Spaces of Identity: Global Media, Electronic Landscapes, and Cultural Boundaries*. New York: Routledge.

Morris, Lydia. 1997. "A Cluster of Contradictions: The Politics of Migration in the European Union." *Sociology* 31, no. 2: 241-259.

Mouzelis, Nicos. 1978 *Modern Greece: Facets of Underdevelopment*. New York: Holmes and Meier.

_____. 1995. "Modernity, Late Development and Civil Society." In *Civil Society: Theory, History, Comparison*, ed. J. A. Hall. Cambridge: Polity Press.

_____. 2002. "Poios Fovatai tous Metanastes?" *To Vima*, 7 July: A45.

Mukerjee, Chandra. 1983. *From Graven Images: Patterns of Modern Materialism*. New York: Columbia University Press.

N.a. 1992. "Mikra Asia-Nauplio 1922-1992: Skorpies Mnimes Prosfigon." *Apopeira Logou kai Technis* (fall): 27-30.

New York Times. 2000a. "Resenting African Workers, Spaniards Attack." 12 February: A3.

_____. 2000b. "Europe's Migrant Fears Rend a Spanish Town." 8 May: A1.

Nodarou, Maki. 2003. "Oi Simaies tou Ratsismou." *Eleutherotipia*, 21 March: 52.

Ouli, Thoma. 1965. *Midea*. Athens: Sillogis ton en Athinais Mideaton.

Papadokostaki, Anna. 2003. "Zitisan Auxiseis, Piran...Lintsarisma." *Eleutherotipia* 5 February: 62.

Papadopoulos, Apostolos. 2001. "Farmers and 'Rurality' in Greece: The Evolution of their Strategic Relationship and their Responses to European Integration." *EKKE Working Paper* 2001, no. 14. Athens: National Centre for Social Research.

Pavlou, Miltos. 2001. "Oi 'Lathremporoi tou Fovou': Ratsistikos Logos kai Metanastes ston Tipo Mias Ipopsifias Metropolis." In *Metanastes stin Ellada*, ed. A. Marvakis, D. Parsanoglou, and M. Pavlou. Athens: Ellinika Grammata.

Pentzopoulos, Dimitri. 1962. *The Balkan Exchange of Minorities and Its Impact upon Greece*. Paris: Mouton.

Pepelasis, Adam. 1963. *Labor Shortages in Greek Agriculture*. Athens: Center of Economic Research.

Piore, Michael. 1979. *Birds of Passage: Migrant Labor and Industrial Society*. New York: Cambridge University Press.

Portes, Alejandro. 1998. "Divergent Destinies: Immigration, the Second Generation, and the Rise of Transnational Communities." In *Paths to Inclusion*, ed. P. Schuck and R. Munz. New York: Berghahn.

Potts, Lydia. 1990. *The World Labour Market: A History of Migration*. London: Zed.

Poulantzas, Nicos. 1976. *The Crisis of the Dictatorships*. London: NLB Press.

Pred, Allan. 2000. *Even in Sweden: Racisms, Racialized Spaces and the Popular Geographic Imagination*. Berkeley: University of California Press.

Psimmenos, Iordannis. 2000. "The Making of Periphractic Spaces: The Case of Albanian Undocumented Female Migrants in the Sex Industry of Athens." In *Gender and Migration in Southern Europe*, ed. A. Floya and G. Lazaridis. New York: Berg.

Richmond, Anthony. 1994. *Global Apartheid: Refugees, Racism and the New World Order*. New York: Oxford University Press.

Romaniszyn, Krystyna. 2000. "Clandestine Labour Migration from Poland to Greece, Spain, and Italy: Anthropological Perspectives." In *Eldorado or Fortress? Migration in Southern Europe*, ed. R. King, G. Lazaridis, and C. Tsardanidis. New York: St. Martin's Press.

Rose, Nikolas. 1996. "Governing 'Advanced' Liberal Democracies." In *Foucault and Political Reason*, ed. A. Barry, T. Osborne, and N. Rose. Chicago: University of Chicago Press.

Roseberry, William. 1996. "The Rise of Yuppie Coffees and the Reimagination of Class in the United States." *American Anthropologist* 98, no. 4: 762-775.

Salapatas, Anastasios. 2000. "To Onoma, Stoicheia, Istorias kai Vivliographika tou Horiou Merbeka." In *Naupliaka Analekta*, vol. 4. Nauplio: Dimou Nauplieon.

Sassen, Saskia. 1983. "Labor Migration and the New International Division of Labor." In *Women, Men and the International Division of Labor*, ed. J. Nash and M. P. Fernandez-Kelly. Albany: State University of New York Press.

_____. 1996. *Losing Control? Sovereignty in an Age of Globalization*. New York: Columbia University Press.

_____. 1998. *Globalization and Its Discontents*. New York: New Press.

Schirm, Stephen. 2002. *Globalization and the New Regionalism*. Cambridge: Polity Press.

Schlesinger, Philip. 2002. "Media and Belonging: The Changing Shape of Political Communication in the European Union." In *The Postnational Self: Belonging and Identity*, ed. U. Hedetoft and M. Hjort. Minneapolis: University of Minnesota Press.

Schmidt, Vivien. 1999. "Convergent Pressures, Divergent Responses: France, Great Britain and Germany between Globalization and Europeanization." In *States and Sovereignty in the Global Economy*, ed. D. Smith, D. Solinger, and S. Topik. New York: Routledge.

Schneider, Jane. 1971. "Of Vigilance and Virgins: Honor, Shame, and Access to Resources in Mediterranean Society." *Ethnology* 10, no. 1: 1-24.

Scott, James. 1998. *Seeing Like a State*. New Haven: Yale University Press.

Seremetakis, C. Nadia. 1996. "In Search of the Barbarians: Borders in Pain." *American Anthropologist* 98, no.3: 489-491.

Sider, Gerald. 1992. "The Contradictions of Transnational Migration: A Discussion." In *Towards a Transnational Perspective on Migration*, ed. N. Glick-Schiller, L. Basch, and C. Blanc-Szanton. New York: New York Academy of Sciences.

Silverman, Max. 1996. "The Revenge of Civil Society: State, Nation and Society in France." In *Citizenship, Nationality and Migration in Europe*, ed. D. Cesarani and M. Fulbrook. New York: Routledge.

Simeonidou, Hari. 2002. "Gonimotita." In *To Koinoniko Portraito tis Elladas*, ed. A. Mouriki, M. Naoumi, and G. Papapetrou. Athens: National Centre for Social Research.

Skiadas, Eleutherios. 1993. *Istoriko Diagramma ton Dimon tis Elladas, 1833-1992*. Athens: Mikros Romios.

Smith, Gordon. 2003. "The Decline of Party?" In *Governing Europe*, ed. J. Hayward and A. Menon. New York: Oxford University Press.

Solomos, John, and John Wrench. 1993. "Race and Racism in Contemporary Europe." In *Racism and Migration in Western Europe*, ed. J. Wrench and J. Solomos. Providence: Berg.

Soysal, Yasmin Nahoglu. 1994. *Limits of Citizenship: Migrants and Postnational Membership in Europe*. Chicago: University of Chicago Press.

_____. 2002. "Citizenship and Identity: Living in Diasporas in Postwar Europe?" In *The Postnational Self: Belonging and Identity*, ed. U. Hedetoft and M. Hjort. Minneapolis: University of Minnesota Press.

Stevenson, Nick. 1997. "Globalization, National Cultures and Cultural Citizenship." *The Sociological Quarterly* 38, no. 1: 41-66.

Stoianovich, Traian. 1960. "The Conquering Balkan Orthodox Merchant." *Journal of Economic History* 20, no. 2: 234-313.

Stoler, Ann. 1992. "Sexual Affronts and Racial Frontiers." *Comparative Studies in Society and History* 34, no. 3: 514-551.

Stolke, Verena. 1995. "Talking Culture: New Rhetorics of Exclusion in Europe." *Current Anthropology* 36, no. 1: 1-24.

Storper, Michael. 2000. "Lived Effects of the Contemporary Economy: Globalization, Inequality, and Consumer Society." *Public Culture* 12, no. 2: 375-410.

Sweet-Escott, Bickham. 1954. *Greece: A Political and Economic Survey, 1939-1953.* New York: Royal Institute of International Affairs.

Swyngedouw, Erik. 1989. "Neither Global nor Local: 'Glocalization' and the Politics of Scale." In *Spaces of Globalization*, ed. K. Cox. New York: Guilford.

Taguieff, Pierre-Andre. 1990. "The New Cultural Racism in France." *Telos*, no. 83: 109-122.

Thompson, John. 1995. *The Media and Modernity: A Social Theory of the Media.* Stanford: Stanford University Press.

Tilly, Charles. 2002. *Stories, Identities, and Political Change.* Lanham, MD: Rowman and Littlefield.

Tsakalotos, Euclid. 2001. "The Political Economy of Social Democratic Economic Policies: The PASOK Experiment in Greece." In *Social Democracy in Neoliberal Times*, ed. A. Glyn. Oxford: Oxford University Press.

Tsarouha, K. 2002. "I 'Odisseia' tou...Hasan." *To Vima*, 14 July: 38.

Tsoukalas, K. 1987. *Kratos, Koinonia, Ergasia stin Metapolemiki Ellada.* Athens: Themelio.

Tsoukalis, Loukas. 1997. *The New European Economy Revisited.* New York: Oxford University Press.

Turner, Terence. 2003. "Class Projects, Social Consciousness, and the Contradictions of 'Globalization'." In *Globalization, the State, and Violence*, ed. J. Friedman. Walnut Creek, CA: AltaMira.

Tzilivakis, Kathy. 2002a. "Living and Working in Greece without Papers." *Athens News*, 8 February: 12.

———. 2002b. "Who's Going to Do the Dirty Work?" *Athens News*, 12 July: 12.

———. 2003. "Asylum in Disarray." *Athens News*, 28 February: 18.

———. 2004a. "The 'Ensima' Question Mark." *Athens News* 9 July: 15.

———. 2004b. "'Frustration, Injustice, Insecurity.'" *Athens News* 18 June: 15.

Tzortzopoulou, Maria. 2002. "I Thesi ton Metanaston stin Ellada." In *To Koinoniko Portraito tis Elladas 2001*, ed. A. Mouriki, M. Naoumi, and G. Papapetrou. Athens: National Centre for Social Research.

Verdun, Amy. 2002. "European Integration, Theories and Global Change." In *The Euro: European Integration Theory and Economic and Monetary Union*, ed. Amy Verdun. New York: Rowman and Litchfield.

Vernier, Bernard. 1984. "Putting Kin and Kinship to Good Use: The Circulation of Goods, Labour and Names on Karpathos (Greece)." In

Interest and Emotion: Essays on the Study of Family and Kinship, ed. H. Medick and D. Sabean. New York: Cambridge University Press.

Vincent, Joan. 1974. "The Structuring of Ethnicity." *Human Organization* 33, no. 4: 375-379.

Vlavianos, Haris. 1992. *Greece 1941-49: From Resistance to Civil War.* London: Macmillan.

Vryonis, Speros. 1971. *The Decline of Medieval Hellenism in Asia Minor and the Process of Islamicization from the 11th through the 15th Centuries.* Berkeley: University of California Press.

Waisbord, Silvio. 1998. "When the Cart of Media Is Before the Horse of Identity." *Communication Research* 25, no. 4: 377-398.

Wallerstein, Immanuel. 2003. "Citizens All? Citizens Some! The Making of the Citizen." *Comparative Studies in Society and History* 45, no. 4: 650-679.

Weber, Eugen. 1976. *Peasants into Frenchmen: The Modernization of Rural France, 1870-1914.* Stanford: Stanford University Press.

Whyman, Philip. 2001. "Can Opposites Attract? Monetary Union and the Social Market." *Contemporary Politics* 7, no. 2: 113-127.

Wilk, Richard. 2002. "Television, Time and the National Imaginary in Belize." In *Media Worlds,* ed. F. Ginsburg, L. Abu-Lughod, and B. Larkin. Berkeley: University of California Press.

Wilpert, Czarina. 1998. "Migration and Informal Work in the New Berlin: New Forms of Work or New Sources of Labor?" *Journal of Ethnic and Migration Studies* 24, no. 2: 269-294.

Wimmer, Andreas. 1997. "Explaining Xenophobia and Racism: A Critical Review of New Approaches." *Ethnic and Racial Studies* 20, no. 1: 17-41.

Wolf, Eric. 1981. "The Mills of Inequality: A Marxian Approach." In *Social Inequality: Comparative and Developmental Approaches,* ed. G. D. Berreman and K. M. Zaretsky. New York: Academic Press.

_____. 1982. *Europe and the People without History.* Berkeley: University of California Press.

_____. 1999. *Envisioning Power: Ideologies of Dominance and Crisis.* Berkeley: University of California Press.

Zakopoulou, Ersi. 1999. "Poliapasholoumenoi kai Georgia: Pros mia Nea Anihneusi enos Poludiastatou Fainomenou." In *Ipaithros Hora: I Elliniki Agrotiki Koinonia sto Telos tou Eikostou Aiona,* ed. C. Kasimis and L. Louloudis. Athens: Plethron.

Zegkini, Ioannou. 1968. *To Argos Dia Mesou ton Aionon.* Pirgos: N.P.

INDEX